INTERIOR
LANDSCAPES

GERALD VIZENOR

INTERIOR LANDSCAPES

SECOND EDITION

AUTOBIOGRAPHICAL MYTHS AND METAPHORS

Published by
State University of New York Press, Albany

Printed in the United States of America

For information, contact State University of New York Press, Albany, NY
www.sunypress.edu

Production by Ryan Morris
Marketing by Michael Campochiaro

Library of Congress Cataloginig-in-Publication Data

Vizenor, Gerald Robert, 1934-
    Interior landscapes : autobiographical myths and metaphors / by Gerald
Vizenor. — 2nd ed.
        p. cm.
    Includes bibliographical references and index.
    ISBN 978-1-4384-2982-3 (pbk. : alk. paper)
    1. Vizenor, Gerald Robert, 1934– 2. Authors, American—20th
century—Biography. 3. Indians of North America—Mixed descent—
Biography. I. Title.

    PS3572.I9Z466 2009
    813'.54—dc22
    [B]   2009018969

10 9 8 7 6 5 4 3 2 1

In memory of my father

Clement William Vizenor

Long before I wrote stories, I listened for stories. Listening for them is something more acute than listening to them. . . . Listening children know stories are there. When their elders sit and begin, children are just waiting and hoping for one to come out, like a mouse from its hole.

Eudora Welty, *One Writer's Beginnings*

Childhood is give to us as ardent confusion, and the rest of life is not time enough to make sense of it or explain to ourselves what happened.

Michel Tournier, *The Wind Spirit*

If one lives in a compact, serried group, as bees and sheep do in the winter, there are advantages; one can defend oneself better from the cold and from attacks. But someone who lives at the margins of the group, or actually isolated, has other advantages; he can leave when he wants to and can get a better view of the landscape.

Primo Levi, *Other People's Trades*

By his very nature the half-blood epitomized the integration . . . of the red and the white races, provided a dramatic symbol of the benign possibilities or malign probabilities inherent in this encounter.

William Scheick, *The Half-Blood*

What is true for writing and for a love relationship is true also for life. The game is worthwhile insofar as we don't know what will be the end.

Michel Foucault, *Technologies of the Self*

C O N T E N T S

INTERIOR
LANDSCAPES

Families of the Crane

━━━━━━━━━━━━━━ When the earth was new six
tricksters posed as humans on a wild landscape; one revealed
the power of a trickster stare, a mortal wound to humans, and
then returned to the sea. The others abided on the earth as
totems and endured as the crane, loon, bear, marten, and cat-
fish clans. There are other totems in tribal narratives, but
these five were the first woodland families. The crane is one
of the original five totems of the Anishinaabe.

Alice Mary Beaulieu, my paternal grandmother, was
born more than a century ago on the White Earth Reservation
in Minnesota. She inherited the crane totem, a natural tribal
pose, but we were crossbloods, loose families at the end of
the depression in the cities.

Clement William Vizenor, my father, was a crane descendant. He was born on the reservation and murdered twenty-
six years later on a narrow street in Minneapolis. My tribal
grandmother and my father were related to the leaders of the
crane; that succession, over a wild background of cedar and
concrete, shamans and colonial assassins, is celebrated here
in the autobiographical myths and metaphors of my imagination, my crossblood remembrance. We are cranes on the rise
in new tribal narratives.

My grandmother did not hear the beat of the crane in the
cities. She was concerned with other measures of survivance,
those marginal revisions of personal pleasures and familial
travail in a secular tenement. My father died in a place no
crane would choose to dance, at a time no tribal totem would
endure. One generation later the soul of the crane recurs in
imagination; our reversion, our interior landscapes.

Keeshkemun, grandson of the first leader of the crane families, must have beamed when he presented his George Washington Peace Medal and told the British military officers that he was a bird; indeed, he was a man who inspired compassionate stories, a tribal man with a new avian trickster vision. Keeshkemun resisted the influence of the crown colonies. Later, when the territorial wars had ended and the woodlands had been opened to white settlement, the tribes were amended with political ironies, racial aspersions, traducements, and held behind new colonial boundaries. The crane, bear, and other totems would prevail in narratives.

The people of the crane are "noted as possessing naturally a loud, ringing voice, and are the acknowledged orators of the tribe," wrote William Warren, the nineteenth-century mixedblood legislator and historian, in *The History of the Ojibway Nation*.

The crane totem, *ajijaak* in the oral language of the Anishinaabe, is the sandhill crane, but the modern totem seems to embrace the more common great blue heron. The nuances that separate the crane and heron as totems are considerable; our leaders and the moods of families are heard in treaties, narratives, even the worst translations. The sandhill crane is gregarious, a tribal bird that soars, walks, leaps, and dances; the crane has a distinctive wingbeat, a rolling voice, and a stretched neck in flight. The great blue heron is one more mood as a totem: a solitary figure in tribal narratives, but never lonesome in my remembrance. Sentries at the shoreline, herons move at dusk in shallow water. There, shiners rush the sunbeams, the last warm host between the reeds. We are crossbloods, or mixedbloods, now, and we are heron and crane totems in the wild cities.

The crane leaders in "former times, when different tribes met in councils, acted as interpreters of the wishes of their tribe," wrote William Warren. "They claim, with some apparent justice, the chieftainship over the other clans" of the Anishinaabe. The crane "loves to soar among the clouds, and its cry can be heard when flying above, beyond the orbit of human vision. From this 'far sounding cry' the family who claim it as their totem derive their generic name" of *passweweg*, the echo makers. The crane and the bear families were the first to remember the white strangers, the French explorers and fur traders, at Michilimackinac, the Great Turtle Island.

Englishman, said Keeshkemun, "You ask me who I am. If you wish to know, you must seek me in the clouds." Michel Cadotte, a mixedblood who was a member of the crane clan, was the interpreter at the time; he reported this encounter to William Warren.

"I am a bird who rises from the earth, and flies far up, into the skies, out of human sight; but though not visible to the eye, my voice is heard from afar, and resounds over the earth."

Englishman, said Keeshkemun, "You wish to know who I am. You have never sought me, or you should have found and known me. Others have sought and found me. The old French sought and found me. He placed his heart within my breast. He told me that every morning I should look to the east and I would behold his fire, like the sun reflecting its rays towards me, to warm me and my children. He told me that if troubles assailed me, to arise in the skies and cry to him, and he would hear my voice. He told me that his fire would last forever, to warm me and my children."

Englishman, "You have put out the fire of my French father. I became cold and needy, and you sought me not. Others have sought me. Yes, the Long Knife has found me. He has placed his heart on my breast. It has entered there, and there it will remain."

"You say true," replied the British officer. "I have put out the fire of the French men; and in like manner am I now putting out the fire of the Long Knife," the Americans. "With that medal on your breast, you are my enemy. You must give it up to me, that I may throw it away, and in its stead I shall give you the heart of your great British father, and you must stand and fight by his side."

Englishman, said Keeshkemun, who wore the George Washington Peace Medal, "The heart of the Long Knife, which he placed on my breast, has entered my bosom. You cannot take it from me without taking my life."

"Tell him, sir," the British officer told the interpreter, "that he must give up his medal, or I shall detain him a prisoner within the walls of this fort." Keeshkemun heard the threat in translation and held the medal in his hand.

Englishman, said the leader of the crane, "I shall not give up this medal of my own will. If you wish to take it from me, you are stronger than I am. But I tell you, it is but a mere bauble. It is only an emblem of the heart which beats in my bosom. . . . You are stronger than I am. You can do as you say. But remember that the voice of the Crane echoes afar off, and when he summons his children together, they number like the pebbles on the Great Lake shores."

"Your words are big, but I fear them not," said the commandant of the fort. "If you refuse to give up the medal of the Long Knives, you are my enemy, and you know I do not allow my enemies to live."

Englishman, responded Keeshkemun, "You are stronger than I am. If you consider me an enemy because I cherish the heart which has been placed on my bosom, you may do so. If you wish to take my life, you can take it. I came into your strong house because you sent for me. You sent for me wishing to set me on to my father the Long Knife, as a hunter sets his dogs on a deer. I cannot do as you wish. I cannot strike my own father. He, the Long Knife, has not yet told us to fight for him. Had he done so, you Englishman would not now be in this strong house. The Long Knife counsels us to remain quiet. In this do we know that he is our own father, and that he has confidence in the strength of his single arm."

"Your English father has not sent for you to take your life. You have refused to accept the badge of his heart. You have refused to join him in putting out the fire of the Long Knife who are stealing away your country. Yet he will not detain you. He will not hurt a hair of your head. He tells you to return to your village in peace," said the commandant. He placed tobacco and other gifts in front of the tribal leader. Your English father says remain quiet, and "remember if you join the Long Knives, we shall sweep your villages from the earth, as a fire eats up the dry grass on the prairie."

William Warren wrote, "Keeshkemun, without answering a word, accepted the presents and returned to his village. To his influence may be chiefly attributed the fact that the Ojibways of Lake Superior and Mississippi remained neutral" during the wars.

Kechenezuhyauh, the first recorded leader of the original crane clan, lived at La Pointe du Saint Esprit on Madeline Island in Lake Superior; he died in the late seventeenth century. Akeguiow, his eldest son, succeeded his father as leader of the crane families at La Pointe. Shadawish, the youngest son of Kechenezuhyauh, became a leader at the headwaters of the Wisconsin River.

Keeshkemun, son of Shadawish, continued the distinguished role as leader of the crane families; he settled at Lac du Flambeau. Warren pointed out that "Keeshkemun was not only chief by hereditary descent, but he made himself truly such, through the wisdom and firmness of his conduct, both to his people and the whites. During his lifetime, he possessed an unbounded influence over the division of his tribe with whom he resided, and generally over the Lake Superior bands and villages." Waubishgangauge succeeded his father, Keeshkemun, as leader of the inland familes of the crane.

Ogemaugeezhigoqua, daughter of Waubishgangauge, married Basile Hudon dit Beaulieu, who was employed in the fur trade by the North West Company. Ogemaugeezhigoqua had been baptized Margaret Racine; she was the granddaughter of Keeshkemun and became known to the crane families as Margaret Beaulieu.

Pierre Radisson and Medart Chouart des Groseilliers were fur traders at La Pointe du Saint Esprit in the middle of the seventeenth century. In 1693 Pierre Le Sueur and his soldiers established the first white fur trade post at La Pointe on

Madeline Island. In 1763 New France was ceded to the British; a generation later they established a trading post on the island.

William Warren wrote about a sacred copper plate with marks that represented the tribal generations on the island. "By a rude figure of a man with a hat on his head, placed opposite one of these indentations, was denoted the period when the white race first made his appearance. . . . This mark occurred in the third generation, leaving five generations which had passed away since that important era in their history." The Anishinaabe had established communities on the island more than "two hundred and forty years since they were first discovered by the white race," which would be at least the turn of the fifteenth century.

Basile Hudon dit Beaulieu was born May 18, 1785, at Rivière-Ouelle, Province of Quebec. The Treaty of Paris was signed two years earlier by Great Britain and the United States; territorial boundaries were established at the end of the Revolutionary War. Basile moved to Madeline Island in 1804 and was active in the fur trade; he died on September 9, 1838, at La Pointe. His grave is located on the island at the Baraga Catholic Church. Warren wrote that Basile Beaulieu, William Morrison, and others were mentioned with the principal traders John Baptiste and Michel Cadotte. "These early pioneer traders all intermarried in the tribe, and have left sons and daughters to perpetuate their names." Basile and Margaret raised nine mixedblood children at La Pointe.

Julia Beaulieu married Henry Oakes, who worked for the American Fur Company. Elizabeth married Charles Borup, an immigrant from Copenhagen, Denmark. Oakes and Borup became bankers in Saint Paul, Minnesota. Henry Hudon was a veteran of the Civil War. Paul Hudon married Marie-Margaret Fairbanks. Catherine married Robert Fairbanks. Sophia married a man named Henderson. Margaret married Martin Bisson. Abraham, a popular name at the time, is remembered on a monument at the Baraga Catholic Church cemetery on Madeline Island: "To the Memory of Abraham

Beaulieu, born 15 Sept 1822, accidentally shot, 4th Apr 1844, As a mark of affection from his brother."

Clement Hudon Beaulieu, the eldest son, was born at Lac du Flambeau in 1811. He attended the government school at Mackinac, where he met Elizabeth Farling, the mixedblood daughter of a missionary. Clement was twenty-seven when they married. He was an agent for the American Fur Company in Chequamegon Bay. Elizabeth established a home at old Crow Wing, Minnesota, a new trade center with a vision of the future. Beaulieu and Allan Morrison were the prominent traders in the area; they had proposed a townsite on the shores of two rivers, but the railroad line and station were built farther north. The mixedbloods lost their land and economic incentives. Colonel Clement had underestimated the power of the banks, corporations, and politicians. In 1868 the families of the crane were removed to the White Earth Reservation.

Elizabeth Ayer, the first school teacher at old Crow Wing, wrote to her son, "Crow Wing is quite dilapidated. The Beaulieu house in which so many gentlemen of rank, and ladies too, have been entertained is empty; the yard fence is much broken and hogs and other animals have destroyed what they can that is valuable on the premises."

Clement and Elizabeth raised ten children. Julia Elizabeth married a second cousin and retained her surname. Robert George married a cousin and she retained her surname. Clement Hudon, the mixedblood namesake, attended the Seabury Divinity School in Faribault and departed from the canon of his father; he was ordained a priest in the Episcopal Church. The Beaulieu families had been members of the Roman Catholic Church.

Reverend Clement Beaulieu wrote that when General Henry Hastings Sibley was elected the first governor of Minnesota, "he commissioned some of his old fur trading associates. . . . My father was made a Colonel of a Guard in the Northern Counties of the state. As the military status of the Pioneer Guards was more or less nebulous, its real function for the greater part was social." Colonel Clement held the highest commissioned rank of any mixedblood on the reservation. He participated, with his son, Augustus Hudon, and his nephew, Theodore Hudon Beaulieu, in the publication of *The Progress*, the first newspaper on the White Earth Reservation. Theodore, editor of the newspaper, was married to his second cousin, Julia Elizabeth Beaulieu, daughter of Clement Hudon Beaulieu. Colonel Clement died on the reservation in 1892.

Theodore Hudon Beaulieu wrote an editorial salutation in the first issue of *The Progress*, dated Thursday, March 25, 1886. "With this number we make our bow to the public. The novelty of a newspaper published upon this reservation may cause many to be wary in their support, and this from a fear that it may be revolutionary in character. . . . We shall aim to advocate constantly and without reserve, what in our view, and in the view of the leading minds upon this reservation, is the best for the interests of its residents." I am related to the editor, and to the mixedblood families of the crane who published the first newspaper on the White Earth Reservation.

The United States Indian Agent at White Earth saw the newspaper as a threat to his control of tribal people on the reservation. He wrote to the publisher that the newspaper was circulated "without first obtaining authority or license so to do from the honorable Secretary of the Interior, honorable Commissioner of Indian Affairs, or myself as United States Indian Agent."

In March 1886, "we began setting the type for the first number of *The Progress* and were almost ready to go to press, when our sanctum was invaded by T. J. Sheehan, the United States Indian Agent, accompanied by a posse of the Indian police," the editor wrote. "The composing stick was removed from our hands, our property seized, and ourselves forbidden to proceed with the publication of the journal. . . . We did not believe that any earthly power had the right to interfere with us as members of the Chippewa tribe, and at the White Earth Reservation, while peacefully pursuing the occupation we had chosen. . . . We were restrained and a guard was set over our property. We sought the protection of the courts. . . .

"The United States district court, Judge Nelson in session, decided that we were entitled to the jurisdiction we sought. The case came before him, on jury trial. The court asserted and defended the right of any member of a tribe to print and publish a newspaper upon his reservation just as he might engage in any other lawful occupation, and without surveillance and restriction." *The Progress*, which became *The Tomahawk* two years later, was the first tribal newspaper to be seized by federal agents. The editors published controversial stories and opposed the Dawes Severalty Act, or General Allotment Act, the federal legislation that allotted collective tribal land to individual reservation members.

Colonel Clement testified at a hearing of the Subcommittee of the Committee on Indian Affairs on March 8, 1887. The committee had resolved to examine the conditions and capricious decisions of the agent at the White Earth Reservation. Senator Morgan asked the first questions:

What is your age?

I was seventy-five years old last September.

What family have you living with you?

I have my wife living with me. . . .

Is your wife Indian or white?

She is half Chippewa and half Scotch.

Are you Chippewa? asked Senator Morgan.

Yes, sir, responded Clement Beaulieu.

Full blood?

No, sir; half French and half Chippewa.

What other members of your family have you living in the house?

My children are all grown up; there is only one living with me. My oldest son, Charles Beaulieu, has been in the Army.

Which Army?

The Union Army. In 1862 I raised up a company for him of mixedbood, Indians and French. I got him a hundred men.

And he took them into the Army?

Yes, sir, said Clement Beaulieu.

He was a captain of the company? asked Senator Morgan.

Yes, sir; he was captain of the company. . . .

Where do you reside?

I reside at the White Earth Agency.

How long have you lived there?

For fifteen years. . . .

What other sons have you?

I have another, a minister. . . .

What church is he minister of? asked Senator Morgan.

The Episcopal Church, answered Beaulieu.

How long has he been in that calling?

He was confirmed about four or five years ago.

What is your religion?

Catholic; we are all Catholics except that one. . . .

Are you a citizen of the United States?

I was born in what is now the State of Wisconsin, said Beaulieu. My mother was a member of the Chippewa tribe, and my father was a Frenchman. I was born before any treaty was made between the Chippewas and the United States. The first treaty was made in 1837. No removal of the Indians was made to any tract, but we had a right to occupy the land and to hunt as usual. . . .

When did you move to Minnesota?

I was two years in Canada and in 1838 I came to Wisconsin and have remained there just on the edge of Minnesota ever since until 1846, and then I removed as an agent for the American Fur Company to Minnesota. . . .

When did you first join the body of Indians of which you are now a member, the White Earth Indians? asked Senator Morgan.

I joined them under the treaty of 1854, when there was a separation between the Lake Superior Indians and the Mississippi Chippewas. I joined that band because I could not go so far back as Lake Flambeau. Under the provisions of that treaty we were allowed to go either with the Mississippi Chippewas or with the Lake Flambeau Indians. . . .

Have you held office or paid taxes?

Yes, sir. . . .

Where was that? asked Senator Morgan.

That was in Duluth.

In what county?

We had no county. . . .

Under what law did you do all these things?

I thought I had the law of Minnesota, or Wisconsin as it was then, to go by . . . the law of the Territory. I had a few pieces of the printed laws; I do not know where I picked them up or whether they were the laws of Michigan or Wisconsin, and I used them to dictate to me what to do. But it was all a mistake, I suppose. . . .

What was your reason for wanting all this power?

To keep the peace; that was the only motive, said Clement Beaulieu.

Was there much trouble with the Indians up there?

There was a good deal of stealing. . . .

Are your children educated people? asked Senator Morgan.

My children pass to be educated. They are the best educated boys, I think, there on the reservation, my boys are.

Where did you educate them?

When I was at Brainerd. . . . I sent for a teacher and kept him there as long as I could, and then sent them down to Saint Paul, and then, after they were there, I thought they hadn't enough, hadn't but a small education, and I sent them down to New Jersey and kept them there as long as I could.

All of your children?

No, sir; four of them. The other one didn't want to be educated, he wanted to be a farmer, and I could not get him to go away from home.

Which one was that?

That is the one now living with me, Theodore B. Beaulieu. . . .

Are there many white people on the White Earth Reservation who are not connected with the Chippewa Indians by ties of kindred, and who are not connected with the offices of the Government of the United States?

No, sir; there might be a few sometimes to do some kind of work we cannot do ourselves. We just hire some man to come in on our reservation, provided he is a good man, and we generally inquire about that, and a great many are looking for work and they come in there and they get some work too, said Clement Beaulieu.

Paul Hudon, son of Basile Hudon dit Beaulieu and the younger brother of Clement Hudon, became a government interpreter. Paul, Marie-Margaret Fairbanks, his mixedblood wife, and their five children were the first settlers on the White Earth Reservation. He was allotted forty acres of land according to the treaty between the United States and the Chippewa Indians of the Mississippi, concluded March 19, 1867. John Hudon, their eldest son, was promoted to lieutenant in the Ninth Minnesota Infantry, a veteran of the Civil War. Truman, their last born, is my great-grandfather.

Major J. B. Bassett, the agent at the time of removal to the White Earth Reservation, wrote to Alvin Wilcox, author of *A Pioneer History of Becker County Minnesota*, that Paul Hudon Beaulieu was "sent by me to White Earth in the spring of 1868, before the removal to explore the county and meet me on my arrival there, which was to precede the arrival of the Indians." The removal agent concluded that the "attempt to civilize a people and at the same time prevent them from adopting any of the arts or advantages of civilization, is to my mind absolutely absurd and ridiculous. Give the benefits of law and the work is down at once. Abrogate law amongst the white people and we would soon relapse into barbarism."

Truman Beaulieu was born August 15, 1859. Minnesota was a new state, and John Brown, the radical abolitionist, was tried, convicted, and hanged for treason. Truman married

Josephine Turpin; their six children were born on the White Earth Reservation. Rose Belle married John Spratt. William Robert married Rose French. Ellen married Matthew Miller. Paul married Emma Earth. An Indian Land Certificate for forty acres was issued to Truman on August 11, 1881, and signed by Commissioner Henry Rice. Truman was a hauler of logs; his breath was hard, and he was a gentle man with common ambitions. Later, the family lived in a large house in Calloway, a small town on the reservation, and served as the first telephone exchange in the area; the switchboard was located in the house.

John Clement, the youngest son and my granduncle, was a great story teller, one of the best on the reservation; he even knew where the best stories lived and were remembered. Once we drove around the reservation to visit friends that he had not seen for more than twenty years; he looked over some of his best stories, and he even remembered some of the first telephone conversations on the reservation. We found one of his stories at a small farm on a warm afternoon. We parked near the house, shouted and honked the horn, but no one responded. The doors and windows were open; we tried again, and when we were about to leave, an old woman, a distant cousin, moved out from behind the barn. She wore rubber boots, a black apron covered with blood, and carried an ax in one hand. The wooden handle and blade were stained with blood. Her face and arms were spattered with blood. Our cousin was dazed and dragged her feet as she walked; she was not able to speak. I smiled, nodded, and moved back to the car. "Yes, yes, these were the good old days on the reservation," said John Clement. Our cousin had butchered more than two hundred chickens behind the barn that day, each head chopped by hand on a blood soaked stump. She bathed and appeared later in a print dress with bright red flowers; we ate dinner and told stories, but she never did seem to be there with us that night. "Our women never missed a chance to butcher chickens, the ax has settled the reservation and sobered some men," he said.

John Clement was born May 12, 1893, on the White Earth Reservation. He married Elsie Rabbit from Two Points on the Leech Lake Reservation, and together they lived in various reservation communities. When his wife died he moved to Bena; he lived there in several small houses that he repaired, and then gave away to tribal families. Bernadine Kirt and her daughters lived in a nice red house in Bena; their good humor was honored in that wild reservation town. Bernadine worked with John Clement on the histories of the Beaulieu families.

Alice Mary Beaulieu, my grandmother, was born January 3, 1886, in the same year that the Statue of Liberty was dedicated in New York, and the same year that Geronimo, the spiritual leader of the Chiricahua Apache, was deported as a war prisoner to Florida. Alice, daughter of Truman Beaulieu, married Henry Vizenor on the White Earth Reservation. Three years later she was issued a land allotment, signed by President Theodore Roosevelt on May 21, 1908.

"Whereas, There has been deposited in the General Land Office of the United States an Order of the Secretary of the Interior that a fee simple patent issue to ALICE BEAULIEU, a White Earth Mississippi Chippewa Indian, for the east half of the southeast quarter of Section twenty-four in Township one hundred forty-two north of Range thirty-seven west of the Fifth Principal Meridian, Minnesota, containing eighty acres:

"Now KNOW YE, that the UNITED STATES OF AMERICA, in consideration of the premises, HAS GIVEN AND GRANTED, and by these presents DOES GIVE AND GRANT, unto the said Alice Beaulieu, and to her heirs, the lands above described; TO HAVE AND TO HOLD the same, together with all the rights, privileges, immunities, and appurtenances, of whatsover nature thereunto belonging, unto the said Alice Beaulieu, and to her heirs and assigns forever."

The "fee simple patent" was printed on bond paper, ten by sixteen inches, with the watermark of the Crane Paper Company of Dalton, Massachusetts. The handsome document bore the red embossed seal of the United States General

Land Office. Alice tried to understand the description but she never located the land on the reservation. President William Taft signed a second land document on September 18, 1910, for eighty more acres to my grandmother.

Peter Vezina, my second tribal great-grandfather, was a mixedblood born in Canada. Peter was métis and not embraced by treaties because his tribal mother had married a white man. In Canada, land rights were based on race and gender. He, and hundreds of other métis, moved to reservations in the United States. The Indian Agent recorded his surname as Vizenor, a despotic transcription, when he moved, before the turn of the last century, to the White Earth Reservation. The Vezinas were related to the Vezinat families in the Province of Quebec. Peter married Sophia Trotterchaud, the mixedblood daughter of Peter Trotterchaud and Angeline, a tribal woman.

Henry Vizenor, my grandfather, was born June 20, 1883, one of fourteen children, on the White Earth Reservation. He married Alice Mary in November 1905. Sixteen years later he abandoned his wife, seven children, and the families of the crane on the reservation. He married Margaret Porter and moved to Chicago, where he died in 1942. Small, round Vizenor Lake, located on the county maps in the western part of the reservation, was named for a family allotment that touched the shoreline.

Alice Beaulieu Vizenor sold her government land allotments and moved with her eight children to Detroit Lakes, Minnesota, and later to Minneapolis. She held this new world on a sideboard, but the tribal beams were checked and the wind was cold. Two sons were convicted of felonies in the same year. Our families of the crane were down, marooned in a winter depression, mixedbloods nicked with racial abasement. Joseph, the eldest son, whose nickname was Jeek, and Truman, whose nickname was Bunny, were sentenced to one year in the Minnesota State Reformatory at Saint Cloud.

The Detroit Lakes District Court records indicated that Joseph Henry Vizenor, born July 24, 1906, "then and there

being at said time and place, did willfully, wrongfully, unlaw-
fully, and feloniously carnally know and abuse one Ona
Peck." The Honorable Carroll Nye sentenced Joseph to "hard
labor" for one year on a plea of guilty. Jeek and Ona were in
love. She was white and seventeen years old; he was a mixedblood who ended his public school education in the sixth
grade and wanted to be a baker. A few years later he was
married and a house painter with his brothers in Minneapolis. Joseph died on October 18, 1982. He was survived by his
second wife, Ethel Love; his daughter, Mary Oehler; and his
son, Robert Peck.

Truman Paul Vizenor was convicted of grand larceny. He
had stolen candy and cigarettes worth about sixty dollars
from a store near Detroit Lakes. Alice wrote to the warden of
the reformatory, "Please do something to get Truman out for
he knows his mistake and I know he has learned a good lesson and will be not so full of mischief as before." Bunny was
twenty years old, three years younger than his brother Jeek.
"Some boyfriend would happen along to coax him to go with
him and he'd come back not the same Bunny at all and my
heart would just sink," my grandmother wrote to the warden. "So it's the use of intoxicants that turns the mind into
false doings like one in a dream. Just like an insane man does
things which lands him in the insane asylum. Their body fol-
lows their crazy mind what another crazy mind suggests."
Truman died on June 1, 1936. He had fallen from a railroad
bridge, struck his head, and was found in the Mississippi
River.

Alice lived in Detroit Lakes, about a hundred and thirty
miles northwest of Saint Cloud. She made frequent trips to
visit her boys at the reformatory; the records indicate that my
father and other relatives visited several times that year. Jeek
and Bunny were trustees assigned to work at the institution
farm. My grandmother brought Timmy, the family mongrel,
along on one visit. Naturally, Timmy was left behind with the
boys on the farm; he was hidden in the barn that first night.

"Dear Madam," the warden wrote, "our day turnkey informs me that upon your recent visit to this institution that you lost a dog belonging to your son. The dog has been found and is here. . . . You may have him by calling here."

Alice responded that her boys loved their dog and that she would soon return to the reformatory. Timmy, meanwhile, became the mascot at the farm. When the boys were released at the end of the year the dog stayed, the first canine lifer and trustee at the reformatory. Several years later the warden wrote to my grandmother that Timmy had died and had been buried at the institution.

Thirty years later I was behind those same bars at the Minnesota State Reformatory in Saint Cloud. In 1961, a few months after my graduation from the University of Minnesota, I became a social worker and corrections agent at the institution. The reformatory was not my first choice, but there were only two positions open in social services at the time. The preference accorded military veterans and a high score on the state examination had placed my name at the top of the civil service list. I was determined to be a social worker at the Cass County Welfare Department in Walker, Minnesota. The welfare director at Cass County discovered several relations with my surname on their case load and refused to hire me. He asserted that there would be a conflict of interest. Moreover, he said that my religious tastes, Unitarian at the time, were uncommon, and that my personal aversion to game hunting would cause some problems in a reservation area. "We're hunters, that's what we do together here, you'd be out of place." Roman Catholics ruled the reformatory, but no one asked me about my religion there.

Naturally, in the first week of my profession, a college educated social worker, I checked the cumulative record of prisoners at the reformatory. There, much to my surprise, were the names of my two uncles. No one ever mentioned that they had been convicted and sentenced as felons. I studied their records, read letters from my grandmother, copies of letters from the warden about the family mongrel, and notes from my father to his brothers. Jeek and Bunny were photographed in striped prison uniforms.

That moment was concealed, a chance encounter in a secret mood with my relatives, the unusual manners of the crane families on the hard road to the new urban world. I was touched by the humor of my grandmother and uncles, and mettlesome when the warden observed my responses. Peculiar, he said, and then he ordered an instant hearing on the matter of my felonious relations. We were tribal, and that would represent a racial weakness to the warden; more than that, we were mixedbloods, a double weakness, he would consider. Convicted criminals were one generation removed from me; we were together then, behind the bars when the warden pressed me to be a racial felon with my uncles. No consideration or humor would unburden the warden of his bent and bias; he turned a rubber band on his stout hand and invited my resignation to avoid a certain investigation, an institutional embarrassment.

The warden snapped the rubber band and withdrew his invitation when I promised a lawsuit, at least one civil rights complaint, and a mordant news release on the matter. My mixedblood career had begun, but a college education, the first baccalaureate in our families of the crane, would not secure tolerance, mitigate malevolence or institutional racialism. At those wicked intersections there were courageous and compassionate women and men who would overturn the harsh realities of the moment. This was true even at the reformatory. The associate warden who was responsible for custody in the institution supported me in an unusual manner; he did so with several stories. "I remember your uncles," he said. "They worked at the farm, good boys, hard workers, they always had a laugh on being here." He had been hired as a guard in the same year that my uncles were convicted and sentenced. He remembered the mascot, Timmy. "That dog's buried here, outside the wall," he said. "The name's gone, but the wooden marker's still there."

January 1934: Thank You, George Raft

━━━━━━∿∿∿∿∿∿∿∿∿George Raft was an inspiration
to my mother and, in a sense, he was responsible for my conception. She saw the thirties screen star, a dark social hero
with moral courage, in the spirited manner of my father, a
newcomer from the White Earth Reservation.

"The first time I saw your father he looked like George
Raft, not the gangster but the dancer. He was handsome and
he had nerve," my mother told me. "The first thing he said to
me was, 'I got lots of girls but I always like new ones.' He
came by in a car with one of his friends. Nobody would talk
like that now, but that's how we got together."

I was conceived on a cold night in a kerosene heated
tenement near downtown Minneapolis. President Franklin
Delano Roosevelt had been inaugurated the year before, at
the depth of the Great Depression. He told the nation, "The
only thing we have to fear is fear itself." My mother, and millions of other women stranded in cold rooms, heard the new
president, listened to their new men, and were roused to remember the movies; elected politicians turned economies,
but the bright lights in the depression came from the romantic
and glamorous screen stars.

George Raft appeared in four movies that year: he
danced with Carole Lombard in *Bolero*; as a paroled convict in
All of Me, he and his lover leapt to their death from a hotel
window; in *Limehouse Blues*, he played a mixedblood Chinese
racketeer; and he portrayed a Mexican bullfighter in *The
Trumpet Blows* and received some of the worst reviews of his
career. My mother might have seen him in three movies the
year before she met my father and became pregnant: Raft was
a romantic detective in *The Midnight Club*; in *Pick-Up* he was a

taxicab driver who gave a paroled woman shelter in bad weather; and he was a nineties neighborhood gang leader in *The Bowery*. The Italian mixedblood actor and my father were swarthy, and they both wore fedoras. My father must have smiled on screen; he might have flipped a coin and overturned the depression in the winter tenement of my conception. My mother remembers the romantic dancers in the movies; that night she might have been Carole Lombard.

LaVerne Lydia Peterson, my mother, was seventeen years old, a white high school dropout. Lovey, as she was known to her best friends, was tall, thin, timid, and lonesome that winter. She was the eldest daughter of Lydia Kahl and Robert Peterson of Minneapolis. Her father was a bartender on the northside.

Clement William Vizenor, or Idee, a nickname and a tribute to his eyes, was twenty-four years old, a reservation-born mixedblood in dark clothes; he was a house painter and lived with his mother, two sisters, and four brothers. Everett, or Pants, the youngest, was seventeen, the same age as my mother. Idee, Lawrence, whose nickname was Tuffy, Jeek, and Bunny, who had been paroled from the reformatory, worked as painters for the same contractor. When they could not find work as mixedbloods, they presented themselves as Greeks; at last they were hired as Italians. They were told then that Indians did not live in houses and would not know how to paint one. Later, they corrected their identities; their employer was amused but not convinced.

My parents were married in the spring at Immanuel Lutheran Church. My father was a Roman Catholic and my mother was three months pregnant. I was born October 22, 1934, on a clear, balanced morning at General Hospital in Minneapolis. LaVerne remembered the labor and pain of my birth under the sign of Libra that Monday. She was in the hospital for ten days. She said: "My feet tingled when I got up to leave, I could hardly walk. Funny how I can still remember that feeling." My first name was recorded on the certificate of birth, but my second and surname were not entered, for some reason, until eighteen years later. Adoption may have been a consideration, but no one would admit to that now.

George Raft was the inspiration of my conception; he gave his best performance that night, but he was not there for the burdens and heartache that came later. "Clement was a womanizer," my mother confessed to me. "I was out for a walk and there he was at a local bar between two women. Al Jolson was singing 'About a Quarter to Nine.' Whenever I hear that song I still think about what I saw then. I walked home, sat outside, and cried. I wished someone loved me that much." The song, which was a top hit on Your Hit Parade in 1935, ends with these words: "The world is gonna be mine, this evening, about a quarter to nine." My mother and father lived together for about a year.

My mother believed in the love that was promised by families, but her father was an alcoholic and there were harsh memories at home. "We waited in our winter clothes," she remembered, at night with her brother and sister. When her father came home drunk and violent, she said, "we would run out the other door to escape him." I heard these stories, but he was never drunk around me. My mother said he loved me. "He was tolerant in a way he was not with his own children."

Robert, my maternal grandfather, tended bar at the 305 Club, a tavern on East Broadway. I was there several times with my grandfather; the bad breath, of course, but those patrons in the booths were so generous to a child. They gave me their brightest coins, and peanuts to feed the squirrels out back. I remember that tavern, the warm people and rough boards on the porch, and the tame squirrels that ate from my hand. Robert Peterson hated the world when he turned to alcohol, but he cared for me. I might have been the one last courteous measure of his mortality. A decade later, and a few months before his death, I was able to care for him in a way that brought us both pleasure. Lydia, my grandmother, had locked his clothes and other properties in a trunk as punishment. I opened the trunk one afternoon, when the coast was clear; he carried his clothes away in brown paper bags. I walked two blocks with my grandfather and paid his last fare on the streetcar. He pawned his rings and sold his clothes, but he never asked me for money. Robert died a pauper in a transient hotel downtown, poisoned with alcohol. Lydia never knew the trunk was empty when she gave it to the Salvation Army.

LaVerne was insecure and sensitive to trickster stories. She did not understand my grandmother, and she could not appreciate the critical nature of tribal humor. "Alice Beaulieu kidded me about my skinny legs," she told me, "and at that time I was very self-conscious." My grandmother cared for me then; we lived in a tenement downtown. My father painted houses by day with his brothers, and gambled at night; he played poker and other games in backrooms at taverns and cocktail clubs. Some relatives believe that my father gambled at clubs that were owned by organized crime families. Was my father murdered for his bad debts? My mother said that the detective who investigated the crime told her to forget about the whole thing. "You're a young woman, better not look into this." LaVerne took his advice and never said a word about the death of my father. She told me he had died in an accident. My mother had been taught to bear her wounds and burdens in silence. She was worried, curious, and bound to please; these common leads in the depression restrained her memories, a nuisance in the rush to decadence.

F. Scott Fitzgerald's *Tender Is the Night*, the popular novel of tragic hedonism, alcoholism, mental harm, and moral descent, was published in the year of my birth. Fitzgerald, the most gifted writer of his generation, was born in Saint Paul, about ten miles from our crossblood tenement, but he lived in a world removed by economic promises, a natural decadent paradise. The common social pleasures of his characters would have been felonies on the reservation. My uncles were convicted of crimes that would have been comedies of the heart at white parties on Summit Avenue and Crocus Hill.

LaVerne loved the music of the time; she matured in the depression. Some of her memories were tied to the sentimental phrases in popular songs. Alice, my grandmother, would remember the depression on the reservation, almost with humor. Her children and grandchildren lived with her, and her envies in a tenement were comic. My father, and his brothers, told better stories than the nabob novelists. The tribal tricksters in their stories were compassionate, crossbloods, and they liberated the mind.

June 1936: Measuring My Blood

▬▬▬▬▬▬▬▬▬▬▬▬Alice Beaulieu, my grand-
mother, told me that my father was a tribal trickster with
words and memories; a compassionate trickster who did not
heed the sinister stories about stolen souls and the evil gambler. Clement William must have misremembered that tribal
web of protection when he moved to the cities from the White
Earth Reservation.

Nookomis, which means grandmother, warned her trickster grandson that the distant land he intended to visit, in
search of his mother who had been stolen by a wind spirit,
was infested with hideous humans, "evil spirits and the followers of those who eat human flesh." Naanabozho was the
first tribal trickster on the earth. He was comic, a part of the
natural world, a spiritual balance in a comic drama, and so he
must continue in his stories. "No one who has ever been
within their power has ever been known to return," she told
her grandson. "First these evil spirits charm their victims by
the sweetness of their songs, then they strangle and devour
them. But your principle enemy will be the great gambler
who has never been beaten in his game and who lives beyond
the realm of darkness." The trickster did not heed the words
of his grandmother.

Naanabozho paddled by canoe to the end of the woodland and took a path through the swamps and over high
mountains and by deep chasms in the earth where he saw the
hideous stare of a thousand gleaming eyes. He heard groans
and hisses of countless fiends gloating over their many victims of sin and shame. The trickster knew that this was the
place where the great gambler had abandoned the losers, the
spirits of his victims who had lost the game.

The trickster raised the mat of scalps over the narrow entrance to the wiigiwaam. The evil gambler was inside, a curious being, a person who seemed almost round; he was smooth, white, and wicked.

"So, Naanabozho, you too have come to try your luck," said the great gambler. His voice was horrible, the sound of scorn and ridicule. Round and white, he shivered. "All those hands you see hanging around the wiigiwaam are the hands of your relatives who came to gamble. They thought as you are thinking, they played and lost their lives in the game. Remember, I demand that those who gamble with me and lose, give me their lives. I keep the scalps, the ears, and the hands of the losers; the rest of the body I give to my friends the wiindigoo, the flesh eaters, and the spirits I consign to the world of darkness. I have spoken, and now we will play the game."

Clement William Vizenor lost the game with the evil gambler and did not return from the cities. He was a house painter who told trickster stories, pursued women, and laughed most of his time on earth. He was murdered on a narrow street in downtown Minneapolis.

"Giant Hunted in Murder and Robbery Case," appeared as a headline on the front page of the *Minneapolis Journal*, June 30, 1936. The report continued: "Police sought a giant Negro today to compare his fingerprints with those of the rifled purse of Clement Vizenor, 26 years old, found slain yesterday with his head nearly cut off by an eight-inch throat slash.

"Vizenor, an interior decorator living at 320 Tenth Street South, had been beaten and killed in an alley. . . . He was the second member of his family to die under mysterious circumstances within a month. His brother, Truman Vizenor, 649 Seventeenth Avenue Northeast, was found in the Mississippi river June 1, after he had fallen from a railroad bridge and struck his head.

"Yesterday's slashing victim, who was part Indian, had been employed by John Hartung, a decorator. One pocket had been ripped out of the slain man's trousers. His purse lay empty beside him. Marks in the alley showed his body had been dragged several feet from the alley alongside a building."

The *Minneapolis Tribune* reported that the arrest of a "Negro in Chicago promised to give Minneapolis police a valuable clue to the murder of Clement Vizenor, 26-year-old half-breed Indian, who was stabbed to death in an alley near Washington avenue and Fourth street early June 27. Vizenor's slaying was unsolved." The murder was never solved, and no motive was ever established. Racial violence was indicated in most of the newspaper stories, but there was no evidence in the investigations that race was a factor in the murder. My father could have been a victim of organized crime. There was no evidence of a struggle; he had not been robbed; the police would not establish a motive for the crime. There were several unsolved homicides at that time in Minneapolis.

The picture of my father published in the newspaper was severed from a photograph that shows him holding me in his arms. This is the last photograph, taken a few weeks before his death, that shows us together. Clement wore a fedora and a suit coat; he has a wide smile. We are outside, there is a tenement in the background; closer, a heap of used bricks. I must remember that moment, my grandmother with the camera, our last pose together.

The *Minneapolis Tribune* reported later that the police had "arrested a half-breed Indian in a beer parlor near Seventh avenue south and Tenth street and are holding him without charge for questioning in connection with the slaying, early Sunday, of Clement Vizenor. . . . The man who, according to police, was drunk, was picked up after making statements that indicated he might know who Vizenor's assailant was. He is alleged to have claimed knowledge of who Vizenor's friends were, and of many of the murdered man's recent activities. . . . The murder was blamed by police upon any one of a growing number of drunken toughs roaming the Gateway district almost nightly, armed with knives and razors.

The killing of Vizenor climaxes a series of violent assaults upon Gateway pedestrians in recent weeks by robbers who either slugged or slashed their victims."

In another report, the police "sought the husband of a former New York showgirl for questioning in connection with the knife murder of Clement Vizenor. . . . The man sought is believed to be the same who left with Vizenor from a cafe at 400 Tenth street south about five hours before the murder. Alice Finkenhagen, waitress at the Tenth street cafe, gave police a good description of the man who called Vizenor to come outside. Detectives partially identified the showgirl's husband as that man. Also they learned this man had resented Vizenor's attentions to his showgirl wife.

"Vizenor was called from the cafe at about 12:30 a.m. Sunday. Later he appeared at his home, then left again. His body was found at 5:30 a.m., his throat slashed, in an alley near Washington and Fifth avenues south. Police also were holding three half-breed Indians for questioning, in the case. Vizenor was a half-breed."

The report continues: "A former New York showgirl and her husband were released by Minneapolis police Thursday after questioning failed to implicate them as suspects in the knife murder. . . . Police learned that Vizenor's attentions to the showgirl had been resented by her husband. But that difference was amicably settled long ago, detectives found out."

The *Minneapolis Tribune* reported later that "Captain Paradeau said he was convinced Clement had been murdered but that robbery was not the motive. The slain youth was reported to have been mild tempered and not in the habit of picking fights. Police learned he had no debts, and, as far as they could ascertain, no enemies."

THE LAST PHOTOGRAPH

clement vizenor would be a spruce
on his wise return to the trees

corded on the reservation side
he overturned the line
colonial genealogies
white earth remembrance
removed to the cities at twenty three

my father lived on stories
over the rough rims on mason jars
danced with the wounded shaman
low over the stumps on the fourth of july

my father lied to be an indian
he laughed downtown
the trickster signature to the lights

clement honored tribal men at war
uniforms undone
shadows on the dark river
under the nicollet avenue bridge

tribal men burdened with civilization
epaulets adrift
ribbons and wooden limbs
return to the evangelists
charities on time

catholics on the western wire
threw their voices
treaties tied to catechisms
undone in the woodland

reservation heirs on the concrete
praise the birch

the last words of indian agents
undone at the bar

clement posed in a crowded tenement
the new immigrant
painted new houses pure white
outback in saint louis park

our rooms were leaded and cold
new tribal provenance
histories too wild in the brick
shoes too narrow

clement and women
measured my blood at night

my father
holds me in the last photograph
the new spruce
with a wide smile
half white
half immigrant
he took up the cities and lost at cards

Clement Vizenor was survived by his mother, Alice Beaulieu; his wife, LaVerne Peterson; three brothers, Joseph, Lawrence, and Everett; two sisters, Ruby and Lorraine; and his son, Gerald Robert Vizenor, one year and eight months old. When my father was murdered, I was living with my grandmother, aunts, and uncles in a tenement at 320 Tenth Street South in Minneapolis.

Twenty-five years later I met with Minneapolis police officials to review the records of their investigation. I was, that summer, the same age as my father when he was murdered.

There was some resistance, some concern that my intentions were not personal but political; the police must be defensive about crimes they have never solved. A thin folder was recovered from the archives. The chief of detectives was surprised when he examined the file; he saw his name on a report and remembered that he was the first officer called to investigate the crime. He explained that he was a new police officer then and defended his trivial report. "We never spent much time on winos and derelicts in those days. . . . Who knows, one Indian vagrant kills another."

"Clement Vizenor is my father."

"Maybe your father was a wino then," he said, and looked to his watch. "Look kid, that was a long time ago. Take it on the chin, you know what I mean?"

I knew what he meant and closed the investigation on an unsolved homicide. The detective must have been the same person who told my mother to move out of town and forget what had happened. She tried to forget and left me with my grandmother in the tenement. Later, my mother placed me in several foster homes.

I hear my father in that photograph and imagine his touch, the turn of his hand on my shoulder, his warm breath on my cheek, his word trickeries, and my grandmother behind the camera. My earliest personal memories are associated with my grandmother and my bottle. She would hide my bottle to wean me in the trickster manner because, she said later, I carried that bottle around all day clenched between my front teeth. She reconsidered the trickster method, however, when I learned the same game and started to hide her bottles of whiskey. She might have forgotten where she placed the bottles, mine and hers, and then told stories, compassionate reunions of our past. I remember the moment, the bottles, and the stories, but not the camera. My father and that photograph hold me in a severed moment, hold me to a season, a tenement, more than we would remember over the dark river.

Alice Beaulieu continued her career downtown in a tenement, poor but never lonesome. She was in her sixties when she married a blind man in his forties. I was eighteen, home on leave from the military at the time, and proud to wear my new uniform to a reception. My grandmother was in the kitchen, in the arms of her new husband. "He's a lusty devil," she whispered to me, "and he thinks I'm beautiful, so don't you dare tell him any different." She was a lover, favored in imagination, and she was plump and gorgeous that afternoon.

Alice and Earl Restdorf lived in a narrow dark apartment on LaSalle Avenue near Loring Park. Earl was pale, generous, and sudden with his humor. He repaired radios, a sacrament to sound, and collected radios that needed repair. Cabinets, chassis, tubes, and superheterodynes were stacked at the end of the small dining room. My grandmother would sit on the side of a double bed, because she had never had a secured, private bedroom in the tenement, and chew snuff when she was older. Earl did not approve of her tobacco habits. Alice stashed soup cans in secret places to catch her brown spit; she pretended that her husband could not smell the snuff or hear the juice. He smiled, folded in a chair near his radios.

My grandmother paid my son a dollar each time we visited to hold her pinches of snuff a secret. Robert was two and three years old when he learned the pleasures of secrets. She loved to tease and praise children, her grandchildren and great-grandchildren, and when she laughed on the side of the bed her cheeks bounced and her stomach leapt under the worn patch pockets on her plain print dresses. Alice Beaulieu was gorgeous. Robert has never told a soul about her juice cans at the side of the bed.

March 1938: Crossing the Wires

LaVerne was taken with the movie manners of another man; married a second time, she was soon separated and divorced. Without me, or her parents, my mother must have renewed a pose of movie independence.

George Raft flipped his last coin to my mother and then he died with my father. Al Jolson delivered the words that raised her sentiments. Clark Gable, the masculine charmer, might have beckoned in the mien of other men. The burdens of the depression were alleviated at the movies, in romantic comedies. Gable was a newspaper reporter in *It Happened One Night*. Claudette Colbert, an escaped heiress, teaches the hero that the "limb is mightier than the thumb" when it comes to hitchhiking. She was assertive on screen, and pursued her man right down to the moment of domination. My mother needed the movies to broach the world.

When my father was murdered, I lived for two more years with my grandmother, aunts, and uncles, in their tenement downtown. Then, with a measure of independence, my mother reclaimed me to begin a new life at the end of the depression.

LaVerne rented a cold and coarse two-room apartment above a trunk manufacturing company located on Washington Avenue, near the streetcar barn in north Minneapolis. The small building, close to the street, was covered with dark asphalt paper; the stairs to our apartment were outside, at the back. There were no screens on the windows; the wind rushed at the broken panes, wheezed between the cracks, and pushed under the door. The sound of the wind in that apartment would have been natural in the movies.

The tenement with my tribal grandmother, aunts, and uncles, was narrow, crowded, and warm. The apartment with my mother, the source of my earliest memories of loneliness, was dark, cold, and desolate.

My mother found a job as a waitress in a restaurant and bar; she worked long hours but her salary was little more than the cost of our rent for the apartment. I was turned over to a neighbor who lived a few doors down the street when my mother was at work, or elsewhere. My first shadow work in the world was being with my mother, and then, without my mother. I remember those long hours in the backyard with no trees or animals; the woman who cared for me did not want me in the house, a miniature frame structure with no more room than our apartment. The earth was hard there. I drove my small metal car for hours between the weeds, down to the mount behind the house. Dandelions bloomed in my hands that spring, my earliest natural pleasure with edible weeds.

My mother was always tearful, especially on birthdays and holidays. No one ever visited us over the trunk company. One warm morning late in the spring, I was at the back window at sunrise. Hungry, I climbed on the rough cupboards and searched the shelves for something to eat. I found a box of prunes, which made that morning memorable over the hundreds of others in that apartment. I ate the whole box of prunes, leaned out of the window, and one by one spit the pits like stones at the empty whiskey bottles behind the building. The earth below was soaked with oil, a landscape of ruin and privation. I am haunted by the wind, by the scent of oil; the real world in my memories must be soiled with petroleum. Later, no summer was ever true without a tar truck that sealed the streets. We were the second generation raised on the lure of oil and tar; we chewed a dose of tar in the summer to clean our teeth. I chewed too much once, stained my teeth, and then turned to other habits.

Christmas over the trunk company began with music, lights, and humor, turned morose, and then the night passed with bold ornaments. My mother came home with a small tree to celebrate the season. The day after we trimmed the tree with one string of lights, electrical service to the apartment was terminated for nonpayment. We sat in the dark, alone; she cried too much, and she must have promised me more than she had known in her twenty-two years. That higher distance in her voice soon turned to silence.

I turned to the windows, to carve the glaciers loose and float them on the lower panes; the ice carried me out on the ocean, back to the woodland, in a burst of light. In "The Snow Queen" by Hans Christian Andersen, the "children warmed coins on the stove and held them against the frosted pane." Gerda might have seen me there, stranded over the truck company, alive and lonesome in that "lovely round peephole."

Sometimes, in that obscure silence with my mother, I would trace the seams and cracks on the rough floor from one room to the next and return. The dirt raised in even rows from the seams was plowed back again with a wedge of cardboard.

On the night before Christmas my mother summoned her courage and broke the seal on the electrical meter; she crossed the wires and called me awake to see a lighted tree. She cried with happiness. That little tree with one string of colored lights, more red than green, was her symbolic triumph over poverty, loneliness, and depression. The apartment was cold, but the ornamental lights were warm, and we warmed our hands on the red bulbs. She sat on the rim of the day bed and cried once more, but this time she touched me, hugged me, and kissed me, and she must have told me her material dreams; once upon a time in the summer of our liberation, how our world would be on the ocean, over the rough wood, over the ice, out the round peephole in the frosted window. We were both so young to be poor and alone in the dark.

My mother placed me with three different foster families during the next five years of my life. These families were poor too, electrical service was terminated more than once, but there were other children in these families. There was violence, but never silence, a sense of abandonment, or loneliness. Two families had children my age, and the third was a widow with an older daughter.

The widow was my first foster mother. I was four and she had food in her cupboard; she read to me from books, and she even tied my shoes in the morning. We lived at the end of the alley and there were always children at the nets, in the box elder trees. I was pleased, too tired from play at the end of the day to remember one episode over another at the end of that year.

My mother, meanwhile, worked very hard for our future, she told me. Later, she learned to live with guilt, and from the widows and my small places in the world then, I learned how to read masks and the worldviews of the depression, and how to endure the needs of families that were not my own. I learned how to hear the hidden sounds of loneliness, the tone of guilt in a salutation, and how to hold open an escape distance from the demands of the land, from evil and human cruelties.

"That's the one trouble with this country: everything, weather, all, hangs on too long," said the narrator in *As I Lay Dying* by William Faulkner. The novel was published at the start of the depression, four years before my birth. The wild tones and tensions of that time are roused in literature, in myths and memories, and in the worldviews that roam between crossblood reservations and the cities. "Like our rivers, our land: opaque, slow, violent; shaping and creating the life of man in its implacable and brooding image."

June 1941: The End of the War

~~~~~~~~~~~~~~~~~~~~ *That* old man with the polished
frown across his forehead, deep and white, never was a soldier. He might have died in the war, a hero to women and his
children, but he was disabled, a warrior deformed by polio-
myelitis, and he was wasted at the bar. He used that shriv-
eled hand and arm to beat his biological son. That man was
my first foster father.

Pierce Elementary School, located across the street from
where we lived in northeast Minneapolis, was my first foster
institution, a torsion of white families, histories, and industrial landscapes. Now, we would review that dominant racialism as a serious detraction in public education, but then, in
my worldview as a six-year-old crossblood, that school was a
sanctuary; my first teachers were a benediction, and students
were the dancers. The demons were in the basement, the
maintenance men at the boilers.

The morning sun bounced down the polished hardwood
halls and burned at the end on the portrait of a past principal.
The floors creaked in winter, and swelled in the spring; we
were never isolated from the seasons. Our wooden desks
held the nicknames, curses, and solemnities of other students. The desks must have been rescued from another
school, from older students, because we did not understand
the literature; the names and signs were our myths, our comic
solace in the first grade.

My teachers praised the clear tone of my voice. I sang religious and patriotic songs in a chorus at school. Music, and
the touch of other voices, was closer to paradise than any
other experience in public education.

There, my remembrance becomes a natural neighborhood trinity: my generous teachers, older women, thin at the bone; the arch evangelist, a wise pragmatist; and a foster father with a wizened arm.

The evangelist established his church next door in a square house at the back of the narrow lot. We could hear religious music night and day. He had converted the living room of his house to a chapel, with wooden theater seats screwed in a curve to the floor. He built a new church that summer before the war, a plain block building on the front of the lot, close to the sidewalk. For several months, an hour or two a day, we hauled concrete blocks to the walls. The evangelist set the blocks in concrete; he licked his finger tips and wagged his tongue with pleasure when he worked. The small children crumpled newspapers and the rest of us stuffed the wads into the holes in the blocks for insulation.

When school started he invited the neighborhood children to the chapel in the house to sing, and to listen to his acute religious stories. I was eager to sing with others for any reason. We stayed for the free red apples and small cartons of milk, the reward for our labor on the concrete blocks and for our attention. We sang high, higher, and even higher, now and then, when it rained, or when we were inspired by other events; later, we mocked his stories.

Biblical stories, milk, and music were certain incentives to us because we were poor and our hunger was real, and because construction sites were natural attractions, but our passion to bear witness at the wall was a more natural association with bare breasts. The wife of the evangelist nursed her child in the open, at the site, as her husband told stories, a natural pleasure. My foster father shamed those breasts in our name. We sang, we listened, we ate, we hauled blocks, and we waited and watched for months, but we never saw those breasts again. The evangelist never mentioned them either.

My second foster mother was a natural with her love and humor. She embraced me by day, as she would her own son and daughter, but at night she retreated with her husband.

She was cautious at dinner, sullen at times, and she tried to save her children from punishment. I was the same age as my foster brother; his sister was a year younger. Our father, the lame warrior, would crash through the back door, call us to the kitchen, and demand that we confess our misbehavior that day; we learned the power of silence and deception. He accused his biological son of various crimes and beat him more and more the closer the nation came to war. When he caught us stealing food, or when we wandered down the railroad tracks near home, or when we cursed, he rolled his shoulder back, turned to the side, and then threw his hand, a wicked motion that his son never resisted.

My foster father watched me in silence; his pale nostrils and his facial muscles moved, but he never hit me with that wizened arm. I was the witness, not the victim of corporal punishment. My fosterage was for the money, not for parental love, salvation, or my moral restoration.

My own world war started on Sunday, December 14, 1941, one week after the Japanese had bombed the naval base at Pearl Harbor. The magazine section of the newspaper carried photographs of the attack, of burned battleships, the ruins of the fleet. Our miniature cars and trucks were transformed to serve the war that morning on the hardwood floor; we made airplanes with sticks at an assembly line in the kitchen and attacked our new enemies at the winter windows, on land and at sea. Later, I backed my tricycle across the continent on the ice and rescued our sailors who were stranded in the alley.

The evangelist enlisted in military service and the church we attended was never completed. Men waited in lines, eager to enlist, and few were turned back. My foster father became more sullen, more abusive, more violent, because he could never serve his country with a deformed arm and hand. He came home later and later, wild, wizened, and drunk. Soon my foster mother joined him at night; he lost his job because of alcohol, and we learned to look after ourselves at the front lines.

Christmas was strained, that somber season in families at war. We were forced to move from the northeast apartment to a smaller, three room unit on the second floor of a house located near the trunk company, four blocks from the place my mother had once rented on Washington Avenue. The evangelist was in military service, we had abandoned the neighborhood, and we were no longer in school. Nothing was the same; that natural trinity had been broken.

One winter night when the electrical service was terminated and the space heater ran out of kerosene, we huddled at the window in our coats and blankets to keep warm. They returned drunk, to a home that was at war but had no enemies. We served in the war as children; we gave so much to that war that lasted so long at night.

My war continued for four years, until April 12, 1945. My mother had remarried and we were living in north Minneapolis. I was playing war with a friend; we made our best assault between the cenotaphs on Memorial Parkway when two police officers stopped their car and summoned us to explain our maneuvers. We thought our combat was patriotic; we were heroes, to be sure, not criminals. Soldiers, we would be soldiers.

"What are you doing over here?"

"Playing war," I answered.

"Do you know what happened today?"

"No, what?"

"President Roosevelt died, and you shouldn't be playing at anything, you should be at home showing some respect for our dead president," said the officer. He confiscated our wooden rifles; he must have hated even the simulations of the war that was near the end. My war ended that afternoon.

Twenty years later my foster brother was convicted of a felony and sentenced to the Minnesota State Reformatory at Saint Cloud. I became his social worker at the time of his incarceration, a chance encounter because new cases were assigned to several case workers at random. The warden would have been thrice worried had he learned that one more relative was a convicted felon; two tribal uncles, and now a white foster brother.

My foster brother waited for his punishment, he did not resist; that much should have been familiar. We met several times in my office to talk about his case, his crime, and his workplace in the institution, routine matters. I did not recognize him, and there were no common associations in his record, but he insisted that we had met somewhere. We told stories about high school, military service, college, reservation identities; we found no familiar intersections or connections in our lives because, at first, we did not reach back into childhood. His intentions became more dubious the more he persisted.

Later, we discovered our common past and adventures; his father, and my fosterage. We shared our memories, lost brothers behind the bars, the church, breasts, and those cold nights at the window. We were equals in remembrance, but then he was reminded that he would return to the cell house. We talked more, and he was troubled by our distance, what we had become in two decades. We decided that violence is what caused the differences in our lives; he was beaten, my fosterage was for the money. We were both somber, brothers for a time, but the war had ended once more in the reformatory.

"Childhood is given to us as ardent confusion," wrote Michel Tournier in *The Wind Spirit*, "and the rest of life is not time enough to make sense of it or explain to ourselves what happened."

October 1943: Silence in the Third Grade

Elmer Petesch was not espied in the movies, not much. He was mean, seasoned, divorced, lonesome, and determined in the chase scenes. LaVerne married him in the summer, her third and most reliable husband, but in the end she needed the movies more than a home. Elmer lost his hair, his pose, his pendant, and inherited a worrisome son. My stepfather never adopted me as his own, but for a time we shared the same house and surname.

LaVerne and Elmer were married in the morning by a justice of the peace. I wore my best shirt, my new Sam Browne belt, and waited for them to return to an informal reception. My stepfather held me once, or was it twice, and encouraged me to be a man. He liked my belt. The chase was over and I was eager to leave with them, to recover the lost trinities. When desserts were down, I climbed into his huge blue Chrysler New Yorker and pressed one finger on the name, traced the letters to the end. My mother leaned through the door and laughed at me in the backseat. "Where do you think you're going?" she asked but never listened. She lighted a cigarette, inhaled twice, and then she said they were leaving, but not with me. I had to stay behind once more, a cruel moment to remember at the curb.

Enormous automobiles remind me of that time, and other lost trinities: Sunday mornings, killdeer at the river, the marble counter at the drug store, boiled horse meat for my dog, slow turns behind the church, narrow rooms, my mother with her friends at poker games, cigarette smoke, white ice at the margin, and my victory garden in the back yard. I rode in the backseat, when gasoline was rationed, with several packages of precious seeds to win the war. The principal at the school said the best vegetables would win a prize and help end the war, but she lied; no one ever came by to praise my carrots, the triumphant red radishes, and the war lasted two more years.

Later, other worlds would be discovered in the backseat. We toured the best automobile junkyards near the river and governed our corners from limousines with no engines, no tires, and some without hoods, fenders, or windshields. Most of my friends were race drivers, but the backseats were mine, sanctuaries on the simulated mohair.

Elmer and LaVerne rented the west end of a small double bungalow at 4101 Humboldt Avenue North. I lived with my maternal grandparents for several months to give my mother time to settle with her new husband. My conversion came later; meanwhile, the backseat was a glorious passage that first month. My grandfather loved me, drunk or not, and he chauffeured me to and from my new elementary school in north Minneapolis. I never said a word; it was the start of my new silence.

My stepfather was born near Bellevue, Iowa. His relatives owned rich farms, and the ice plant, the movie theater, the Ford Motor Company agency, and a beauty salon in the small river town. I was there one summer, the year after my mother married into the family, and learned how blocks of ice were made, how to drive a tractor, cut and bale hay, and ride a horse. The man who owned the new car agency told me the pop in the cooler was free. They were generous people; I drank seventeen bottles of Dr. Pepper.

Elmer and his brother, who was a professional wrestler, moved to Minneapolis. My stepfather was a stationary engineer at a millworking company in the city. He tended the boilers that generated electrical power to run the saws, wood planers, and routers that made hardwood molding and window frames. Two or three times on weekends, he invited me to work with him, to bank the coal fires in the boilers. He would talk then about his brothers, the war, the depression, and conservative economics; a dollar earned was a dollar saved, and more. I was closer to him at work than he was to me at home. I sat in his oversized wooden chair that faced the boilers and listened to him wheeze over the stokers. The room was dark, deep, and warm; the fires were measures of his patriotism. I loved that man in the boiler room; he was secure there, determined, a rural pragmatist who cared for me and powered the industrial revolution at the same time.

My mother worked at a liquor bar and had no interest in machines or revolutions; she would be bourgeois, given the chance, or cast in the movies. She was not aware that her husband could repair automobile engines, build houses, or dock puppy tails, and he made huge crocks of the best sauerkraut on the northside. There were other distinctions that caused tenseness in the house. My mother worked late and slept late, even on weekends. She would seldom see her husband; he was early to bed and early to rise. Her interest in me, and my stepfather, was minimal. We both lived in domestic seclusion and seldom shared a meal with my mother. Memories are bound to sound, taste, and unusual landscapes; for instance, shoe stores and advertisements remind me of shadow labor and that time with my mother. One of my shoes, which had been in need of repair for a month, disintegrated on the way to school. I returned home and awakened my mother. "Oh Jerry, not again, there's five dollars in my purse, that's all I have to my name, so get what you can with that." I walked twelve blocks without shoes. I told the salesman what I needed for the money. He pushed my feet under a fluoroscope, measured, and sold me a pair of plain brown shoes for five dollars even. I thought the leather had a nice shine, but the shoes were made with cardboard. That afternoon my new shoes decomposed on my way home in the rain.

The basement of our double bungalow was scented with cabbage, coal, hardwood kindling, bleach, trunk mold, dog shit, the low measures of that civilization. The basement was my room, my only room, most of the time; I slept there with my dog on a double bed. My friends would peer in the basement windows. The case on my radio was broken and at night the tubes lighted my secluded corner of the basement. My radio received stations from all over the country. In winter my corner was cold.

Elmer had been a cuckoholic, or a cuckolded alcoholic, a nonce word from a past marriage that ended in divorce; a condition he cited in others, once removed. He wore black bluchers and white socks, carved his thick curved toenails with a broken pocketknife, consumed too much boiled cabbage and ring bologna, carried wooden matches to burn off his flatulence, and he was slow, much too slow to show his love to me.

Hamilton Elementary School, my second foster institution, was four blocks from our house. I entered the third grade and do not remember speaking one audible word in class that year. My interior landscapes were never secure, but my silence was solace, a bold mixedblood reservation at the word line. I created new trinities, benign demons, little people and tricksters from the woodland, in my head. My new home had become a crossroads adventure in imagination and there were no true reasons to risk my voice once more, to leave my interior landscapes and answer teachers in school. I had earned the reputation, by the end of that school year, of being a behaved slow learner. I was held back and repeated the third grade, but not in silence. I had started school at age five, turned six in the second month of the first grade, and then turned eight and nine in the third grade. My remonstrance originated in the third grade, the second time; however, the conversion from slow learner to a nine-year-old daredevil was not persuasive to the teachers.

Much later, I read *On Disobedience* by Erich Fromm; he wrote that "to disobey, one must have the courage to be alone, to err and to sin. But courage is not enough. The capacity for courage depends on a person's state of development." To be alone seemed as natural as the seasons and my imagination; my new moves in the third grade were silence and then disobedience. My state of development as a mixedblood descendant of the crane was bound by the river, back-seats, basements, institutions, and my new friends at school.

My interior landscapes were enhanced when we discovered the river and the hollows under two bridges. The Mississippi was our wilderness; we were bold, disobedient, and the most adventurous truants to swim in the cold brown water when the river swelled in the late spring. The eddies turned our bodies, wasted our strokes, but we swam downstream to the wooden railroad bridge and escaped the underwater monsters. The real demons were in the wild train wheels, the crack and groans of the support beams. The bridge shivered, the most portentous power was over our heads, and the demons rained coal dust down on our wet bodies. Twice under a train was our initiation. We told stories about our adventures and boasted that we were blessed by the river hosts. I knew then that my fate would never be sealed in public schools.

Our double bungalow was located on a dirt road, one of the last in the city, across the street from a cemetery, an enormous undeveloped section of the cemetery. We tunneled under the fence and explored the mausoleums, the chapel, and that wicked pond. We had survived the river, but the pond had swallowed animals and birds over the dark water; there was no bottom to the pond. The water held no reflections. That pond might have been a death mirror, a mirror made by the devil as it was in "The Snow Queen" by Hans Christian Andersen. The best landscapes were distorted in the mirror and the "nicest people looked hideous. . . . Their faces were so distorted that no one would know them, and people's freckles spread all over their noses and mouths."

Our shadows were stolen at the pond, and we heard wheezes and moans in the chapel. Rusty, my dog, was cautious, she hesitated near the ominous shore. We whispered and never provoked the demons. We were certain that the cemetery pond and chapel were haunted, but even so, that did not stop me, by and by, from working there as a grass cutter. I trimmed around the markers, determined to overcome my fear of death and the dead.

We built summer tree houses in the wild section of the cemetery, and in the autumn we dug forts in the sand and covered them with woven grass. We burned milk cartons and newspapers to keep warm; once, the wind carried the fire and burned the vast north end of the cemetery. Fire crews were summoned from several stations in the city, but they could not control the flames. The cemetery was blackened, and two months later the demons danced on the ashes and the snow.

My personal cemetery territories were overrun and occupied, from time to time, by the enemies of secrets and childhood sovereignties. That spring and late summer, between the third grades, my enemies became my friends, a custom that would not be limited to cemeteries. My silence ended with these new friends: Myron Game, whose nickname was Frog because he hesitated over certain words and sounded like a frog; Randolf Mullins, whose nickname was Black Foot because he never bathed; Wilbur Wannum, who had no nickname but owned his own revolver. Frog shot me in the lower lip once when we practiced fast draws. My lip wilted from the lead, and blood oozed down my chin and neck.

The leaders of the cemetery legions were the biggest in stature, the toughest, but never the heaviest or the witless. Black Foot never had a chance to lead, but later he owned the first car and we allowed him to be our driver around the city. Naturally, I rode in the backseat.

Frog and I were recruited with hot dogs and corn chips to attend catechism at the Covenant Evangelical Church in north Minneapolis. We ate, waited to eat more, and then we raised more questions than the evangelist cared to answer. Jesus Christ was painted on a slight vault, his arms reached out, at a wide angle, over the room. When the evangelist raised his voice and leaned closer to the lectern light, his short red hair seemed to burn; his hair was a summons that mine was too long. Frog pulled my hair, and we pointed overhead. "My hair is just like his," I told the evangelist. "I'll get mine cut when he does." Frog was forgiven his blasphemies, but catechism in my name was terminated. I had demanded his respect and lost my rights to the hot dogs. The Sabbath became the touchstone, as it were, of my disobedience and liberation; there were more sacred adventures on the river than in the hard hands of an evangelist. The slow currents turn the leaves, cover the stones.

Spiritual music, and the true contrition of sinners, has led me to the rituals of the church, but my crossblood soul is unbound, never baptized or confirmed in the New World.

December 1946: Saturnalia at Dayton's

━━━━━━━━━━━━━━━━━*I* was invisible when we entered the department store late that afternoon, a mixedblood on the margins with wild hair, dental caries, and the unrestrained manners of a child who lived in a basement. The aisles were packed with festive holiday shoppers; we were pushed aside at the counters, at cosmetics, at confections, misruled in the sundries. No one saw me steal the mittens and baubles, but the ski poles, we were seen with the ski poles, and the rest was made visible. We were arrested on the elevator, held in an executive suite, but no one revealed the punishment. The police would separate and humiliate, my stepfather would beat me, and with no heart my mother would shame me, a burden in the blood.

"The principle of moderation in punishment, even when it is a question of punishing the enemy of the social body, is articulated first as a discourse of the heart," wrote Michel Foucault in *Discipline and Punish*. "Or rather, it leaps forth like a cry from the body, which is revolted at the sight or at the imagination of too much cruelty." I was right about the police and my mother, but my stepfather surprised me that night at the saturnalia.

"Zero three, come in," said the radio voice.

"This is zero three, over."

"Two juvenile suspects have removed cartoon films from toys and are leaving the department. They are proceeding to the escalator near aisle seven, zero four out."

"This is zero three, have visual contact with suspects, one in brown coat, fake fur collar, and wild hair, and the other suspect in blue parka. Will pursue on escalator."

"Check, zero three, zero two will intercept on the next floor. Suspects are heading for winter mittens and the sports department, zero four over."

"Check, zero four."

"Zero four, juvenile suspects are leaving winter sports department with ski poles, and mittens. Advise zero one, we plan immediate interception on the elevator."

"Check, zero two, they must think no one can see them."

"The invisible shoplifter, zero two over."

"Suspects on elevator, notify police, zero three out."

"Check, zero two out."

"Elevator closed, zero four out."

"Main floor, please," said Wilbur Wannum.

"We made it," I said with the ski poles at my side.

"The mittens are mine," he said.

"But you wanted the ski poles, you got the skis, not me."

"No, the mittens."

"You already have a pair," I argued.

"Let's get another pair then," said Wannum. He smiled, flashed his cold tooth at me on the elevator. Two men at the back moved closer; we were visible between them.

"Never mind, dummy."

"I see you boys have been shopping for ski poles and mittens," said zero one. Another zero held us by the coat collars when the elevator doors opened on the main floor. "Have you stolen anything else today?"

"Oh shit, you asshole," shouted Wannum. He turned his back to me and pleaded with the zeros, the collar tightened around his neck. "This wasn't my idea, I didn't take a thing, nothing," he continued to plead as we were marched from the elevator to the zero one suite.

Elmer would beat me, and that bothered me more than the zeros and the police. He would stumble at me in his black boots, with his big hairy arms out, and jerk my body around, and beat me on the ass until he was out of breath.

"Mister, anything, I'll do anything, but please, do you have to tell my father, do you have to tell him?" Zero one seemed to listen but he did not answer; he never even moved his head. "He's really my stepfather."

"Are you ashamed for what you have done?" Zero one leaned back in his executive chair and folded his hands on his chest. "We watched you both for more than an hour." He smiled, at last.

"Even in the toilet?"

"Smart ass to boot," said another zero.

"No, I mean yes, but do you have to tell my stepfather?" I pleaded a second time, my heart at the mercy of the zeros. "You don't know what he will do to me when he finds out about this."

"Well, I don't think it is my place to tell your father what to do or not to do," said zero one in dictation tones. "At any rate, we are pleased with your confessions and when the police come along any minute now the whole matter will be out of our hands."

Minutes later, two stout uniformed police officers came into the zero one suite, out of breath. Zero one gave them the facts while they looked us over. Without a word we were hauled to the police car and driven three blocks to the courthouse. I was invisible; the people on the street could not see me in the backseat.

Juvenile officers questioned us in a dark room, they asked us about other crimes, and we were eager to confess to the ski poles, the mittens, and the baubles. Then, the last punishment, the officers called our parents. The scene was not as it should be with parents in the movies. Wannum was an adopted child, and his mother was blue with so much love to lose.

Elmer arrived at the courthouse about an hour later. He smelled of boiled cabbage and sulfur from wooden matches. He was my stepfather and had nothing to lose over me. He breathed hard and moved in silence; we marched out the door, around the corner. I waited for the first blow and ducked when he opened the door on the passenger side of the car. He smiled and seemed to be at ease, the worst sign of the storm that would follow once we were at home.

He started the engine and drove in silence; right turn, followed the streetcar tracks, but we turned right again, not left, we were not going home. My stepfather was taking me out to eat. We had hamburgers, onions, lemon meringue pie, my favorites then, and a man-to-man talk, the first in our three years together. I measured his gentle manner, however, as a new punishment; I was certain he would beat me when we got home. I asked for a second bottle of Dr. Pepper.

"Are you going to hit me later?" I asked.

"No, not this time, and you know I don't like doing that any more than you like getting it," said my stepfather. Parents and children must bear that platitude as their test of truth.

"Does that mean you won't beat me?"

"No," he said in a whisper.

"Not ever again?"

"Well, there might be a time when you'll need it again, but you're old enough now to talk about things man to man." He smiled; the truth had been tested and he survived once more.

"When?" I was eager to talk about punishment.

"You just eat now, and let's talk about this afternoon before I lose my temper and change my mind." He beat the bottom of the ketchup bottle. "You and that kid you were with have to appear in juvenile court and that will be punishment enough for stealing. The judge will be tough, but you need the lesson."

I returned to the basement and listened to my radio. I would travel to those lights and voices in the night, southern, mountain, the great cities on my radio. I ran away at age fifteen to Biloxi, Mississippi, and the Gulf of Mexico, because the south was on my radio and a friend was stationed at a military base near there. I am reminded of that time on the highway now, the glow of the dashboard lights at night, the distant stations on the car radio.

Juvenile Court was cold, the wood had no luster, and parents cried over the phrases of punishment. Wannum wore a new necktie his mother bought for the occasion. I wore my best wool shirt. We stood at the bench to hear our punishment, the sentence for our crimes. The judge looked down from his perch, down at the accused, and said that this was not the first time we had stolen. We took the bait and confessed to more than we had stolen, we wanted to please the judge.

"Do you want to grow up to be criminals and spend the rest of your natural lives in prison, do you?" He never waited for an answer. The scene was too common. "Let me tell you this, young man," he said and leaned over the bench. He pointed at me, "And you too, young Wannum. If it were not true that our two juvenile training schools were filled I would send you both there in a minute for your crimes. You deserve no less, but because Glen Lake and Red Wing are filled to the windows, I will give you a chance to do good by placing you both on probation for six months, and if during that time you ever steal, or do anything wrong again, I will let someone out at Red Wing just to make room to put you in. Do you understand what I have just said?"

We nodded at the bench and listened with our heads back. He was serious, that much was clear, but we never understood what he said about institutions and probation. The movie *Boys' Town* came to mind; Father Flanagan, played by Spencer Tracy, rested his warm hand on my shoulder and welcomed me to his school in Nebraska. Mickey Rooney was there too, and we were honored as reformed juvenile delinquents.

"You will report to your probation officer every Monday afternoon for six months, and you will tell the principal of your school that you are on probation for stealing and he will permit you to leave early to report. Do you understand what I have just told you?"

*Clement Hudon Beaulieu,
1811 to 1893, White Earth
Reservation*

Elizabeth Farling Beaulieu

Paul Hudon Beaulieu, 1820 to 1897, first Native interpreter, White Earth Reservation

Truman Beaulieu, White Earth Reservation, 1917

White Earth Reservation School, 1900

School Band, White Earth Reservation, 1916

Clement William Vizenor holding his son Gerald, Minneapolis, 1936

TOP *Gerald Vizenor, White Earth Reservation, 1936*

LEFT *Gerald Vizenor, White Earth Reservation, 1936*

BOTTOM *The Vizenor brothers, Clement, Truman, and Joseph Vizenor, White Earth Reservation, circa 1932*

Henry Vizenor, married to Alice Beaulieu Vizenor, White Earth Reservation, circa 1932

Joseph Vizenor, Minneapolis, 1962

Alice Beaulieu Vizenor and her brother John Clement Beaulieu

*Gerald Vizenor, Photomatic
Picture, Minneapolis, Snow
Storm, November 11, 1940*

*LaVerne Peterson, Minneapolis,
1933*

Mary Norman Haase

4-401-ty.

The United States of America,

To all to whom these presents shall come, Greeting:

WHEREAS, There has been deposited in the General Land Office of the United States an Order of the Secretary of the Interior directing that a fee simple patent issue to ALICE BEAULIEU, ——————————— a White Earth Mississippi Chippewa Indian, for the east half of the southeast quarter of Section twenty-four in Township one hundred forty-two north of Range thirty-seven west of the Fifth Principal Meridian, Minnesota, containing eighty acres:

NOW KNOW YE, That the UNITED STATES OF AMERICA, in consideration of the premises, HAS GIVEN AND GRANTED, and by these presents DOES GIVE AND GRANT, unto the said Alice Beaulieu, and to her heirs, the lands above described; TO HAVE AND TO HOLD the same, together with all the rights, privileges, immunities, and appurtenances, of whatsoever nature thereunto belonging, unto the said Alice Beaulieu, and to her heirs and assigns forever.

IN TESTIMONY WHEREOF, I, Theodore Roosevelt , President of the United States of America, have caused these letters to be made Patent, and the seal of the General Land Office to be hereunto affixed.

GIVEN under my hand, at the City of Washington, the ....twenty-first........ day of ....May...... , in the year of our Lord one thousand nine hundred and ......eight........ , and of the Independence of the United States the one hundred and ....thirty-second.

By the President: Theodore Roosevelt .

By A S Stump , Secretary.

Recorder of the General Land Office.

Recorded   Vol. 776 Page 240

Patent issued to Alice Beaulieu, 1908

"Yes sir," but my tongue wanted to say the opposite.

"Have you learned your lesson?"

"Yes sir, sir."

"No more, sir," said Wannum with a scared smile. His mother had coached him to say the right things, but his gold tooth turned even his best manners into comedies. His mother blamed me as the evil influence, the cause of his brush with the law. She never knew about his revolver, and the things he stole from the grocery and the drug store. The judge and our parents agreed that we were never to see each other again. Close your eyes, they instructed, and turn the other way when you see each other in school or on the street. We listened, nodded, and went on with the legion and our adventures in the cemetery. Monday afternoons, however, we pretended not to be together when we reported to our probation officer at the courthouse.

Mondays in the courthouse were given over to juveniles. There were no more than two or three probation officers for the entire city of juvenile criminals. We waited in a line with more than a hundred other criminals that circled one end of the building. Shoplifting was minor compared to the crimes the bandits from northeast claimed. They stood in line and boasted about armed robberies, rape, extortion, burglary, and car theft. Pressed, we told them about the ski poles and mittens. Wannum impressed them with his revolver, but we remained pansies on probation. No matter what time we arrived we were at the end of the line, the last to see the probation officer.

His face was ocherous, the color of probation, and his neck was burned and cracked. My probation officer had brown fingernails from cigarette smoke; his teeth were stained and he hacked over his last words.

"Did you go to church?" He leaned to the right and waited with his head down for me to answer; his pencil was aimed at the large yellow card on his desk. His hands were old animals, covered with brown spots.

"Yup," I said and watched his hand move over the card.

"Attending school every day?"

"Yup," I said and wondered what happened to his legs. He sat behind that desk for several hours and never moved. He lighted a cigarette and told me not to smoke.

"Staying away from known criminals and juveniles on probation?" He rubbed his forearm on the edge of the desk. There were several other probation officers in the same large room; they sat in the same wooden chairs, behind the same metal desks, and asked the same questions. He marked the card before he heard my answer.

"Yup," I said and wondered if he had been wounded in the war.

"Staying away from Dayton's?"

"Yup," I said and remembered that my mother warned me that no one would ever let me into the store again, that they would never allow me to work there, or open a charge account.

"Gerald, you are making very good progress and I think in a month or so, if you behave yourself in school, attend church, and stay out of mischief and follow the rules, we may release you from probation early."

"Really?"

"Yes, but don't forget to attend church every week," he said. Then he looked up, the only time during the interview, and smiled, a sudden crack on his face. "Keep your nose clean, kid, you know what I mean."

"Yup," I said and looked under the desk. He had two legs, and two feet, but no shoes. He wore brown socks and one foot was stacked on top of the other. He moved his toes.

"Lose something?"

"Nope," I said and turned to leave.

"Send in the next boy."

July 1947: Many Point Scout Camp

━━━━━━━━━━━ *"I* am my past and if I were not, my past would not exist any longer either for me or for anybody. It would no longer have any relation with the present," wrote Jean-Paul Sartre in *Being and Nothingness.* "That certainly does not mean that it would not be but only that its being would be undiscoverable. I am the one by whom my past arrives in this world."

The White Earth Reservation returned to my past in a most unusual manner. I arrived as a tenderfoot in the Viking Council of the Boy Scouts of America in time to connect with a summer adventure at the Many Point Scout Camp in northern Minnesota. Much to my surprise, the camp was located on wilderness reservation land north of Ice Cracking Lake on the eastern border of the Tamarac National Wildlife Refuge.

I had no idea that the camp was on the White Earth Reservation. Park Rapids darkened, and Fish Hook Lake passed in the last light. The bus moaned on the turns, the narrow road near Two Inlets and crossed the reservation border near Indian Creek. White pines marched on the pale horizon. The bus rumbled on gravel roads for more than an hour through the White Earth State Forest to Many Point Lake. The camp was new and we lived two scouts to a tent. Nils, my tent mate, was from the same elementary school in the city; he was lonesome, and the older boys abused him because he was stout and devoured canned sardines. The smell of fish in the tent reminded me of cod liver oil, the preventive medicine of the depression and the war.

Mary Norman Haase is responsible, in a sense, for my best experiences in Cub Scouts and then as a tenderfoot in the Boy Scouts. She urged me with love and cookies to be part of her den, the primal coterie of the Cub Scouts. She was generous and spontaneous, a wise mother who cared for more than a dozen boys, most of them on familial margins. Walter, her husband, was a scout master, and her son was an Eagle Scout.

Mary would invite me to her house on my way home from school; she never tested me or teased rumors from me about my mother, stepfather, or my troubles. Rather, she praised me as a parent would, and so she praised my best ash coffee table, with a rubbed blond finish, that I made in a wood-working class. Now, my sadness inhibits the truth behind the table. My mother told me she would be home, that she would wait for me to return with my surprise from school. LaVerne lied, she was not there; no note, no reason, no humor, no honor. I worried over my table and then decided that she would never see it; she never even remembered.

Mary was at rest on the porch; she invited me in with my dog and the table. She loved me, my creation, my dog, that warm afternoon, and she loved the light she saw in children. I would be a writer a decade later, a crossblood at the scratch line, and she presented me with my first desk. I am moved and heartened in these memories; she was a humane and honest den mother, closer to being a saint than a mother dared to be with children on the loose. I dedicated *Raising the Moon Vines* to her, my first book of haiku.

The Boy Scouts of America earn the honors and merits that are bestowed on them by earnest adults in the troop, in the best of times at summer camp; however, the behavior is material, political, and dubious ceremonies are borrowed from tribal cultures. That a merit badge, or the Order of the Arrow, represents the measure of a mature course is ostentatious and insincere. The badge is a cultural tribute that has value to other scouts and masters.

Many Point Lake was wild and clean with red pine and roses, with moccasin blooms and water lilies. We were in line early for breakfast, touched by the moist air. I was invited that morning, with another, a tenderfoot, to earn my merit badge in compass reading. We were driven down a dirt road several miles to a remote area south of the lake, but not far from the shore. There, we were provided with one compass, pencil, paper, and packed lunches for our first merit badge test. We had our knives and full canteens. The scout master instructed us to read our compass and find our way back to the camp. We were bored by the instructions because any fool could follow the dirt road and tire tracks back, no compass test there. Six years later, at a night compass course in military basic training, I told that scout story, the crossblood on the trail. We used the compass then because we had to mark the maps, but the real milestones were truck tire tracks.

When the truck disappeared in a cloud of dust, we decided to have a real adventure, liberation from the regimentation of the day. We followed the shoreline to the west and then north, easy enough, and ate our lunch on the far side of the lake from the camp. We could hear the distant sound of scouts in canoes; this was tribal land. The lakeshore was wild then, there were no cabins. We saw beaver, deer, bald eagles in nests near the north end of the lake, and other animals and birds. Ten hours later we walked back into camp, in the dark. We were tired, but pleased with our adventure. We waited for some salute, but we heard no praise.

Walter Haase and the other scout masters were in a panic because they were convinced that we were lost; they had organized several search parties. So, we had at least caused some adventure for other scouts. Several scouts passed the word in the camp that we had been found; we were described as scared and hungry, but unharmed.

"How could anybody get lost with a compass?" asked a senior scout at a marshmallow roast that night. He said we were stupid and gave other scouts a bad name. "All you had to do was follow the road back."

At first we both protested his censure, but later we chose silence. We were wise not to run down the compass test then, or to boast about our real adventures. Our wisdom cost us a

merit badge and some humiliation, but when we told our stories about eagles and beavers, we were esteemed by the other
tenderfoot scouts, if not for our adventure, then at least for
our imagination. Stories are a better past than merit badges.

At the end of the two-week encampment the scout masters produced the Order of the Arrow, an adventitious comic
opera with racialism, wild dancers, shamanic simulations,
and a bearded man who ate fire.

We listened to wild rumors and waited near our tents until dark; no flashlights were permitted. The senior scouts,
those who had been at other summer camps, would not reveal what happened at the Order of the Arrow ceremonies.
At last we were led to a humid clearing in the forest and told
to sit in a circle around a fire pit. Our silence was unnatural,
once or twice a nervous laugh, and then there were animal
sounds and a wild shout from the trees behind our circle. Silence once more, and then a ball of fire flew down from a red
pine into the circle and hit the pit. The fire spread over the oil
soaked firewood. At the same time the stranger with the
beard ran to the pit and spit gasoline on the fire from the four
cardinal points. Later, he spit fire in the main lodge. We were
amazed, a high-risk performance by some of the most conservative scout masters at the camp. Later, we pursued the fire
eater and learned that he had been hired to enhance the Order of the Arrow. The shamanic ball of fire was guided by a
thin wire between the tree and the pit.

The bonfire created wild shadows in the circle. A dancer
leapt from behind the trees, dressed in breechclout and dubious tribal vestments. The dancer pounded the earth around
the fire, between the scouts in the circle. He came closer to
me, wailed and circled me, and then moved to circle another
tenderfoot. I watched his stomach bounce; the scout paint he
used to tone his pink body was streaked with sweat. He was
the scout master who shamed me for being lost. He told me,
"A real scout is never lost." He would not believe that we
were in agreement. I was twelve then, overawed at the circle,

but later, I wondered who these white men thought they were, playing Indian on stolen tribal land.

The purpose of this comic opera on the White Earth Reservation was to scare the tenderfoot scouts, and to initiate certain proud and proper senior scouts into the Order of the Arrow. The pretend warriors raised the novice by the hair and decorated his face with paint. Then the comic warriors presented a marked arrow to the scout; he was touched on the shoulders, a modern chivalric code on a reservation. These men of the arrow were not horsemen, or gallant gentlemen of the woodland; they were pretenders to the land, abusers of gasoline, and artless readers of the compass.

Sunday mornings, in connection with religious services at the camp, we were told to write to our parents. I pretended to write to my mother: You never told me when I left for camp that they were sending me back to the reservation. You should have said something. My father grew up here you know, everybody knows that, we are on the White Earth Reservation.

There are animals and birds everywhere, but I don't like the people very much here. Everybody is always telling me what to do all the time. They think they own this place. I can't even swim when I feel like it, everything is on time, go here and go there, and I am hungry all the time.

I am living in a tent with another scout and he eats sardines all the time and leaves the cans in the tent. He said he can do it because he's a Norwegian. He smells like a fish in the tent. He never gave me any either.

One of the scout leaders started a fire in the big fireplace in the main lodge with his mouth. I was fooled at first but then I saw the gasoline he drank and spit at a match he was holding in front of the logs. But don't worry because he told us never to drink gasoline.

Yesterday they killed a whole pig and roasted it over a fire outside. I didn't eat any because it smelled awful.

Everybody tells us to work all the time. We wanted to explore around the lake but nobody would let us. One kid has all the merit badges they make. He's an eagle scout and everything, but he looks dumb with his thick glasses. He walks like Black Foot, you know, my dumb friend across the alley.

We learned about canoeing and life saving and fire building. In the morning they give us cold toast and cold eggs. They gave us time after church today to write to you.

My mother never cared much about me as a scout; she remembered my crimes, my punishments, but not my victory gardens, or my time at summer camp. I pretended to write a second letter to my mother: You won't believe this but they took us away from the camp yesterday to find our way back with a compass, but we went for a walk around the lake and they said we were lost. The kid with the thick glasses said he hoped we would get lost for the day on purpose. We had a great time. Nobody told us what to do all day. We circled the camp and walked around the lake until dark. We saw a nest of bald eagles. We knew where we were and didn't need a compass. Nobody could get lost walking around a lake anyway. It was really wild.

When we came back they thought we were lost so now we have to stay here all the time. The kid with the thick glasses laughs at us all the time. Nobody believes we were not lost. Another dumb thing here is the order of the arrow when all the scouts pretend they are Indians. Tell the Frog I will be home next weekend.

The Many Point Scout Camp is operated by the Viking Council of the Boy Scouts of America on more than twenty thousand acres of valuable tribal land on the White Earth Reservation. Not many loyal and trustworthy scouts are aware that the land was stolen from tribal people by the federal government.

August 1948: The Titan of Green Lake

The *Minneapolis Journal* hired me to deliver their newspapers on a four-block route in north Minneapolis. That was my first real source of independent income. I had been a shadow worker as a child, bribed by adults, dependent on cash allowances, and nourished by evangelists for the right words, the proper poses. These were not subsistence activities and, with a wider brush on submission, could be embraced in *Shadow Work* by Ivan Illich. He wrote that "unpaid servitude does not contribute to subsistence." We are cast in shadow work and selected for paid labor. "The amount of shadow work laid on a person today is a much better measure of discrimination than bias on the job."

My mother was a shadow worker; she was a waitress, a server at the bar, who estimated the humor of customers by their gratuities. I listened and learned how to overturn servitude and the burdens of an uncertain allowance. For instance, my mother was more sympathetic in the early morning to my entreaties for cash: monies for lunch, locker dues, and other institutional considerations. She would moan and direct me to her purse, my tribute; we had both been trained as shadow workers.

I was emancipated on my newspaper route, free as a bird, most of the time, from shadow economies. The *Minneapolis Journal* was engaged in a subscription war, a wild competition with other newspapers for readers. I was courted, for the first time, by capitalists to sell more and more subscriptions. The carriers who increased the subscriptions on their routes by a certain number were rewarded with a picnic, free hot dogs, and cash premiums.

My first employer lost the competition and one year later merged with the *Minneapolis Tribune*. My service and my route were part of the corporate blend. The same two newspapers that had reported on the front page the murder of my father a decade earlier, now embraced me, the mixedblood survivor, as a newspaper carrier. My route became much larger, about six blocks on the northside, and included morning and evening deliveries. I was up earlier than my friends and gathered with other carriers in the best and worst weather at the corrugated metal shack behind a small grocery on Forty-Fourth and Logan Avenue North, where we received our newspapers. The station manager, a college student, was a trickster, and the humor was rough, but we were independent and the shack was warm in winter. The new carriers were initiated at least once a month, and the humiliation lasted until the bad turns were reversed, or new dupes were hired. We all lost hats and gloves in the trash fires. Once, some of the center sections of my newspapers were replaced with a past edition, but no one on my route complained. Twice the other carriers conspired to lock the station on me; they hid behind the grocery. To be late was an act of treason.

After school we delivered the evening paper and once a week, at dinner time, we collected subscription dues from our customers. I worked an average of four hours a day, seven days a week, for about two years. I earned about ten dollars a week and became a consumer, my liberation from most shadow work. I bought a new Schwinn bicycle with a streamlined fender light and a tank horn my first year, and a Whizzer motor to power my bicycle the next year.

My stepfather was proud of me and in the worst weather, snow, cold, and rain, he would help me on my morning route. My mother became more distant; she left for work earlier and returned later at night. Rusty, my dog, and my friends remained the same.

Frog, my best friend, never worked until he graduated from high school; his father was more protective, and generous. Frog earned wages at home, an allowance based on the hours he worked painting windows, cutting grass, cleaning the gutters, shoveling snow, and more. He was never driven to be independent, to be liberated from shadow labor; his parents were much better at tribute. Frog had an older sister and she promised us the world in pig Latin. We never believed her coded praise, but even so, we were misled, bamboozled, and outwitted at every turn and season. She told everyone that we had been caught at a window, with several other boys, peeping at a girl in a bathtub.

Mary Lou Waight won the honors of being the toughest girl in the neighborhood; she downed me and every other boy on the block with two or three blows to the head and chest. She was wild in the corners, but never wicked or merciless; rather, she was honest and mean, and never held back a proud moment or her temper. Mary Lou was pale and wore thick glasses, never the pose of a warrior. She was a fair street fighter, no eye gouging, crotch kicks, or choke holds, but then she could afford to be fair because her brothers represented a considerable deterrent in the balance of power on the northside. Once she lost a fight with me and her brothers tracked me for more than two weeks to get even. Lost is not the best word; she gave up and went home crying, but that distinction and sense of balance were not important when her brothers found me.

Mary Lou and her mother could have been sisters; they shared the same mettle and determination. Charlotte cornered me in the drug store three years later, after my stepfather had died, and ordered me to be at her house for dinner. "Bring everything and don't be late," she said to me in a loud voice at the magazine rack. "You don't get fed at our house if you're late." Elmer died and I was on my own. My mother had left the state with another man. Mary Lou heard about my situation at school and told her mother to find me, to bring me home. I would have resisted missionaries and abstract liberal invitations, and she knew that about me; so, she ordered me to be at her house and beat me at my own pride.

Frog said, "That's what happens when you beat up on a girl, you have to go live with your worst fears, her brothers."

Charlotte lived in a small house with her husband, three sons, two daughters, and two foster children. I was blessed by her great love and her wise, rough humor; she made me a secure bed in the basement behind the furnace.

Frog was a river dreamer; we were both dreamers, and adventurous. The river in the summer, the islands and woods, were enchanted, ominous, and precarious. We were twelve, sudden to the water and the trees, and we were pleased to torment the titan who lived on the river.

Mean Nettles was born in the back of a hearse near the river; he was a squatter with black hair, and he was a star tackle on the high school football team, but he never practiced. The titan drank hard booze from a jar, smoked two packs of cigarettes a day, had sex with older women before he was fifteen, and owned his own lake below the concrete block factory. He was silent, and very mean, so mean that even the demon mosquitoes on the river circled his head out of reach.

Frog pinched blood from the mosquitoes that landed on his arms; we waited in the moist brush and watched the mean titan build his sailboat. He hauled drums, deck joists, and boxcar siding to his dockyard on Green Lake. The lake was once a huge gravel pit near the river; it filled with sulfurous waste from the concrete block factory up the hill. The lake was chartreuse, clear, and smooth; the water turned flaxen at dusk, as thick as cough medicine, and clotted at the bottom. We tried the water as a mosquito repellent, but it dried our skin into thin white wrinkles. Mean Nettles once threatened to baptize his enemies with water from Green Lake.

The Pitcher brothers, six blond cross-eyed squatters, lived in the house next to the titan, about a mile above the Camden Avenue bridge in north Minneapolis. Mean Nettles was silent, but the Pitcher brothers talked all the time at high pitch, twice as much talk about about what they saw with double vision. They were always talking and never apart, like a pack of reservation mongrels. The Pitchers had equal rights as squatters on the river, but they were not welcome on the lake; the titan ruled Green Lake.

When Mean Nettles was out drinking one night, and having sex with the older river sirens, we entered his dockyard to sabotage the construction of his sailboat; no reason but to torment the titan. Frog punched holes in the oil drums and we set them afloat on the thick flaxen water. The titan had nailed a book, opened to a schematic drawing of a schooner, to a box elder tree near the dockyard. His drum sailing vessel was a rectangle about six feet long. We wrote obscene messages about demons and titans on the book and on his narrow dock.

Mean Nettles rescued his drums from the clotted bottom of the lake, and with the better squatters set snares, pitfalls, and issued a wanted poster for Myron Game, the Frog, and Vizenor, or Petesch as I was known to some people then. They dug deep holes on the narrow path near the river and covered them with sticks, earth, and leaves. In the morning one little Pitcher was placed as a scout on the bridge to signal our arrival. Once we were on the river path, the three biggest Pitchers leapt from the brush and chased us down the river. Two more squatters joined in the chase. At a curve in the path we both dropped into the deep hole, a perfect pitfall. When the dust settled, we looked up and saw the titan against the bright sky; he straddled the narrow hole, looked down at us, and ground his teeth together. What a terrible sound the titan made that morning. Then six heads with crossed eyes leaned over the hole and laughed, that horrible high pitched wild sound of the Pitcher brothers.

"Let's just bury 'em," said the wee brother, out of breath. The Pitchers panted and kicked dirt down on us in the hole. "Bury the fuckers with their heads stickin' out."

"Fuck 'em," said the titan.

"No, let's strip 'em," said a bigger Pitcher. He covered his mouth when he shouted, to hide the black holes in his front teeth. "Nettles, let's dump 'em in the lake."

"Badtize 'em, badtize 'em," the brothers chanted.

"Hey, come on you guys, you know us," I said with a hand gesture to the faces over the hole. "We didn't do nothing, so let us out of here."

"Fuck 'em," said the titan.

"You sonnofabitches. . . . " Frog lost his voice and tried once more. "Shit, goddamit, you sonnofabitches, open this hole and let me out of here."

"Throw it up," said the Nettles.

"Throw what up?" we asked and pleaded with our hands.

"Throw it up," he said and ground his teeth.

"Throw what. . . . " The Pitchers kicked dirt down the hole, into my mouth, and then they stumbled around in wild laughter, a wild dance.

"Shit," I said and spit earth. We knew what to throw up, but protested as long as possible, hoping that what we would throw up might spare us a beating, or even worse, baptismal ceremonies in Green Lake.

"Throw it up," screamed the wee brother.

"My uncle is a cop and he gave me this knife," said Frog. He held his hunting knife over his head and lost his voice over every other word.

"Throw it up, assholes, throw it up like we said," said another Pitcher. He kicked more dirt down the hole. We covered our head with our hands.

"My brother in the army sent me this watch," I boasted.

"What brother?" asked Frog.

"What brother, he says, the same brother as your uncle the cop, you idiot. Give up your goddamn hunting knife," I said to Frog. "Hey, Nettles, how about it, let me keep the watch, just the watch."

"Throw it up."

"Shit." We threw up our hunting knives, my watch, billfolds, coins, rings, belts, sacred stones, and a pair of pigskin climbing gloves. We even turned our pockets inside out.

"Everything," said Mean Nettles. The Pitchers grabbed everything and ran down the river path fighting over the booty. The titan straddled the hole once more and ground his teeth. Then he unbottoned his pants, pulled out his giant pe-nis, and urinated on our heads. We blocked the titan piss with our hands as best we could. We were soused with titan urine and sickened by the stench.

When the titan left we dug our way out of the hole and ran to the river; we scrubbed the urine from our hair and clothes. Frog cursed, the urine ran down his arms, and inside his shirt, when he raised his hands. We had tormented the titan and got caught, but we were convinced that with careful planning we could outwit him and his legion of cross-eyed squatters. We would be pirates and decided to plunder his dockyard once more and capture his sailboat. "No one pisses on me and gets away with it," said Frog.

Mean Nettles finished his sailboat several weeks later. The Pitcher brothers and other squatters cheered when he took her on a maiden voyage around Green Lake. We hide in the moist brush. We planned to capture the sailboat about noon the next day, sail back and forth across the lake, until the titan was too tired to chase us on shore, and then, when he was near exhaustion, we would run her ashore and punch her drums.

Perfect, he performed according to our master plan and was too tired to run to the other side of Green Lake. He was out of breath; his shouts and curses were impotent over the chartreuse water. We were sure he would never swim in that water, but twice he he almost caught us near shore, once when the sail was loose. We had never sailed before and learned, as the best pirates would, under way; we reefed at a turn on one side of the lake and almost capsized. The second time we hit a doldrum with a small board to paddle a drum sailboat into deeper water. We shouted at him as he ran back and forth around the lake. When we cursed his mother and his birth as a squatter, he retreated to summon the other squatters. We had the sailboat and nothing more to lose at Green Lake.

We ran the sailboat ashore as we had planned. Rather than running to the bridge and the security of home, we decided to climb the box elder trees near the river; that was a serious blunder. We were at the top of the trees when we heard the brothers with the crossed eyes on the river path below. We were certain that the titan and the brothers would pursue us deeper in the woods, higher on the river. We were crows perched at the top of the trees. I held my breath, and laughter, as the brothers pounded in the thick brush below, back and forth, on both sides of the river path.

The Pitchers beat the brush and shouted at the river and the trees that we would be baptized in Green Lake. They had not seen the crows, but we heard them chant on the path and threaten to whip the bottoms of our feet, drive soft sumac stakes into our armpits, pound shit in our mouths, and ears, and burn our eyelashes.

We watched from the top of the box elders; the breeze turned the high limbs in the afternoon sunlight. The katydids sounded, the leaves waved, and my right foot was asleep. I dreamed we soared as crows, or eagles, rubbed my wings against the leaves, and sent my eyes above the trees to see danger on the river path. My shadow, wings spread wide, danced between the demons. I turned, descended, and tried to shit on the titan.

Mean Nettles was a silent squatter, but we were soon to discover that he was not stupid at the river. The Pitcher brothers searched deep in the woods, and the titan walked down the river path in search of signs of our escape; he was a wise tracker. He stopped right under us on the path and examined the scuff marks on the soft bark of the box elder trees. Then he shouted to the others, and with their hunting knives, which had once been ours, the brothers chopped down our trees. The crow in me reached into flight but the tree cracked and swung to the ground. The brothers grabbed us on the ground. I was beaten and kicked until I felt as numb, my wings were broken, but never a dead crow.

The wee brother spat at us when our hands were tied behind our backs. With ropes around our necks we were led like leashed animals to the dockyard; the titan told us we would be convicted of piracy by a jury. He smoked several cigarettes and drank from a jar. He held a trial to find us guilty of stealing his sailboat. Point by point, the titan listed the evidence against us. Naturally, we denied everything at first.

"Mistaken identity," said Frog.

"We've been in the trees since dawn," I pleaded.

"Liars," said the titan.

"Have you lost your sense of humor?" We pleaded in the name of humor and then decided the best course of survival was confession, at the mercy of the squatter jury.

"Guilty, fuck 'em," said the brothers. "Guilty as shit." The titan ground his teeth and then sentenced us to be stripped, whipped with leather, and banished to an island in the river for the rest of our lives.

We were embarrassed to be stripped because we had no more than a dozen dark pubic hairs to show. We were whipped and that hurt, each brother took a turn with the leather. The leather burned, but my stepfather had been meaner than the titan. Banishment on the island was much better than being baptized in Green Lake. We were transported to the island on a raft and left there naked with our hands and feet tied to trees.

The late afternoon was hot and humid. Blackflies bit the top of my head. The demon river mosquitoes, bloated with too much blood, rolled over on our shoulders, arms, back, and dropped from our bodies into the moist thick grass. The mosquitoes were grounded on our blood and crawled back to their ponds.

Hours later, at dusk, we were able to loosen the ropes. We swam down the other side of the river, out of sight of the titan, and came ashore below the bridge. The cool dark water soothed the welts and mosquito bites on our bodies. Naked, we ran home through the alleys. We were pirates, and the sailboat was an adventure, but we needed to be punished and tortured by the titan. We would never leave him alone as a squatter near the river. He owned a lake we had discovered. Rusty, my dog, was waiting for me in the basement. We would be crows, cursed by the titan, and we were praised for our courage as little people.

May 1949: The Trickster and Libertina

▬▬▬▬▬▬▬▬▬▬▬▬ *T*ribal tricksters arise in imagination, create the earth, chance, praise, impermanence, humorous encounters, and totems, and liberate the mind in
their stories. The cranes endure these creations, these interior
landscapes, and turn their voices to the seasons, the remembered seasons.

My tricksters are tender on the wild rise in dreams, memories, myths, and metaphors now, and hold their chances
over the wicked seams in ecclesiae. The best stories are survival trickeries on the borders, marcescent blues on the margins, on the colonial curbs; the rest would be simulations.

Erdupps MacChurbbs is a remembered trickster on the
margins; more than inverse benevolence, heroic separations,
representations, and measures of atoned realities, he is a cre-
ator; she is a crane, a man, a woman, a shaman, a clerical
beast in seven seasons, a consumer with no providence, and
wild words, words erased in most translations. Erdupps created me on his rise, the rise in the rough; she became my solace near the burned meadows, down to the printed words in
the concrete cities. She has me in his stories.

Tribal tricksters, benign demons, and woodland atomies
of praise and pleasure, arose in my imagination that year of
silence in the third grade and became stories, metaphors on
the borders, certain names with real stature. Tricksters were
my preparation for one more year in the third grade. The best
world moved in stories at my desk that first year in silence,
and then the crane arose in me and we celebrated tricksters
on the margins. My dreams became stories; tricksters touched
me at the windows, and tricksters overturned boredom,
monotheism, coarse repetitions in the classroom, and lured

me to the river. My tricksters raised me in imagination, and we were remembered in stories; we were wild, wild on the ice, wild banners on a winter bus at night in the cities.

These tricksters and woodland atomies marched with me in the service and held me awake with humor as a military guard. The tricksters sat with me in stories, wavered with me in baronial museums, held me wild in ornamental grammars and untamed in heroic causes. Tricksters eased the pain in stories: when my elbow cracked on a stone, and a rope burned me to the wrist bone, when a relative died. Stories were told to measure lines and liberate my mind at school, at cafeterias, at the court house on probation, on road marches in the military, on the interstate, and at banks. The trickster has been a gambler, a priest, a translator, a poet, and a lover in some stories; once we were gunfighters.

Frog shot between my legs in a fast draw gunfight on a dusty rural road. The bullet ricocheted and wounded me in the lower lip. The blood ran down my chin and neck; my blood sacrifice dried on the way home that afternoon. The lead bullet, flattened on one side, became a talisman that would protect me in other wars. Other wounds would be healed in stories.

The tricksters were with me in stories, and we remembered how to turn pain and horror into humor, how to distract the river mermen with language games and contradictions. Evangelists wounded our imagination and demanded our best humor, renunciation on the run; the tricksters and our stories liberated the mind. When those wicked warlocks promised the new world, the newer, and then the late world, their objective complements were overturned by woodland tricksters.

Frog built a fort with uneven boards and we watched the weather from there: the cut of the sun through a crack near the peak, the rain on a chicken house at the side, and the movement of our enemies in the alley behind the garage. The world buzzed around me in stories, the sound of animals, beasts, and insects. The woodland turned on the wind, the ancient trees creaked in the beams, the joists, and the shiplap siding; the moans that haunted the wood enlivened our stories. The woodland tricksters came to me that year under a velvet throw in the loft of a garage.

Erdupps MacChurbbs leaped from the pine boards and walked across the red velvet throw. His rise in the rough was a game, a language game, his introduction a lecture. MacChurbbs said, "We have been traveling together in dreams for a long time, and now we are one and know our names as little people. You are me, and I am you. You have become a little person and I have become you." He knitted his fingers, little hands, and bowed several times, the gestures of a trickster. He mocked me and terminal believers, those who believe in one vision of the world and hear no humor in the corner.

"But I am not a little person," I demanded and moved my hands and toes to validate the great space between them. He would mock me that summer in the loft but we were not the same.

"You are a little person when you free yourself from the customs of civilized measurements," said MacChurbbs. He extended his arms and told me that tricksters were without measure in stories. "You are so big, and so little at the same time. You have learned only one way to measure our stature in the world. Little people disappear when civilization and terminal believers surround them. Imagination and humor expire and people grow too big for their eyes when they seek cultural perfection and permanence from the past. Civilization is a burnished skull to those who will never know the space between dreams. I will show you now." He stood on my shoulder with his head cocked right in front of my left eye. "We are flowers and birds," he declared, a modest examen. "Sometimes we are numbers but now I am in your eye and you are in mine, and I see you back again as a little person. I will disappear when you think about what you will be in the future, by the measures of the past. What will you be when you grow up?"

"Nothing, just me."

"What civilized attention will you demand from the world?"

"Nothing, just me."

"Who will you be in the future?"

"Nothing, just me."

"Nothing?"

"A famous writer, then."

"Nothing then," said the trickster. Erdupps MacChurbbs snapped into late dust; in an instant he had vanished. I searched the velvet throw, patted the folds, and called his name. My movements were huge, mechanical; my hands were numbers, massive and mistaken on the throw. The trickster was gone. I had been tricked that afternoon in the garage, tricked by my own stories; I laughed at myself, stupid and isolated. Who cares what I would be? I said, nervous, and lost in the folds. I will be nothing then, no matter what my name becomes in stories.

I leaned back on the boards in the fort and changed my mind once more. The window at the peak was open, and on the warm breeze pollen, great flowers of dust, floated through the pillars of sunlight. I was on dust when a dragonfly hovered at the opening of the window. Her shadow reached to the boards, uneven, folded over the craters in the wood. Then the dragonfly entered the garage, closer to her wild shadow. My warm wings spread and moved with her over time and space. The garage turned with no shadows, my eyes marbled the light in greens and violets.

MacChurbbs was there with other little people, in a spiral a hundred times my size. He and the others turned in place, compounded in pillars of sunlight. My wings bounced, huge shadows waved over the boards.

The Right Reverend Bishop Baraga, the missionary, Old World linguist and grammarian, was there on the throw in several images. He was dressed in a scarlet gown, a black satin hat with a ragged tassle, and carried a sprig of white pine as a bookmark in his *Dictionary of the Otchipwe Language*.

We worried that people who carried books would be lone-some, but here we are associated with the same words.

"There are so many of you here." I tried to blink away the many images of his stern white face in the garage. "Which one of you is the real you?"

"The one you see," said the missionary.

"But I see you everywhere."

"Then you must be everyone to see me everywhere."

"Did you come through the window?"

"Yes, always through the windows in this new world." Bishop Baraga moved over the throw with his right elbow in one hand. He chanted, "I am burdened you see, see, see, with five glorious centuries of terminal believers in celibacy and the virgin birth, and I am not able to pass through time and cross common thresholds. My life is waiting at the edge of time in the past. I can move as a spirit, spirit, spirit, through open windows."

"But you could fly over the thresholds."

"Only windows."

"But why?"

"Thresholds are the wilderness, demon fires."

"So, would you burn up if you crossed?"

"No, my spirit, the internal fires would go out."

"So, why do you carry that white pine?"

"Bald eagles always have a fresh sprig in their nests."

"So, your nest is in a book?"

"The better nests," said Bishop Baraga.

"Never the better, better, best," mocked Erdupps Mac-Churbbs. The wild trickster bounced on the throw, a hundred tricksters in my vision as a dragonfly. He returned with a dark and beautiful woman; she was dressed in white linen and leathers. Her black hair was plaited with silver and tur-quoise beads. Sophia Libertina wore gold rings and tiny bells on her fingers; her skin was moist.

MacChurbbs said she cornered him in the mountains where he had gone to meditate and to seek the mysteries of translation. She told him that men overturn the world with translations because they cannot bear children, because they cannot tolerate their own impermanence, because they have not learned how to listen to animals. I could understand animals, but the problems of translation did not interest me at the time. The trickster listened with his head cocked and then heaved his maw; he became a bear. Libertina touched me; she pressed her hands on my face, moved her fingers and rang the tiny bells; she was warm and clean in the sunlight.

"Famous writers spend too much time alone with their style, carving their experiences with the past," said the trickster. MacChurbbs rubbed his black shoulders on the boards. "No one has ever come alive in blank verse, or as an objective complement," he said and leaped to the rafters. He poised there with one eye closed. "Love and passion are never left to dull men who create histories from their collection of tame words, or from their grammars. Some people put things together, and others take things apart, but tricksters and little people float between words and dreams. Maybe that was seams."

My shadows gathered on the throw. The little people in the loft came back to my vision one by one in a glance of light from the window at the end of the garage. I leaned on my elbows over the velvet and listened to the trickster and the missionary. Bishop Baraga moved his thick eyebrows higher, a divine gesture, and told me that tricksters were comic, even tricked by their own humor. Tricksters are moored in language games, in their own contradictions, he said, an instance when passion enlivens reason, and when reason holds an animal by the tail.

MacChurbbs leaned over the boards in a beam of light and wigwagged his tail but there were no shadows on the throw. "Grab hold of this tail," said the trickster. He searched the folds in the velvet for his shadow. "Tricksters are shadows, the bones of contention between terminal believers, between men and women, dogs and cats, night and day, up and down, words and then silence."

"Men contend, women are tricksters," said Libertina.

"Tricksters tell fathers they are sons, criminals they are victims, men they must be women, saints they are sinners, and he hides shadows on the run," said the trickster.

Bishop Baraga signed a shadow cross over the throw. We held hands and danced on the boards in the fort, down the narrow rafters, and soared home in the last sunlight. Mac-Churbbs, Libertina, and Baraga have been with me in dreams since that afternoon in the garage. I would remember to leave a window open for those who cannot cross thresholds, for those who hold their shadows too close to the internal fires.

Frog waved me down from the loft and closed the garage doors. The sun was low behind the thin leaves on the birch. I heard the sound of finger bells in the alley, on my way home to dinner. I climbed through a basement window; later, the tricksters held their distance in the dark.

July 1950: Masturbation Papers

The Minnesota National Guard issued new uniforms and paid their defenders of freedom once a month. I was sixteen years old and lied about my age to enlist as a private in a field artillery battalion, a proud uniformed soldier between the wars.

I learned how to march and count cadence, turn about on command, how to order arms, parade rest, and salute with several hundred other men, and how to operate a carbine, disassemble machine guns and other weapons, one night a week at the Minneapolis Armory.

We marched behind the lines on the hardwood, our sounds echoed under the dome; lonesome men leered over the rails in the balconies. I was a mixedblood featherweight, more trickster than warrior, more earnest than comic; the headband in my helmet liner rested on my ears. Six months later we were prepared for intensive summer war games at Fort Ripley near Little Falls, Minnesota.

The first invitation to a military uniform, seven years earlier, was my Sam Browne belt. Since then my essential uniforms have included those issued by the military, a movie theater, a drug store, a meat company, a hospital, and universities; most borders were easier to cross in the right uniform. I padded my helmet, polished my boots, and preened in oversized fatigues that summer of the war games.

Sunday morning, our second day of training, deer flies bounced on the warm canvas inside the tent; we lazed, a precise martial back-formation, but our pleasures were violated by the rude voice of the first sergeant over the loudspeakers. Even worse, he called my name more than once. "Private

Vizenor, Vizenor, Vizenor, get your ass to the orderly room on the double."

"Private Vizenor reporting," I said and saluted the sergeant. I was there on the double in the company command tent, my boots were untied, trousers unbloused, and my shirt was loose.

"At ease, soldier," said the sergeant with practiced disdain. He looked down and moved several folders on his desk. "I have been going through your service file, soldier, and I have not found your masturbation papers."

"My what, sir?"

"Your masturbation papers, soldier."

"Sorry sir, but. . . . "

"But nothing, soldier, get your sweet ass over to headquarters and get your masturbation papers right now," said the sergeant. He waved a folder at me. "On the double, soldier."

"Yes, sir." I was unstudied in masturbation, and that particular noun was not in my language then; the associated documents seemed to be critical at the time. I tied my boots and hurried to the headquarters tent, worried that someone would discover my age. I was determined to be an honorable soldier in the Minnesota National Guard.

"Private Vizenor, sir, reporting for my masturbation papers," I told the sergeant at the headquarters company. He frowned and returned my salute. Black flies circled his hands and a sugar donut on his desk.

"Where the hell have you been, soldier? Your masturbation papers are at the command post. Look smart and get your skinny ass up there," he said. His voice was strained, histrionic, an obtuse act that was directed by my ignorance. "Ask for the colonel, he's got your papers."

"Yes, sir." My last salute disturbed the black flies on the donut. The cozenage ended with the sergeants; the colonel, or base commander, and his aide-de-camp, were not aware of the wild masturbation papers chase.

"Private Vizenor, sir, requests permission to see the colonel, sir." I was nervous and held my salute. The blond captain was casual; he leaned back in his chair, smiled, and studied me. I should have noticed his mood, that he was not prepared, as the sergeants were, to see me.

"At ease, soldier," he said and returned my salute. "What could be so urgent that you must see the base commander, soldier?" The captain leaned forward in his chair and waited for my response.

"My masturbation papers, sir."

"Your what?"

"My masturbation papers, sir." I raised my voice the second time to avoid the appearance of being uncertain, or evasive. "My service file is not complete, sir."

"Who sent you here?"

"My company sergeant, sir."

"I think the colonel will want to talk with you about this, soldier. Just a minute," said the captain. He cranked a field telephone and talked to the base commander. Later, the colonel entered the command tent. I imagined him to be more eminent, but he was mean and distant; he could have been a probation officer. I stood at attention and saluted. He gestured with his nubby swagger stick. His brow was marked with shallow lines.

"Private Vizenor, sir, reporting for my masturbation papers," I said a second time in a loud voice. I was certain that my papers were at hand and the problem would be resolved.

"Where did you lose your papers, soldier?"

"I don't know, sir, I don't remember ever having them."

"Soldier, do you know what masturbation means?"

"No, sir."

"Then how can you find your papers?"

"I don't know, sir."

"Have you ever used the word masturbation?"

"No, sir."

"Soldier, do you know what onanism means?"

"No, sir."

"Jacking off?"

"What?"

"Do you know what jacking off means?"

"Yes, sir." I was hesitant and embarrassed, to be sure, encumbered in a military uniform. I was a soldier, and the escape distances were closed in the summer war games.

The captain held back his laughter; he turned his head to the side and covered his mouth with one hand. The colonel could have been debauched; instead, he touched me on the shoulder, disabused me of the inane search, and taught me a new word at the same time.

"Masturbation means the same thing, soldier," said the colonel. "You can pick up your jacking off papers from your company sergeant, and you can tell him that I sent you."

"Yes, sir."

"Hang in there, soldier."

"Yes, sir."

"Do you know what I mean, soldier?"

"Yes, sir."

"Carry on then."

"Yes, sir."

"How old are you, soldier?"

"Eighteen," I said with assurance.

"Old enough," said the captain. "This enlisted man has completed with distinction his papers," he wrote to the sergeants. The note was signed by the aide-de-camp.

The sergeants were not pleased with me when they learned that the colonel knew about their scheme, that they had sent me in search of my masturbation papers. My company sergeant ordered me to clean the urinals for three days as punishment. I had earned the dubious distinction of being the most credulous survivor because the masturbation paper chase had been dormant for several years.

June 1951: One More Good Home

~~~~~~~~~~~~~~~~~~~~~ *E*lmer Petesch, the last of my stepfathers, returned home from work on schedule one summer night and found a short departure and disunion note from his wife of eight years. My mother was inspired by a new man who once bought me two bacon, lettuce, and tomato sandwiches. He could have been in movies; his voice was rich and sensuous, and he had a winsome manner.

LaVerne wrote to her husband that she would never come back; she had moved to a warmer climate and a better life that very afternoon. The note was concise, written with care, in a poised cursive hand, as she would a sentimental message on a birthday card, and placed in the center of the kitchen table. The gesture was petulant and sarcastic because her husband prepared most of our meals.

I came home from school earlier than usual that afternoon. The scent of perfume warmed me at the back door; that special essence was associated with celebrations. Once, in the eighth grade, I borrowed that same perfume to touch a card on Saint Valentine's Day; my mother traced the scent, found the card attached to a shoebox loaded with candy hearts, and read outloud my first love letter to a secret sweetheart.

My mother was in the bathroom blotting her lips with a tissue. She wore her best clothes and jewelry, and her suitcase was near the front door. I asked her what happened, "where are you going?" She stared into the bathroom mirror and plucked hairs from her eyebrows. LaVerne was tall, handsome, and nervous.

"California," she said. Her breath steamed on the mirror.

"Who lives out there?"

"Nobody," she said from the side of her mouth.

"Why you going then?"

"Jerry, I'm leaving for good."

"Why?" I pretended to be surprised.

"I'm leaving Elmer."

"Are you going with someone?"

"Do you want to come along?"

"Where would we go?" I had no interest in going anywhere, but she was worried so we talked more about me. I was at home, a better home than fosterage, and there were no good reasons for me to leave.

"California," she said to the mirror.

"No," I said to the doorjamb.

"Why not?" My mother would pursue conversations to resolve her worries, but she hesitated the closer we came to maternal responsibilities. Her invitation was insincere; she would have been gone before school ended at the regular time.

"Because, my friends are here."

"I'll send you postcards," she promised.

"Thanks, mother."

"I'm going to be late," she said as she put on her shoes. When she turned one last time at the door, there were tears in her eyes. "I wish you could come with me."

"You'll be all right," I assured her with a wave and a sudden smile. My mother chose to be lonesome in the movies, in her marriage, even in her own home. The scent of her sweet perfume lingered in the bathroom for several weeks.

LaVerne said she was leaving him with the mortgage, a secondhand piano, most of the modest wedding presents, and as a parting gesture of ironic trust and affection, she also left behind her only son. I became a mixedblood fosterling overnight; once more my home was surrendered in the wars of blood and pleasure.

Elmer had no legal responsibilities; he had not adopted me, but he was burdened to remember my mother in me. I renounced his bad memories, denied his power, and escaped, a few weeks later, from his house, his kitchen, his basement, and his garage, lonesome, hurt, and very angry.

We had just finished another boiled dinner, ring bologna, potatoes, and onions, when he struck me on the back. I was washing the dishes and talked back to him about the spilled water on the floor under the sink. In his book of manners, children would never talk back to adults, not even expressions of pain over punishment. He cursed me over the sink because of my mother, and then he hit me again. I left his house in silence, without a word of pain, determined never to return.

Elmer was alone in his house for four days with his memories of my mother. He punished himself with alcohol, and then on the fifth day he started to search for me. He left considerate messages with some of my friends and selected neighbors, that he wanted me to return home; he said our home, but that word had lost value in my survival language. I avoided his rapprochement and peddled my own stories to friends and their parents: stories about his violence to me and my mother, stories that would gain an advantage in the fosterage wars. My mother mismeasured his sentiments because he was older; his emotional distance was cruel, and he blustered at times, but he was not a violent man. He was much wiser in the material world, a pragmatist with machines; but he lost power when he turned, as a last resort, to passion and adoration.

Frog invited me to stay at his house. I was pleased because his father told great stories about his adventures in the wilderness, about the time he was shot in the leg in a gunfight at a mining camp in the mountains, and he had a scar, and the gun, to prove the wound, and how he ran bootleg corn whiskey down on rural roads from North Dakota. He told us stories in the basement, in the car, and in the garage, his sacred territories, and winked at us when his wife complained. We were his best listeners and eager conspirators in his great boyhood memories. I pretended he was my father for a time.

Elmer found me in the backyard. I was playing basketball when he drove down the alley and stopped by the garage. I told him to leave me alone. "I will never listen to you again," I said and passed the ball. Frog dribbled in a circle and pretended that my stepfather was not there.

"Let's just talk it over," said Elmer. I refused to answer him, or even gesture in his direction. Later, he told my friends that he would return the next night to talk with me again. He was defensive, and his appeals to me gave me a sense of personal power.

"Here he comes," someone shouted from behind the garage. Elmer met me in the alley on the sixth night. Frog and several other friends were there with me. I told him to listen to my conditions. Elmer said he would stand across the alley, and he agreed that we would listen to each other without interruptions. He was the first to speak that night.

"I am very sorry, please believe me," he said from behind his car on the other side of the alley. "I know you want to be with your friends now, but I want you to know how sorry I am for taking your mother out on you. I have been very lonely since you left and I know it was wrong to hit you. It was not your fault, but sometimes we hurt the people we love the most. You know what I mean?

"I want you to come back home. We need each other now. I have never had a good home, and you have never had a good home either, now we need to make one together."

Elmer cried. Tears ran down his fat cheeks. He took his glasses off and pleaded to me with his stout hands. I was moved and wanted to reach out to him, but I had been hurt too many times in the past to yield so easily to tears and promises. My thoughts were overburdened with his violence and his weakness. He cried on one side of the alley, and we were silent on the other side; embarrassed to watch a mean, bald man break down with a stained handkerchief.

"I wish I could take back all the times I have hurt you," he said and dried his eyes. "Leaving home was the best thing for you to do, and I have no right to expect you to trust me now and come back home, but I do want you to believe me this time." He blew his nose and his voice was a normal tone.

"I don't believe you," I said in a cold tone of voice. "You have said all those things before, when I was home. Go take it out on my mother, not me. Go away." I must have sneered too much because my friends were troubled by my mood and manner.

"Can we talk tomorrow again?"

"Maybe." I would bear the moment but never surrender to tears and sentiments. Frog was there, my best friend, and his father was mine that night; he encouraged me to return home.

Elmer faced not only my best friends the next night, but their parents and other neighbors who had learned from gossip about such unusual family negotiations in the alley. He parked near the garage as he had the two previous nights, and stood on the other side of the alley. He wore a starched white shirt, brown suit trousers, and black dress shoes. The women stood behind their children with their arms folded over their breasts. The men stood in the shadows of open garage doors; some chewed toothpicks and looked down at the cement. I was silent; the audience was tense. My mother would have been humiliated by the tableau in the alley; she lacked the courage to face an audience, and she missed the best movie scene of the season.

"I will come every night to tell you I want you to come home, but not the way it used to be. I promise you, and you have your friends here listening, that I will never again mistreat you," he said with his hands in his pockets. He was sincere, and eager to taste his promises in public; he was more at ease in the alley, a rural place he must have trusted that night. "We both need a good home, please come back home."

"Let me think about it," I said and turned to my friends. Neighbors and friends looked at each other in silence, husbands and wives walked home with their children between them. Screen doors banged closed and lights were turned on in kitchens and bathrooms. I was outside, alone. The trees were hushed, the leaves were moist. The first fireflies blinked in the dark grass. My hands were clenched, my fingers swollen. No one called my name that night.

Elmer was home; his car was parked near the house.

The night air was blue, and shadows bounced under the chokecherry tree in the back yard. I circled the house and saw him in his overstuffed chair, asleep with a western novel. I could hear him snore, a primal sound at the windows. I waited in silence near the front door. Mosquitoes landed on my shoulders, out of reach, but I was not ready to open the screen door and return home.

I walked toward the river later that night, down the alleys, between houses to avoid the police, and a possible curfew violation. I bought fresh warm sweet rolls from the back door of a local bakery and ate them on the way. I caught the sweet centers in my hand. I was loose, alone, and free that night, a dubious pleasure without a home. I measured my uneven breath with the river, held summer over the thick dark water, and waved moon slivers to tame the shore. I made a bed under the bridge. Overhead demons thundered on the seams, and the animals of the night lettered their escape distances. The tricksters soared in magical flight over the woodland, and the crane must have sounded in my dream that night.

I returned home the next morning when my stepfather was at work. The air hummed at the back door, the floors creaked and the halls cracked with excitement. I walked through the house and touched handles, cabinets, and furniture, to be sure there was a home there. I imagined my mother in the bathroom, lipstick prints remained in the basket, and my stepfather at the stove, over cabbage steam, over me at the sink. I forgave them both and their problems ended in me.

Elmer would be home on schedule for dinner. I cleaned the house, emptied the baskets and trash, washed the dishes, cut the grass, and baked a blueberry pie, his favorite, and then waited on the front steps for him to return. He parked the car and smiled when he noticed the grass, smelled the pie. Without a word he took me by the hand, pulled me from the steps, and embraced me. We both cried and never remembered my mother in our conversations.

At last, he was a very compassionate man; his caution was connected to past memories and experiences. He learned to show his love in new ways. I believed the promises he made to me in the alley. I trusted him once more, and learned to share his gentle humor. My trust in him, and his courage to trust me, a mixedblood adolescent son left over from a bum marriage, made me a better person.

We decided to share the house, to live together, no hard rules. He paid me an allowance to maintain the house. I would never be his son, and he would never be my father, we agreed; we would be brothers and friends at the same time. We had a great time together for about five months and then he died in an accident.

December 1951: Death by Elevator

━━━━━━━━━━━━━━━━━━━Elmer Petesch asked me if he
could work at the millworking company on Christmas Eve.
He explained that a new employee, a young man with two
children, had been scheduled to tend the boilers that night. I
agreed, and said we would have our celebration when he returned at midnight. We ate an early dinner at the kitchen
table; he packed a sandwich and told nostalgic stories about
his brothers and cousins at the farm on the holidays.

Elmer must have banked the fires when he first arrived at
the mill; then he might have read a few pages from a western
novel, or he might have watched the fires and remembered
other holidays. He was nostalgic that night. On the hour he
would begin the watch and turn the key in the security clocks
at numerous locations in the buildings. He used a flashlight,
the route was as familiar as the back of his hand. One of the
mill mongrels followed him through the machines, stacks of
window frames and molding. He turned the clocks in a prescribed pattern; first floor end to end and then the stairs to the
second floor. He turned the last clocks on the third floor,
walked down to the second floor and decided to take the
open industrial elevator to the basement. He flashed his light
on the elevator button and noticed that both the floor and
safety gates were raised. The elevator should have been
there, the safety gate would not have been raised otherwise;
but when he stepped under the gates he tumbled to the bottom and crushed his pelvis. The safety gate mechanism had
been interrupted by an impatient workman at the end of the
day; the elevator was on the third floor.

Elmer was determined to live. He pulled himself out of
the pit, hand over hand, and slithered on the cold floor to a

pushcart; with his hands over the side he pushed the cart to the nearest security clock, but he could not reach high enough to insert the key. The security inspectors would be summoned on the hour that the clocks had been interrupted or not turned. He was found several hours later.

I washed the dishes and then watched a holiday program on our black and white television, a small table model that my mother left behind. She owned the first set on the block, a distinction that raised our stature, but she never watched much television then. The programs ended, even the test pattern was out; he had not called and it was past midnight. I was insecure when there was no answer at the mill. I waited and worried in his chair; he chewed snuff and the scent surrounded me.

Christmas, early in the morning, the doctor called and asked for my mother; then he told me about the accident. Elmer was in critical condition with a crushed pelvis and internal injuries. I telephoned several relatives in both families and then hurried to the hospital. Someone would be able to locate my mother.

Elmer was on his back, wired to a wooden brace. He smiled, touched my hand, but he was pale, broken, and bloated; the perspiration on his arms and in the black hair on his chest held the natural light at dawn. No one ever heard him complain about pain. The first thing he told me was not to inform my mother that he was in the hospital. I lied at his bedside; he must have known she would learn about the accident from her relatives. He told the nurses to leave his black bluchers and white socks near the bed, close at hand. Elmer trusted me once more; he trusted me with his wallet, black, thick, and worn on the corners, and his car keys; he told me to cash his last check and how to pay the mortgage and utilities, rare responsibilities at seventeen with a man who had been double-crossed by my mother.

I opened a savings account at the Camden State Bank that morning with his cash and a payroll check from the A. T. Rydell Company, plus a small holiday bonus. The bank president was curious and praised my mature prudence; later, he would become my protector.

My mother called that night. I told her the truth, how critical his condition was, but tried to dissuade her from returning. More determined than ever, she demanded that money be wired to her for travel. I stood alone on paternal ground, my honor, and refused to spend his wages to bring her back from Los Angeles. Our silent wars were declared in that conversation, the protracted hostilities worsened, and lasted more than a decade; the revisions have not ended.

Early in the morning two days later the doctor called to tell me that my "daddy" had died from massive internal injuries. I was calm at first, the relatives were notified, and then the loss of my best friend was too much to bear. I was overcome for hours, and hours, and the loss overcomes me now in these words about his death. We were so close those last five months; we survived the harsh measures of fathers, sons, and surrogates, and then our great friendship was tested by his death.

The Industrial Commission of Minnesota reported that Elmer Petesch "sustained a fatal accidental injury arising out of and in the course of his employment on December 25, 1951 while in the employ" of A. T. Rydell, Incorporated, "under a Minnesota contract of hire, at a wage of $81 per week." Under the Workmen's Compensation Law the medical and hospital expenses were paid, and a funeral allowance was provided. Six months later the Commission paid me $736 as a survivor, less $300 to H. L. Nehls for legal services. The balance of $436 was deposited in my account at the Camden State Bank.

My mother arrived by train, on her own money, later that day. They were not divorced. She would inherit the estate, and she had nowhere else to live, but my heart was turned with resentment when she moved back into our house and reproved my best friend on the day of his death. She was my mother and she weakened me with her demands, and her refusal to honor my responsibilities. I brooded and cried in the basement. My mother caused a desperate and cruel loneliness in that house; she belittled my friend and the trust we shared in her absence.

The funeral had been arranged in two days and my mother, once again, demanded the money. This time she wanted proper clothes to mourn the burial of her estranged husband of eight years. I pointed out the debts that must be paid and refused to turn over the money, no more than a few hundred dollars. She threatened me and then the bank president who would not transfer the money or close the savings account in my name. I was a minor, and she had a legal right to my account, he told me later, but she never challenged his confidence and the debts were paid as my friend had directed.

LaVerne and her mother claimed the house, the car, which had been stored in a garage, and everything in his name. Elmer had a son from a previous marriage. Milton had served in the Marine Corps. He lived with us once, when he was home on leave; my mother washed his uniforms, and then she complained that he had propositioned her over the ironing board. His mouth was heroic, and he convinced me at thirteen that alcohol and cigarettes were masculine. He was right, but not for long. Milton honored my responsibilities to his father, and he tried to reason with my mother, but in the end he hired a lawyer to represent his legal interests. LaVerne had abandoned her husband and now she would possess the entire estate.

Elmer would be punished by my mother even at the grave; he was buried near the house in the cemetery across the street. She told his best friends to stay away from the burial, and she told me that my friends, most of whom were in the eleventh grade, would not be allowed at the funeral or the reception at the house. My emotions were run down as punishment. I organized my friends with stories about my mother; even more students attended the funeral. Later, my school friends gathered in front of the house and waited to see who would attend the reception.

LaVerne and her mother turned the blinds, worried at the windows. We waited more than an hour on the sidewalk that cold afternoon; but no one came by to comfort the widow. Their bitter sandwiches, and wicked remembrance, were wasted in a cold, cold house.

I stayed with my friends that afternoon; later, on my return to the house, the backdoor, which had never been locked, not even at night, was bolted from the inside. I went around to the front door and discovered that my mother had changed the locks, and that my clothes were on the front steps in a plain brown box. Once more that wild moment of abandonment was at hand, but there was some humor in that cold moment. I was sure that my personal properties could not be contained in a single box. I smiled and pretended to plead with my mother who was at the window. "There must be more than this, my shirts, my socks," but she turned the blinds in silence.

I moved in with a friend who lived a block away. He was a year older, in his senior year, and lived with an uncle because his mother had vanished when he was a child. His uncle was an automobile mechanic, disciplined, ethical, religious, and he never asked me once to explain my urgent need for a place to live. He was generous and good-natured. I was certain he would have taken me in for any length of time.

I returned to the house the next afternoon to collect my electronic equipment and other things in the basement that my mother had neglected to pack on the front steps. My interest in electronics started with a crystal set, the same as most boys. I built my own superheterodyne radio receiver from drawings and was amazed that it worked at first power. I had declared a basement radio repair business at age fifteen with my knowledge of basic electronics and new testing equipment. The printer who accepted my order for business cards handed me my first official repair job because he was so impressed with my ambition. The radio needed to be cleaned, the tuner plates were shorted with lint, nothing more, and he was even more impressed that the repairs were free. In return, he did not charge me for my first business cards: Jerry's Radio Repair Service.

I removed a basement window to enter my business because the doors were locked. LaVerne and her mother were in the kitchen, their voices were at a great distance. I heard my mother pound a cigarette butt into an ashtray on the table. I gathered my equipment, tubes, and electronic parts into boxes. I had built a special work bench; it would be left behind with chassis, motors, and heavier parts. I threw the last of my business cards into the furnace.

They must have heard me close the furnace door, or else my mother sensed my presence, because they shouted at me and threatened to summon the police. I went upstairs to call my aunt when my mother told the police there was an emergency. She described me as a wild criminal with a gun, "You must arrest him before he hurts someone." She told the police that I had threatened her in her hour of mourning for her dead husband. "That boy is violent, and his friends tormented us after the funeral."

Betty Petesch, who was married to Ed the wrestler, brother of Elmer, was told not to attend the funeral. She did anyway and reminded me to call her if there was ever trouble at home. Trouble indeed, and the trouble scared me. Betty heard me say my name before my mother pulled the telephone cord out of the wall and stood there holding the wires, defiant and absurd. LaVerne and her mother stood at the door, they wanted to hold me for the police. I pushed past them and struggled out the front door, but my mother had a firm grip on the left sleeve of my winter coat. I leaned and tugged, she resisted, and the sleeve was torn loose. That was my only coat and it was a cold winter. The scene, however, was comical: my mother, dazed with anger, stood at the door with my sleeve in her hand, her breath steamed, as wild as a horse, and her mother was holding her from behind, when the police roared up to the house.

That comic moment came to a sudden end when one policeman told me to close my mouth, to get back into the house. He followed me through the door; the keys on his belt clicked as he walked. The other policeman opened a narrow notebook and prepared to record the domestic scene.

"Gerald, is that your name?"

"Yes, sir."

"Stand against the wall, now."

"I didn't do anything, nothing." I protested that nothing had happened because my mother pulled the cord out of the wall. "I didn't do it," but no one listened and there was no hope. The end was at hand, the state training school would be my new home. Social workers would have my soul in the end.

"He's a liar and a cheat and he steals cars, money from my purse, and he's got a loaded gun in the basement." LaVerne screamed at the policeman with the notebook. He seemed to listen and recorded one or two words.

"I'm in the National Guard, and that's my hunting rifle."

"I told you once, against the wall, and shut your mouth, now," said the tough one. Mention of my military service did not attract his attention. He aimed one hand at me, but his eyes never touched me when he talked.

"Yes, sir."

"He threatened my mother, and he stole our money." She continued to shout and waved her hands at me. The room was encroached with hand waves and pointers.

"Never did," I whispered to the ceiling. My mother was obsessed with fear, death, and loathing. She was wicked that winter; she sputtered her hatred, seethed, and scorned my independence and responsibilities to the man who trusted me more in five months than she had ever dared to care in seventeen years.

LaVerne and her mother shouted more and more lies about me. No one would hear my pleas of innocence. My fears were confirmed when the tough policeman ordered me to the police car. My mother was victorious, but she continued her invectives.

"Lady, that's enough," said the policeman.

"He's a criminal, no good, he'll never be any good, he should be in jail, teach him a lesson," she shouted and then folded her arms high on her chest. Her mouth was a fist, her face was twisted with rage.

"Lady, that's about enough from you."

"He's never been worth anything, never. . . . "

"You've said enough to hurt this boy," said the policeman.

"He's a criminal," she pleaded.

"I'll run you in too, lady," said the tough policeman.

"Who do you think you're talking to," she responded

"Shut up," shouted the policeman who took the notes. I was cushioned but not vindicated. My mother was stunned; her arms drooped and her mouth closed on the furies. I whistled and walked past her to the police car.

The back seat was cold. The tough policeman radioed that the scene was under control. I was worried when a radio voice asked about me, by name, and wondered how much they knew about me. I was certain that someone would remember my probation for shoplifting five years earlier.

"Where are you taking me?"

"Take it easy, kid," said the tough policeman.

"Betty Petesch, we're taking you to her house."

"My mother pulled the phone out."

"She's crazy."

"Betty's worried about you."

"I knew she would be."

"Who is this Betty Petesch?"

"She's my aunt."

"You're lucky," said the tough policeman.

"My uncle's a wrestler."

"Ed Petesch?"

"Yes, do you know him?"

"Sorry about your dad, kid."

"My mother wouldn't even let his best friends come to the funeral." My arm was cold, the sleeve had been torn away at the shoulder. Thin bits of insulation stuck to my wool shirt. I leaned back in silence and shivered on the cold seat.

LaVerne disposed of my electronic equipment, radio tubes, parts, and my work bench. She sold the car, the house, the furniture, and tried to end the memories of that time in a bungalow near the cemetery, but she never claimed my savings account at the bank. My mother made arrangements for me to live in a foster home, once more, and then she returned to California. Six months later, however, at the end of my junior year in high school, she had not paid one cent for my care. The foster family held my clothes and meager properties until they were paid, and told me to move out at the same time. This was the first time, and the last, that my fosterage became a bad debt.

I rented a room that summer on Willow Street, near the intersection of Penn and Plymouth in north Minneapolis, and worked as a painter to reclaim my clothes. I learned later that my mother had received monthly Social Security checks in my name as a survivor. My mother had cashed the checks but never paid for my fosterage.

The National Outdoor Advertising Company was located, at that time, on Plymouth Avenue, not far from my room. I had no natural interests in advertising, but the company was ninth on my random list of potential summer employers, west to east down the avenue. My connections were chance; my direct approach impressed the company secretary because she insisted that the president interview me. "I need work, and I expect to start at the bottom," I told him. He was tall, thin, pensive, and nostalgic about his own struggles as a youth. "I'll give you the chance," he told me and then asked, "How far down did you have in mind?"

"I could clean the floors."

"Gerald, start tomorrow, eight sharp." He bolstered my confidence when he told his secretary to prepare a time card in my name. She was pleased, she must have seen the president in me. So much depended on a time card then: identity, money, and the need to be distracted by labor. My families have arisen at unusual times, and my careers have been enlivened by chance and coincidence. I had delivered papers for two years, and later held temporary jobs as a movie usher, and a candy store stock boy. The summer my mother moved out of the house, I worked downtown as a sundries stock clerk at the Earl Partridge Company.

The National Outdoor Advertising Company opened as usual on that humid morning, and my nose was at the door, too eager to begin. I punched in, cleaned the main offices, emptied the trash, and then in the afternoon cleaned the sign storage areas. The president would check on me, engage me in conversations about my families and ambitions, once or twice a day. He was paternal, attentive to details, and he even took the time to direct my attention to seven usable nails in a mound of trash. I smiled, but never complained; the salvaged nails and other metals became an enormous pile in a few days. He promoted me to a road crew and raised my wages in my third week at the company.

I was a painter in crude practices, but not the smooth methods of my father and uncles. I retouched the rough backsides of advertisments, a one color painter on the road. The commercial artist enhanced the front of the signs, the obvious commercial announcements.

We would meet at the company early in the morning, load the truck, and then drive out of the city for an hour or two on rural roads to paint and repair signs. We traveled on new roads in different directions every day. We ate lunch in the weeds and wildflowers at the side of the road, my solace in the wide shadows of the signs. The artist drove and painted in silence; he was never very personal, but he was humorous over lunch at the roadside. He told me ironic stories, smart stories about the business, about signs and other painters, the lies of advertising, and about adventures on the road, but unlike most other men in the company, he never told stories about women. He was married, a conservative family man, and never boasted about his sexual conquests or asked me about my sexual experiences.

I lived alone that summer, worked in peace on rural roads, praised the president of my company, and remembered, with a wide brush behind the advertisements, my insecurities, past miseries, and humors. The fosterage had ended; no one haunted the loose seams in my mixedblood identities, and my memories were moved by a new sense of adventure and liberation.

September 1952: The Pink Flamingos

Superior, Wisconsin, was a petit opera once upon a time in our breach of manners and espied remembrance. I crossed the moral boundaries there and undressed for my first performance in a city of lonesome women, tired seamen, and pink flamingos.

We had learned about prostitution in stories; the debaucheries and customs were mythic variations on moral sins, prohibitions, and licentious adventures. The material connections were pictorial, carnal, pornographic, the shadow touch of women; we were aroused by the hidden, curious of the most forbidden, and motivated by what was suppressed. Besides, we could wait in the dark for hours under a bedroom window to see a naked woman.

The tricksters would have embraced our dedication to the erotic beat, but we were burdened with the lessons of missionaries, and censured by erotophobes. We assumed that our pubescence was natural, but at the same time, we worried that erotic and obscene stories might have been printed on cursed pulp; overnight, it seemed, the paper disintegrated in our hands.

Then, at a crucial moment in our adolescent pornopsies, we heard an actual address mentioned by an older student at school, the secret street address of a brothel at 314 John Street in Superior. That number was a pass to a sensual court, a demimonde in our imagination, a prime number to the real; we were counted by day in high school, and our passions and humors were chaperoned to bear the truth at night. To hold the secret location of pleasure was an adolescent measure of power.

"Yet there is nothing seductive about truth. Only the secret is seductive: the secret which circulates as the rule of the game, as an initiatory form, as a symbolic pact, which no code can resolve, no clue interpret," wrote Jean Baudrillard in *The Ecstasy of Communication*. "There is, for that matter, nothing hidden and nothing to be revealed. . . . We can wear ourselves out in materializing things, in rendering them visible, but we will never cancel the secret."

I paid my debts and earned enough money that summer to buy my first car, a 1934 Ford with running boards, mechanical brakes, and a flat windshield that cranked open. My car cost less than a hundred dollars; the eight-cylinder engine burned so much oil, about a quart to fifty miles, that I bought used drain oil by the gallon from service stations.

Candidate, one of my best friends in the eleventh grade, convinced me one weekend to test the truth of our secret, the pass number that we had venerated for more than two years. We bathed, and dressed to appear as mature as possible for the prostitutes. Candidate, who had earned his nickname because he boasted too much and laughed like a politician, crowed over his women, his wild manners on porches, in automobiles, and theaters, for more than a hundred miles, and two quarts of oil, closer to that mythic neighborhood in Superior, Wisconsin.

"No shit, at the movies?"

"Back row," he assured me and turned to the window. He waved to a crowd of boys playing baseball in the street and asked them for directions to John Street.

"314 John Street?"

"That's the number," said Candidate.

"Who do you want there?" asked the pitcher for the street team. He smiled, slapped a scuffed softball into his mitt, and snapped his wad of pink gum.

"Just a friend," I shouted out the window and squeezed the steering wheel to flex my triceps. The pitcher backed away from the car and aimed his mitt toward the west.

"Two blocks that way," he shouted the directions.

"Down and at 'em, boys," the team chanted and then they doubled over in laughter. The pitcher bounced in the street and simulated masturbation. The team laughed, and laughed at our secret.

"Fuck you too," we shouted back. I raced the engine and our voices were lost in the exhaust, and peeled rubber on bald tires over home base. We headed west and shouted out the street names.

John Street was not a red-light district, not a row of criminal brothels, but an established residential neighborhood. The great frame houses were hushed and clean; the boulevard was lined with elm trees. Here and there a lawn jockey waited at a painted curb. We counted the numbers on the doors and searched the streets for signs of prostitution: harlots, hookers, fallen women, corrupt men in their limousines, and the police. At last, we found the house, a duplex that resembled other houses on the block; painted white with black shutters, and there was a wooden swing on the front porch.

"This can't be the place." I was convinced that we had entered a proper neighborhood by chance, that the brothel was on the other end of the street, that we had been taken by trickster stories, or duped by a secret.

"Look, there, we're in the right place," said Candidate. He pointed at a man in a business suit, convinced that he was a satisfied customer. The man walked to the curb, unlocked his car, and sat there in the dark for several minutes; then he drove down the street with no headlights.

"Your grandmother could live there."

"Not mine," said Candidate.

"Your sister then," I said. Candidate punched me on the shoulder and pretended he had a sister. We drove around the block several times and then parked a few blocks from the house. We were curious, and suspicious at the same time; we hid our billfolds, rings, and watches in the car, under the dashboard. We approached the house with no identification.

Candidate peered in the window on the porch but the thick drapes were drawn. He took a deep breath and pounded on the door. We waited, and waited; he pounded once more. A boy ran down the street. Two cars parked near the end of the block. My hands sweated and my neck seemed to vibrate. Then, we heard a voice; a sweet grandmother appeared in a print dress and apron. She smiled behind the screen door.

"May I help you, boys?" she asked.

"Well, we were. . . . " Candidate hesitated, and then scratched his arms, a sign that he was very worried and anxious. He moved his shoulders and waited for the old woman to understand.

"Are you boys collecting for the paper?"

"No," said Candidate. He pressed his hands on the screen. "We were wondering if you by chance had any propositions tonight, you know what I mean?"

"Propositions?" she mocked.

"Shit," I whispered, persuaded that we were at the wrong house. We had a bad address, there was no other explanation. Candidate scratched his arms more and more. His head turned back and forth, from the street to the screen door, and then down to her feet. The old woman wore pink slippers.

"How old are you boys?"

"Twenty-five," said Candidate.

"Twenty-three," I said with my head down.

"I see," said the old woman. "Well, come in now, but be sure not to get your noses out of joint." She opened the screen door and told us to stand to the side. At last, the right house, a real madam with two new customers.

We followed her into the house, into a room where there was a wide ascending stairway right out of the movies. Candidate scratched his arms; we were both nervous. The old woman told us to sit down and wait, and to obey the rules of the house.

"What rules?"

"Cash in advance, enter by one door and leave by another," she said and then pointed at a special light. "When you see the red light, stay out of the hallway."

"Why?"

"Because," she whispered, "that means that someone is leaving who does not wish to be seen." The old woman watched me for a short time and then she left the room.

Candidate bounced his elbows on the arms of the leather chair. "The girls must come to us," he said. I nodded and picked at a blackhead in my ear. We faced the stairway and waited our turn.

"How much will it cost?"

"Five dollars," said Candidate.

"I only have three."

"You can hold hands for that."

"Propositions, who told you that word?"

"Do they come down the stairs?"

"She said from the stairway, and something about the light."

"This is it," said Candidate. He leaped out of the chair and bounded over to the stairs to meet the first woman, a big blonde with large breasts. She laughed as they walked up the stairs; a door closed and then the house was silent again; no moans, no screams, nothing but the certain sound of doors. My hands sweated and squeaked on the arms of the leather chair. The red light blinked once or twice. I closed my eyes and unbodied the house, the chair, the stairs, but the erotic was lost in an opera with no music, no imagination.

"Waiting for me?" she teased at the foot of the stairs. She posed, one arm on the balustrade, in a pink strapless prom gown. She had narrow hips, long brown hair, small breasts that pitched under the erect bodice. She smiled and waited for my response.

"Well, yes, but. . . . "

"But what?" she said in a southern accent.

"Nothing, but which way do we go?"

"Up the stairs, follow me." She led me into a narrow room with a window that overlooked the backyard, three pink plastic flamingos, and the unpaved alley. The flamingos were pressed into a garden that was covered with weeds, maple and elm leaves. The room was overheated; there was a scent of lilacs on the chest, roses near the night table. I turned from the window to explain about the three dollars. She undressed in one move and waited, naked, at the side of the bed.

"Do you want to talk or play?" She mounted the low bed, turned the spread, rolled over on her back, and opened her thighs. The mattress was raised to an ornamental brass headboard.

"Yes," I answered. I loosened my belt and watched her stomach move to the beat of her heart. My trouser leg caught on my shoe, and then the right shoelace turned to knots. I sat beside her on the bed, undressed at last. She rested her head on my thigh, and touched my penis and testicles. She was so close, her hair teased and tingled on my thighs.

"How much?"

"How much am I worth?"

"Three dollars?"

"We better hurry then." She hummed as she ran her fingers down my back to the breech. Her touch, breasts, thin hair, the scent of roses, the brass headboard, and pink flamingos in the abandoned garden, were sensual, new distractions, literature. I would have praised the trickster scenes, the words that turned erotic down to the creature naves, and our bodies to the maw, the wild maw.

"How did a nice girl like you. . . . "

"No words," she said and touched my mouth; her hand was moist and sweet. She pushed me back on the bed and held me down by the shoulders. She kissed my ear, the one with the blackhead. The ceiling light was too bright. She whispered, "Is the little man ready?"

She undressed too soon under a bare bulb to reach that sudden end, but my carnal fantasies were tied to the earlier games. I would need more than three dollars to start over at the staircase, to turn down the lights, to unhook her gown, and roam in the garden with the pink flamingos.

"Erotic reality begins less sharply than it ends," wrote Murray Davis in *Smut*. "It is one of the peculiar characteristics of the human condition that a person can be knocked out of erotic reality by the actual activities of sex itself."

I was in the military seven months later with an overnight pass, the last night on the continent, and then we boarded a troop ship bound for overseas duty. We were serious, defenders of freedom, and we boasted about our encounters with prostitutes. The house at 314 John Street came to mind, and my friends were amused by the address, and the pink flamingos.

Fort Lewis, Washington, swarmed with soldiers. Most of us were eighteen or nineteen, and wild on that last night in Seattle. The city was wide open, age was no barrier; saloons were eager to serve warriors. We drank too much, and then ordered a taxicab driver to find us four clean prostitutes. He was amused; there were more than ten thousand soldiers in the city that night. Our bounce and arrogance cost too much, but it was our last night in the country; we were driven to a clean neighborhood, and that was the last of our order. He turned down an alley, and there we were at the end of a line; more than thirty brash and blue soldiers waited for hours to spend fifteen minutes with a white prostitute.

"Turn around," I shouted to the driver.

"Wait a minute," he said and then parked the taxicab near the rear entrance of the house. He returned with a wide smile. "The front end of the line costs twenty bucks," he said as he leaned into the back window.

"Each of us?"

"Twenty bucks, total, four fucks."

"Deal," we agreed and paid the price.

"Shit, look at this." Inside, we marched to the counter at the side of the room; an older woman, the madam of the house, established our carnal turns. The house had been a speakeasy once; booths surrounded a hardwood dance floor.

Seven small rooms were located behind the booths; on one end, behind the counter, a message was painted on a mirror: We Serve Only Women. A booth opened and we waited for our names to be called. The doors opened and closed, military belt buckles rattled, water splashed, but we never heard an erotic sound.

One of our four fake names was announced, but we hesitated, no one wanted to be first, or last in line; our fantasies would be enhanced later with stories. I was seated on the end, and pushed out when the name was repeated; heads turned, someone hooted when the prostitute led me to the room. She wore a thin bathrobe and cloth slippers, no need for a gown.

"Lower your pants," she demanded and then left the room to fill a metal basin with warm water. She washed my penis too hard, tossed me a paper towel, and then lighted a cigarette. "How old are you anyway?"

"Does it make a difference?"

"You're too young to be in the Army."

"How much?"

"Twenty dollars."

"What does that cover?"

"Whatever you want," she said and then frowned.

"Nothing."

"What?"

"I don't want sex."

"You a talker?"

"Nothing, but here's ten bucks anyway, because I can't leave yet." She took the money, frowned, inhaled a menthol cigarette, and then sat on the end of the bed. She checked her watch several times.

We waited in silence. She moved her feet in and out of her slippers. Her feet were small, but her toes were enormous; her big toes were huge, and twisted from the pressure of narrow wedgies. I buckled my belt and returned to the booth.

I read *Visions of Excess* by Georges Bataille, several decades later, and remembered those enormous erotic toes. "The big toe is the most *human* part of the human body," because humans are erect on the earth, down from the trees.

"That was fast. How was she, soldier?"

"Faster than a speeding bullet."

"Too much down there to eat in one night?"

"Quiet, quiet." I told stories about sudden passions, and masturbation papers, but not with my name. "Some prostitutes are too eager, you have to slow them down a bit." Later, our trickster stories enhanced the sexual fantasies in the booth. "She moans, and pleads, the wild animal moans for more, more, more, mean and smooth, and the juice runs down her thighs.

"She has small firm white breasts with hard wild nipples that reach out and beg to be sucked. Her thighs move when you suck her nipples, she moans even more, and her big toes are beautiful, as big as two hard cocks." I leaned closer and whispered at the end. "She does a wild dance with her tongue, right down your thighs." The second fake name was announced and no one hesitated in the booth.

"We use the term prostitute metaphorically to describe collaboration, libertinism, selling out," wrote Susanne Kappeler in *The Pornography of Representation*. "The willingness of the prostitute is obscured by the factor of money." The prostitute is paid in cash, wages in advance, and the patron receives a service in return; this is not shadow work, but there is no real economic exchange. She sells her part of the common carnal connection, but "his seems to be for free."

We paid prostitutes and told stories that last night on the continent. The next day we boarded a troop ship with more than three thousand other tired soldiers; some lied at sea, some boasted, but those who worried about venereal diseases were the best measures of truth and boredom. Thirteen days later we docked at Yokahama, Japan.

The solicitation and the reception of sexual intercourse are modern in manner and studied positions, but the most common prostitution, the stories that embodied carnal adventures, would be postmodern as literature. The overtures, striptease, masturbation, random chance of disease and violence, the last hard breath, death, come down to stories, remembrance, a narrative. The prostitutes in some stories are at home with madams and no surnames; in lobbies, and on the streets in other stories. Prostitution is comic, or so it seemed late one summer in a postmodern western hotel.

The prostitutes of madams, lonesome women, communal houses, and gardens with pink flamingos are operas in an obscure mother tongue, comic operas and carnal literature from my memories with prostitutes in Superior, Seattle, and Billings, Montana.

"Opera concerns women. No, there is no feminist version; no, there is no liberation. Quite the contrary: they suffer, they cry, they die. Singing and wasting your breath can be the same thing," wrote Catherine Clément in *Opera, or the Undoing of Women*. "I have seen these operas at work; if I am touched by them it is because they speak of women and their misfortune."

The Golden Belle Restaurant in the Northern Hotel was a comic opera, a western simulation of a sensual empire raised on an old railroad line in Billings, Montana. The restaurant was flocked in felt fleurs-de-lis, heraldic kitsch, and cowhand ambiance; the waitresses wore wigs and prom gowns to serve rare meat, lobster, prawns, and flambéed shish kebab, the speciality of the house. The booths near the padded bar were bound in bright red plastic.

The Northern Hotel would never sanction madams or concede to the wicked wiles of prostitution, but on one occasion, two adolescent prostitutes cornered me in a booth at the bar. I was there with many other tribal people to attend a national meeting of the Indian Education Committee.

The booth was curved at one end of the bar; the restaurant was on the other end. The prostitutes, no more than seventeen, sat down and pressed closer to me on the red plastic, one on each side. I was seventeen that night with the pink flamingos; my memories rushed back twenty years and the prostitutes on the plastic seemed more mature. Their clothes were too tight; the one on my right was nervous, she sweated in a thick wool sweater.

"The angels descend." I leaned closer and smiled.

"Are you looking for a good time?"

"Why would you ask?"

"You a cop or something?" asked the one on my left.

"Never, never." I invited them to order beer, and then withdrew my invitation because they were not old enough to drink in public. The two nodded, winked, and frowned at each other; they sorted out these signs in silence and seemed to reached a tactical decision. The one on my right was the most aggressive; she was the talker.

"Where are you from?"

"Minnesota."

"Would you like a good time?"

"How much?"

"We can send you to great heights of pleasure, two are much better than one," said the prostitute on my right. Her presentation was practiced, no pauses or hesitation, but she was nervous; she shivered and dried her hands on her thighs. The scent of wet wool hit my nose.

"Great heights?"

"Yes, more, twice as much excitement."

"How much is that?"

"Greater than you have ever known."

"That great?"

"Even more than that," said the one my left.

"Can you give me some idea of what you have in mind, what you might do to me?" The prostitutes were troubled by my question; what they promised was obscene, a simulation, but they could not imagine words with lust, or erotic literature. The prostitute on the right moved her wet hand to my thigh; she never moved a finger and then her hand was gone.

"We'll both take your clothes off."

"That's a good start."

"We both do that, get your clothes off in slow motion."

"How much?"

"We'll both touch you in places, and with great pleasure."

"Where?"

"God, in your hotel room, stupid."

"Where on my body?"

"Everywhere, and everywhere," said the one on my left.

"How much would that cost?"

"One hundred dollars." The one on the right hesitated, the first time in our conversation; she told me the cost in a lower tone of voice. She turned back the sleeves on her sweater. Her forearms were moist and covered with black hair. The two women waited in silence.

"Both of you?"

"You bet, a hundred fingers on your balls."

"That's too much."

"We don't come cheap," said the one on my left.

"Listen, I'll send you, both of you, to ecstatic heights for only fifty bucks, and that's half of what you would charge me, and that's for both of you, but that price is good for only one more minute," I said and leaned back on the plastic. I counted the seconds on my watch, certain that the two prostitutes would never hold me to the promise.

"Stop it, forget it, asshole," said the one on the right.

"Fifteen seconds more, last chance."

"You're crazy."

"Maybe, but neither of you can describe what you would do to me, or with me, not even one carnal notion, not one word or metaphor of pleasure," I told them. "No words, no sex, no heights, no cash, no nothing."

"Shit, let's get the fuck out of here."

"Not so fast."

"What now?"

"I'll give you great heights of pleasure for nothing, forget the fifty bucks, nothing, free sex, free pleasure, all you have to do is listen." The prostitutes were bored; one turned and searched the bar for another man, and the other dried her hands once more.

"Shit, hurry up then."

"I'll pinch your nipples hard, one by one, two by two, and then my tongue will wet your stomach, wet your thighs, inside, closer and closer to the rim until you shout out all the dirty words you know, shit, cunt, suck, fuck, fuck, fuck. . . . "

"Man, you're fucking weird."

"Dogs mount the bitch and get stuck on the run. . . . "

"Man, that's fucking porn."

"You hate men."

"Fuck you."

"You can't even stand words about sex."

"Fuck you."

"Five bucks, fuck me with your mind."

"Fuck you."

"Listen, you wasted your time on me and it's getting late, so point out someone at the bar and I'll invite him over for a drink to make up for your lost time." At last, the prostitutes leaned back on the plastic and smiled; the one on the right was not nervous.

I invited a businessman to the booth, imagined two names for the prostitutes, introduced them, and then returned to my hotel room. I had pandered in public and could have been arrested. I saw the man the next morning in the restaurant; he turned in his chair to avoid me. Our night was not a great height, but it was western and postmodern, our best petit opera, a comic simulation, and pornographic.

"Pornography is one of the branches of literature— science fiction is another—aiming at disorientation, at psychic dislocation," wrote Susan Sontag in "The Pornographic Imagination." Moreover, "Pornography is only one item among the many dangerous commodities being circulated in this society and, unattractive as it may be, one of the less lethal, the less costly to the community in terms of human suffering."

April 1953: The End of an Alphabet

Patrick Henry High School could have been the end of the world for me; some teachers, most administrators, and that insidious social worker counter-mined the humor of minorities, crossblood identities, the credence of students who were poor and lived in faulted families.

I turned eighteen in the autumn of my senior year when the social worker closed in on me, a vulturous summons, but there were no recitals by me, no weakness rendered to the chosen cause; she recorded my silence, the condition of my clothes, the signs of poverty, blemishes, ruled that my troubles were unnatural, and presented me with a basket of used clothes. Moreover, she paid my senior fees, a despotic resolution of my ethical objections to the high cost of graduation ceremonies, the last humiliation. Liberation from the missions of that school, a rescue from social workers, had been on my mind for months, even on snow days, and those good days in spring and autumn when the river runs brown under the railroad bridge. I was eager on my eighteenth birthday to enlist in the Army.

"You might be killed," insisted the social worker.

"Not me," I protested. Later, my responses would have been much more severe. I might have said, "Maybe right here, mind mauled and heart dead in this school, but not in Korea."

"How can you say that?"

"Because this school is dead, graduation is death, and compared to that, the military is my liberation," I might have told her on my last day in high school. I loathed that social worker, her cold hands, her twisted mouth, her distance as she pretended to be concerned; I resented her racialism, her needs to end our independence, our simple pleasures of humor.

December 2 was cold, not the best time to leave; the chartered bus roamed on rural roads and main streets that night, loaded with tired recruits. We arrived about three in the morning at Fort Sheridan, Illinois. Two stout corporals must have waited for hours, even days, to demean and humiliate those few of us who had enlisted for three years of service; we were not draftees. I was spared the humble pie because of my service in the National Guard. We were issued new boots, shoes, underwear, and several uniforms; sizes were estimated by a sergeant as we moved nude down the cold line in a warehouse.

My other uniforms came to mind when we waited in line to stencil our duffel bags. I had been an usher at the Orpheum Theater in downtown Minneapolis. I was sure the patrons respected my uniform, a dark blue suit coat with a theater monogram, or at least they depended on my flashlight several hours a week at movies and live performances. Johnnie Ray was there once in his uniform; the ushers held back the wild girls when he sang his most popular song, "The Little White Cloud That Cried." He cried on stage over his sad melodies.

I was lonesome that first week at the reception center; the military chaplain would have been bored with my memories, had he been on duty, but my humor was on the rise when we reached Fort Knox near Louisville, Kentucky.

Basic combat training was a rude adventure, a test of not much more than the absurd. I pissed behind a tree once, without permission, when we were on maneuvers; a piss can was presented to me at reveille, in front of the entire battalion, with orders to bear the can, night and day, for two weeks. Otherwise, the sixteen weeks were marches, machine parts, guerrilla tactics, combat simulations, guard duty at the gold deposit, and secret rendezvous in Louisville.

I had earned a high score on the military intelligence test, the first time ever a test was in my favor. I was so surprised that they retested me to be sure; there were interviews, and then, at last, an order to report to the base commander, a lieutenant colonel. I had been selected for officer's candidate school, to become an officer, and for military security training, but no one told me. I reported as ordered, and remembered the masturbation papers chase two years earlier at summer camp in the National Guard.

"Private Vizenor, sir." There were several officers seated behind a wide table covered with a blanket; they seemed to be prepared to punish or negotiate. I had no idea why they wanted to see me.

"Private Vizenor, one year in the National Guard, and why do you want to be an officer in the United States Army?" When the commander smiled the other officers turned the same expressions.

"I don't, sir."

"What did you say?"

"I don't want to be an officer, sir." The commander frowned and then he turned to the other officers in search of an explanation for my response. They could not imagine who would not want to be an officer.

"Why not, soldier?" asked a captain.

"I just want to be with the men," I said and then blushed. My stupid response ended the invitation to become an officer and came close to ending my career as a private, in one sentence. The commander could not bear to see me in his unit, a reminder of my spontaneous renunciation; when we completed our sixteen weeks of basic training he ordered me to combat in Korea.

The United States Steamship *Sturgis*, with more than three thousand soldiers on board, was bound for the port at Inchon, South Korea, an industrial center on the Yellow Sea. General Douglas MacArthur, commander of United Nations forces, carried out an amphibious landing from the same port, behind the lines of the North Koreans.

Panmunjom, in the demilitarized zone between the nations, seemed so far removed from our troop ship, but we were certain that our fate would be traded over a blanket there; peace negotiations were down and there were no indications that the war would end before we docked. We were the counterpoise, the new warriors of democracies, but we were worried, and hushed by heroic rumors. Wild waves crashed over the bow, washed the decks, and the phosphorescence of the sea bears traced our course; we heard the thunder and waited for a sign of peace.

Most of the soldiers were urban, landlubbers to the core, and motion sick; explosive vomit from more than a thousand men held to the bulkheads, ladder wells, covered decks and rails. The anchor capstans were our sanctuaries at sea, and there were others.

Moses, the prophet and leader, appeared near the port bow at dusk, in the vision of one vigilant combat soldier near the anchor chain. My ends were never bound that tight, but his visions were an inspiration, and a liberation from the realities of the sour stench of puke. He talked, we listened to the sea.

I was never sick and ate my meals on time, but there were moments of consequent nausea, for instance, when a soldier on the top bunk leaned over and belched on our boots, three bunks below. I slept with my boots and a damp towel over my face until the seas were calmed. My pose by day was a writer for the ship's newspaper, because anyone could write for the daily mimeographed edition; this pose allowed me to enter a special library reserved for officers and their dependents. I remember *Killers of the Dream* by Lillian Smith, the southern novelist and social worker. She wrote about her home, "its main street lined with great oaks, heavy with matted moss that swings softly even now as I remember. A little white town rimmed with Negroes, making a deep shadow on the whiteness. There it lies, broken in two by one strange idea. Minds broken. Hearts broken. Conscience torn from acts. A culture split in a thousand pieces. That is segregation."

My sea bloom at eighteen was a dubious virtue at meals; the mess needed puke-immune bodies to wash the counters and the decks. It was too late to pretend we were sick; later we commended a petit insurrection. We mutinied on the hour and vanished in the crowds on deck. In a few minutes the captain announced over the loudspeakers how serious was our action and ordered us back to the mess. Our identification cards were returned, our names had not been recorded; we were invisible, in a state of military grace. I learned not to be seen, or heard, and adopted the officer's bakery as my work station. The duties were reasonable and the pastries were delicious, and suitable barter. The master baker, a civilian, was never critical of my work and never doubted my assignment; however, he was an atheist with no tolerance for religion.

"This is a galley, not a church," the baker shouted and bashed from my hands the Bible. Moses had inspired me to read sacred stories and biographies, but the baker was more persuasive. "Fucking lies, scared of death in combat?"

The *Sturgis* anchored near Tokyo Bay; we could hear the city at night and smell the burned charcoal. We waved to the sailors on sampans, and no one remembered the war a decade earlier, or their surrender. We waited for two days on the bay, and then with low rations after a rough thirteen-day voyage, we docked at Yokahama. Later, we learned that a hospital ship was held in the last berth at Inchon.

We were billeted at a reception center on wire bunks, no mattresses. Thousands of soldiers were mustered at dawn and dusk; from the top of the alphabet about three hundred names were called each day for military flights to Korea. The slow muster to combat was unbearable and became more worrisome the closer the list came to my name; then, near the end of the tees, no more musters. We waited and waited and silence turned rumors to paradise; there were no command performances, not even a lecture to ease the boredom.

One week later, by chance, the ends of the alphabet were marched to a special troop train in a shroud of military se-

crecy, and by sunrise we were on our way to the northern island of Japan.

The *Toya Maru* ferried the train across Tsugaru Strait between Honshu and Hokkaido. Chitose was our destination, a
small town cornered by two military bases near the city of
Sapporo. The names at the lower end of the alphabet, about
two hundred combat infantry soldiers, were assigned to the
Seventieth Tank Battalion, First Cavalry Division, a celebrated
unit that had been decimated in Korea.

The next morning at reveille my name was high on the
list because most of our company was new, we had come on
the train. There was an Adams, an Anderson, a Baker, a
Cooper, Gross, Martino, several surnames in the tees, then
Valentine, Vandenberg, Vincent, Vizenor, and the last of the
alphabet, names with double and triple consonants from
Eastern Europe.

Three months later, by the time we had learned how to
move a tank and honor certain combat stories, the war had
ended. An armistice was signed, after two years of negotiations, by officials of the United Nations and North Korea at
Panmunjon on July 27, 1953. To celebrate peace, and other
more common conditions, the enlisted club announced that
drinks were a dime; sloe gin was the pleasure of the warriors
that night.

The war had ended but we trained harder, sustained
more humiliation, and pressed the natural limits of our confidence. The celebrated battalion became a heroic emblem for
displaced career officers who had been trained for combat, to
lead a war that had ended over a blanket, lines on a map, and
razor ribbon. Some of these officers pretended that enlisted
men were their enemies, or at least agents provocateurs.

Major Brown, for instance, seemed pleased to hear the
call to attention when he entered a communal toilet area.
Once, he pushed closer to a row of toilets in the shit house
and a compeer shouted attention. I refused to move from the
stool, but others leapt to their feet, trousers down, and saluted the major in search of a war.

"Soldier, are you at attention?"

"No, sir," I shouted and looked down at the floor. His clean polished boots moved into my low vision; the laces were tied in double bows. The major held his hands behind his back and wagged his fingers.

"And why not, soldier?"

"I'm taking a shit, sir." I shouted and then pretended to strain, a simulated movement. "This is our crapper, sir, not an orderly room." The other soldiers laughed at attention.

"As you were," said the major in a contemptuous military manner. He roamed around the toilets, inspected the seats, then moved to the sinks and tested the water. He saluted at the door and departed.

I remembered the stories about a recruit in our basic training unit at Fort Knox who fashioned turds from peanut butter and dropped them into a clean toilet bowl; minutes later when the officers arrived in the barracks for an inspection the recruit leaned over the toilet and began eating the smooth brown simulated turds. He was discharged in three days. I wondered what happened to him, how he could eat a peanut butter sandwich; his name was high on the alphabet and he might have seen combat.

Major Brown would remember my name and responses to his toilet tour; he was a career officer, a trained avenger. Months later, he would march in a snow storm at midnight hoping to catch me out of uniform, to catch me in some violation of the military code. Our tank company was encamped in the mountains for a week on combat maneuvers. One night the duty guards gathered in a large tent to avoid a blizzard. More than a foot of wet snow had fallen before dark. We played poker, mocked and reasoned that the war had ended and that the foul weather would dishearten even the most evil snow demons. No officer would brave the cold and snow; we were protected by a wild winter storm.

The normal tour on guard duty was two hours, with four-hour rest periods. No one would venture into the mountains in a winter storm, we agreed, and passed the duty clock around the poker table. Our tour of duty was the game. At midnight the clock was mine for two hours.

I drew a straight, teased the bets, and won a large pot, but even that rush did not overcome my apprehension that we would be raided by some paranoid officer in search of a private war. I tied my boots, buttoned my parka, and loaded my carbine.

I pushed into the drifts, snow blind, never more than a shout from our tents; close enough to hear voices at the game. I was at peace in my parka, the snow brushed the wide hood, a gentle sound; snow would be seductive, a familiar meditation, and a generous invitation to death. I remembered other storms at home. My memories were tied to the weather, interior landscapes: the spring snow storms that closed the schools and stopped the trains; under the white pines, the red pines, the sound of winter water, an opening in the ice on a river in northern Minnesota.

I heard the crunch and swish of snow in the distance, the sound of someone walking toward me. I worried, Was that the crunch of an officer or the lurid swish of the ice woman? The crunch came closer and closer to me. The crunch halted, but the swish continued; we listened to each other, and then the crunch resumed. I could not see more than a few feet in the dark and wild snow storm. The swish had moved behind me and the crunch seemed too close to avoid.

"Who goes there?" I shouted but my voice was muffled inside the wide hood of my parka. I opened the hood, turned the wire in the seam, and shouted once more. The crunch came closer, closer. "Who's there?" The crunch slowed but no one answered me. I cocked my carbine and aimed in the direction of the cruncher. "Who's there? I'll shoot if you don't answer."

"Not who's there," said the cruncher.

"Who's there? Identify yourself."

"Whom is there, you should say, not who is there."

"Cut the grammar or your ass is dead."

"Wait, wait, don't panic," the cruncher pleaded.

"Advance to be recognized."

"Major Brown, checking the guards."

"Come closer and show me some identification," I said and pressed my carbine to his chest, once, twice, harder. He raised his hands and cursed me. My responsibilities and duties as a guard were absolute in this instance; no one had the right to pass without identification, not even a general. The major was aware that the guards had been issued ammunition.

"You know me," he said and removed his mittens. Our parka hoods touched in the storm. He was in there, behind the wire seam, but he could not see me smile in the dark. At last, he handed me his identification. I held the wet card close to my flashlight and read out loud his name, rank, service number, and authorized signatures; enunciated in a loud monotone each word and number printed on the card.

"Yes, sir, the major from the toilets," I said at last and returned his card. I stepped back two paces in a military manner, cleared and shouldered my carbine, and saluted. "You may pass, sir."

"Sonofabitch," he muttered and turned to leave. The cruncher had lost his war; he wanted to catch me in the tent, at the poker table, but the tables were turned in a snow storm.

Chitose, the town with dirt roads between two military bases, was named the "sex circus" of the world in several news reports. My worldview embraced prostitution, the circus, and comic operas, but not as comparative moral prohibitions. The stories, however, were unvarnished, and there were truisms in the local signs.

The population of the town, for instance, grew from about six hundred in the third week of the month to more than a thousand the first week of each month when soldiers were paid. Young women from rural areas on the island came to town by train to earn cash with their bodies. One, two, or three hundred yen, less than a dollar then, were the various prices for a few minutes with a peasant woman.

The venereal diseases scores were other signs of the circus. Each company in our battalion posted, on a sign board outdoors, the number of cases of venereal diseases contracted each month; a competition for the lowest number of men treated each month encouraged some soldiers to avoid medical attention for gonorrhea and other serious infections. In fact, the commander of the battalion held the record for the most treatments in one year, the record was unofficial; the housekeeper in the officers' quarters had infected several officers for more than six months. The penicillin prescribed for the treatment of officers was considered a state secret.

Even the medical officer had treated himself for gonorrhea; we learned this from the orderlies. He was so rude and unclean that we were convinced he was infected by masturbation. He would surprise us at least once a month with "short arm" inspections. Early in the morning he would awaken the barracks and order each soldier to "milk" his penis; the medical officer and his aide leaned down with flashlights to examine each urethra for signs of disease. The medical officer used the "scare technique" to fight most diseases; once a month each unit was ordered to attend his slide presentation of enlarged photographs of infected penises. The horror method had no real effect on the rate of infections. We cheered the post chaplain, as we never had in the past, when he recommended "character guidance" and more positive materials prepared by military chaplains. At least there was some humor in the films that would guide our character.

Chitose was once closed to the military for more than a month; we were told that the town was being inspected top to bottom by politicians and religious leaders. Tamaki Uyemura, a member of the Japanese Public Safety Commission, had asked military leaders a year earlier to ban prostitution and "isolate immoral United States troops." She was concerned about the seduction of women who became prostitutes and mothered illigitimate children; many of these mixedblood children had been abandoned. These crossbloods hold my temper and imagination to the end. Chitose was soon opened, and the sex circus was back to normal; however, at critical crossroads in the town the medical corps maintained "prophylactic stations" in trailers and the backs of trucks.

The Japanese have had a rich tradition of brothels, teahouses, geishas, and courtesans; prostitution had never been a crime. Chitose bloomed on the margin of these traditions, centuries removed from samurais, the literature and manners of geishas, the music and dance, but never so rude as soldiers, or wild as a western town. The peasant women blushed, sucked suimono, or soup, from the side of the spoon, a delicious sound, and collected screen magazines. Our similarities to movie actors were eminent to some of the prostitutes; we were remembered in the names of actors. Tony Curtis moved in me once at the House Tokyo.

Matsuo Basho, the founder and master of modern haiku, encountered two prostitutes on one of his haibun journeys in the seventeenth century. He listened to their miseries and then wrote a haiku: the prostitutes were sleeping, the bush clover and the autumn moon, under one roof. The poet and the women are transcended in natural scenes on their way to a shrine. "The prostitutes are no mere specimens of humanity," wrote Daisetz Suzuki in *Zen and Japanese Culture*. "They are raised to the transcendentally poetic level with the lespedeza flowers in their unpretentious beauty while the moon impartially illuminates good and bad, comely and ugly."

I pretended we were in a teahouse, that the women were geishas in a comic opera, but with no severities, and few restrictions. My geisha would be dressed in a silk kimono with a broad sash, an obi; she waited on her favored man, out of season at the end of the month. We would eat at the kotatsu, the charcoal brazier, in winter, our feet covered with a blanket. The madam served tea, and later we pretended that her narrow bunk was our court. My geisha could not pronounce my names; she was spontaneous and laughed at my nose, poems, and passions. I was a liberated crossblood, she was a peasant, and we would remember our generous poses.

Edward Seidenstricker pointed out in *Low City, High City* that the literal meaning of geisha is an "accomplished person," but the word is one of the most difficult "to grasp and define." Chitose was a town that tried; we supported the accomplished peasant geishas. That town became our new histories; we were not the best at music or dance, but we were comic singers and turned the world we had made into humor.

"From midnight on 31 March 1958, public prostitution was officially banned for the first time in Japanese history," wrote Ian Buruma in *Behind the Mask*. More than fifty thousand girls "all over the country found themselves out of a job. The first reaction to the new law was rather charming and very Japanese: just before the midnight deadline prostitutes and their customers all over Tokyo began singing 'Auld Lang Syne', a hugely popular song in Japan, appropriated for those deliciously sad occasions, so dearly beloved by the Japanese people, of saying goodbye."

I had arrived at Chitose by chance, a combat infantry soldier, and in a few months moved from a tank cannon loader to driver to gunner, and then tank commander. This rapid rise in responsibilities ended in the orderly room as a clerk and driver for the company commander. The captain wore risers in his boots because he was an inch below military standards. His father was a career officer with some influence and the critical inch was set aside. The captain loved a parade, but he was forever out of step because his legs were too short to march in normal time. The first sergeant had an unusual stride that must have been a natural practice on a farm; he gave meaning to the expression "clodhopper." I carried the company guidon in parades and road marches, and tried to find a natural pace between the beat of the captain and the sergeant.

The captain would stand in his jeep, with one hand on the windshield, as we drove behind the company tank column. The dust and exhaust in summer turned to snow and exhaust in winter. The day after a heavy snow storm, when the roads had been plowed, the captain ordered me to pass the tank column.

"Not wise, sir."

"Why?"

"Loose snow over the ditch."

"Pass, that's an order." He loved to repeat his orders as much as he loved to pose like a general standing in his jeep. I sounded the siren and followed my orders at high speed, pulled out to pass, and the jeep dropped four feet and plowed into the snow that covered a trench. The captain was catapulted head first into the snow. The column stopped, everyone was out of the tanks to see their commander up to his ass in snow, head buried and humiliated. We brushed the snow out of his helmet and pockets; his pride was bruised, and he had lost his crop in the snow.

One Sunday afternoon in the spring he ordered me to drive around the countryside so we could talk. "But sir, what's country here is a rice paddy." He was bored with his wife and two children.

"Drive, that's an order."

"Yes, sir." I drove on the narrow paths between paddies and then through several small villages. We talked about families, careers, "normal futures in the service." I was nineteen at the time, acted in plays at the post theater, and pretended to be with a geisha who remembered haiku poems.

"Vizenor, you're a smart kid. What the hell are you going to do with yourself, what's in your future?" He seemed urgent, too eager to discourage me from my interest in literature. "How can you support a family?"

"Not the Army."

"What then, if you're so dead set against the Army."

"I want to be a writer." I was embarrassed because no one had ever heard me admit my interest in being a writer. I wanted to take it back, the idea was private, too vulnerable to praise and admonition, but there it was, loose in a jeep with a captain between rice paddies.

"You can't be another Carl Sandburg, you know." He warned me and then became silent. He had planned to lecture me on the merits of a military career, no doubt. He never discussed personal matters with me again; no more weekend drives in the paddies. He lost interest and abandoned me.

I had come to realize that officer's candidate school was much better service than driving a jeep and typing letters for a short captain. Once the normal selection was over at the end of basic training, any reconsideration needed a petition, several official recommendations, and the successful completion of the First Cavalry Division Noncommissioned Officer's School, an intense ten-week leadership course. The captain approved the special school because he was certain that I would never survive the rigorous training and discipline. We were both surprised when I finished third in the class, with a solid recommendation for officer's school.

The captain denied my petition for officer's school, but to mitigate his grudge he supported my application to attend a four-week program at the Far East Entertainment Theatre Workshop located near Tokyo. If not an officer, then an actor. I studied dance, music, stage direction, and learned how to organize entertainment activities on military bases. That experience led to an envied appointment as one of the directors of entertainment at Camp Schimmelfennig, near Sendai, Japan. The first sergeant and the company commander both refused to authorize my transfer, but the battalion commander, the one with the venereal disease record, agreed in the end to sign the orders.

My transfer from a combat tank battalion to entertainment was a series of coincidences and chance encounters. I was named, for instance, the supernumerary guard several times, a competition with other soldiers on the roster to serve the battalion commander as an orderly for the day, rather than stand guard duty. The commander said he liked me and promised to support my military career, should the need ever arise. His humor was rich, his temper was wild, and he was diseased and corrupt; several months later he was arrested with a stolen pistol and reduced in rank, but not before he signed me into special services.

The chance encounter involved a civilian hired by the Department of the Army to supervise entertainment programs in northern Japan; she was impressed with my completion of the entertainment school, appreciated my interests in theater and acting, and recommended my transfer to special services. However, hope was dashed when the captain refused to release me from the company; not only that, but my good connections were lost when we moved, at last, to a new camp near Gotemba, with a view of Mount Fuji.

"The most beautiful sight in Japan and certainly one of the most beautiful in the world, is the distant apparition of Fuji on cloudless days," wrote Lafcadio Hearn, "more especially days of spring and autumn when the greater part of the peak is covered with late or with early snows." Hearn made his ascent to the mountain from Gotemba: "The least picturesque," he wrote, "but perhaps also the least difficult of the six or seven routes open to choice."

Mount Fuji over my typewriter was indeed an inspiration; the view from a military base was the most picturesque, and the most troublesome for me that autumn because my choices had ended. I had resigned myself to be a clerk for a short captain, a mean sergeant, and with a clear view of the mountain; eighteen more months to my discharge.

Then, one night a marvelous coincidence restored my humor and the world turned around: the colonel was drunk at the officer's club, the civilian had my orders in her purse, and the next day my military career came down the mountain to entertainment. I was on my way, with a cold stare from the captain and a curse from the first sergeant, by train to Sendai, in northern Honshu. I had moved in two years from death and separations, to tanks, jeeps, forests, clerical work, and a mountain view; afterward, what a deal, special services, theater, and associations with professional performers, vocalists, and musicians on tour from the United States.

I had decided, when my enlistment ended, to be discharged from the service in Japan. There was nothing at home, not even the memories of a home, to balance my sense of liberation and independence. The University of Minnesota would not consider my application then because of my poor high school record. Japan became my home when Sophia University in Tokyo accepted me as an undergraduate student. I would have studied Japanese language and literature, tea ceremonies, haiku poetry, the soul in the crane.

I might have pretended to be the modern crossblood Lafcadio Hearn at Sophia University. I listened as he had done to the sounds of Japan, the wooden clogs in railway stations, and a crowd, he wrote, "will sometimes intentionally fall into step." I might have studied musical insects in his footsteps. "It would not be easy," wrote Hearn, to convince a foreigner that in the "aesthetic life of a most refined and artistic people, these insects hold a place no less important" than the pleasures of canaries and birds in other cultures.

Hearn was born Irish and Greek, and at the turn of the last century he was a teacher at Tokyo Imperial University. He became Japanese, and he could have become Anishinaabe; we were brothers with the trees and stones. "Until you can feel, and keenly feel, that stones have character, that stones have tones and values, the whole artistic meaning of a Japanese garden cannot be revealed to you." Naanabozho, the Anishinaabe earthdiver and tribal trickster, is related to the wind, and his brother is a stone.

I changed my mind at the last minute and decided not to be a student at Sophia University. I was worried that my past would be unforgiven, that my temper and experience would be abandoned. I would consider the Pasadena Playhouse in California, but changed my mind about that too, because of my insecurities about families and identities. I reasoned that an actor lived in the role, and in my case the role would have become my home. I praised the trickster, our comedies, the turn of egos in a stern word, but there must be more to me than a mere pose.

I would regret my decision to leave, and over the years told stories and wrote poems to remember the sound and scent of Japan. These stories and moods of impermanence overturned the burdens of racialism and the hard rind of ideologies, and terminal creeds, but not my passions, curiosities, rage, and resistance as an insecure undergraduate at two universities.

Japan was my liberation, and the literature, the haiku poems, are closer to me now in imagination, closer to a tribal consciousness, than were the promises of missionaries and academic careers. My stories are interior landscapes.

Japan was much easier than the rest of my life; there were lovers and separations, but no real moral pain, no death, no tribal sacrifices in the poses and comic resolutions of entertainment at military bases. "Perhaps all of us learn to love that which we train ourselves to make sacrifices for, whatever pain it may cause," wrote Lafcadio Hearn. "Indeed, the question might be asked whether we do not love most that which causes us most pain."

Japan was my lover in the mountains, at the snow mounds on the water wheels, at the gates, gardens; haiku on a journey to the bears, stones, these interior landscapes were never sacrifices, neither were the moons footloose near shore at Matsushima. My crossblood remembrance, lost tribal souls, uncertain identities, and wounded cranes in the poisoned cities, cause me the most miseries. I learned to remember these stories, and to honor impermanence, tribal tricksters on the run, run, run, run.

September 1954: The Trees of the Emperor

━━━━━━━━━━━━━━━━━*T*he schemes and reasons nego-
tiated on high in the command seemed to be chance resolutions at the bottom echelons; space heaters, a measure of our
existence, moved in this manner between privates, colonels,
generals, and the Japanese.

The diplomatic maneuvers to turn over our combat
equipment to the national police were a scandalous violation
of the new constitution, but by the time the news hit bottom,
and turned in our rumors, we had been promised a vacation
in paradise, two months in the Imperial National Forest in
central Hokkaido.

The First Cavalry Division turned over tanks, trucks, can-
nons, Quonset huts, and space heaters. The Japanese Security Forces moved into our mess, held the toilets, transformed
the theater and clubs, and packed the bunks by the hour,
three men to our one in the same space. Our rude departure
was mitigated by the return of the space heaters. The military
had contracted with a local company to manufacture hundreds of kerosene heaters for the barracks; the metal was thin
and fire pots burned out. As a result, we had to stand fire
guard once a week. The guards checked the fires, slept for an
hour, and then passed the clock on to the next guard, who
would do the same. I was punished once because properties
were stolen on my watch; we hated those heaters.

The Japanese inherited their own hazardous space heaters; poetic justice, but regrettable. Homeless, we moved to a
virgin forest, and cut down the trees of the Emperor. The
move, however, was neither a pleasure nor common adventure.

The First Cavalry Division was scheduled to move to a new base near Mount Fuji. The train would depart that morning, but at the last minute our battalion and several other units were ordered to remain on the island; we would move south at the end of autumn. We camped in pup tents, the true test of the combat readiness of a cavalry unit without horses or tanks, for about a week on a meadow near the base. We were depressed because the other units in our division were on the train ferry bound for the sacred mountain.

Sunday, September 26, 1954, there was a curious calm as we ate an early breakfast; our voices echoed in the warm mist, a portentous sign that morning. I had been named with nine other soldiers and one officer to a reconnaissance platoon; we were to locate bivouac areas about seventy miles to the west in the Imperial National Forest.

The mist was warmer and held an unnatural light; then, a sudden pulse of warm wind, one beat, a wheeze, but not the last, and a wild silence. We loaded the vehicles, the weather was in my hands, my heart; that warm wind turned on the canvas, and the demons moaned under the trucks. These were not the winds related to the trickster.

We were on the road when the mist turned to cold rain and the winds increased. I was in the front seat of an open jeep. The canvas covers billowed and the gusts moved the trucks on the road; then the canvas tore loose and whipped on the wind, a wild demonic sound. The drivers pulled over to the side of the road, unable to control the trucks. We continued, the jeeps ran closer to the narrow main road, but we were bounced and sheered in the crosswinds.

The wind carried leaves and weeds, the bad weather bloom, and burned my hands and cheeks. A sudden bluster raised the poncho over my head and covered my eyes. I released the chin strap on my steel helmet and the wind bounced it down the road and over the weeds. We were caught in our own motion and continued a few more miles to a town. The wind punched me in the chest, rushed my ears. The jeep was turned and beaten on the road.

The town, once a hundred or more traditional wooden houses, was overturned and flattened; the panels and beams were broken, dismembered, and blown over the rice paddies. We turned on a narrow mound between paddies and circled the remains of the town, the splinters and shreds of houses. The people were gone; they must have taken cover in the woods to the west.

A small mongrel waited in the middle of the mound between the paddies; he barked and sneezed when we approached. The dog came to me, licked my hands, and settled inside my wet field jacket. He never made a sound in the jeep. Lucky was his natural name, and when we were back on the road a few minutes later the storm had passed, the wild wind was calmed. Once more there was a warm mist. That wind was vulpine, more treacherous than a woodland thunderstorm, more than the side of a tornado. We had been on the road for several hours. The trucks had turned back; six of us continued in three jeeps. We were tired.

Lucky was silent inside my jacket when we stopped to piss and smoke near the woods. We had nothing to say about the weather then because the demon winds were too close to praise or mock; we had survived with humor and our stories.

The Imperial National Forest was too far to reach before dark, so we located an intersection deep in the forest. We took cover from the storm there, close to the trees of the Emperor. We were out of radio contact and had no information about the storm. When the wind returned we were on a dirt road deep in the woods; the tall pine trees leaned and the high branches rushed the current, but on the road the wind teased my hair and the smaller trees in the shadows. We stopped at a tee in the road at dusk and staked three tents. My tent was in an open area near two enormous trees. I slept and the wind screamed overhead, high overhead in another world. The wind had turned at sea, double-crossed the seasons, and then twisted and moaned in the pines. That primal sound roared down to our ancient roots.

Lucky pushed my hands, and then he licked my cheeks; he barked to awaken me. I moved to the side and rolled over to hide my face, but he persisted. I worried, at last, that he would wet in the tent. He hurried me to the opening in the tent, but would not go outside. I thought he was afraid that the tent would vanish when he returned; so, with my flashlight in hand we walked toward the vehicles. No more than a minute after we left the tent, one of the trees twisted, cracked in the middle, and impaled the tent.

Lucky had earned his name, my care, devotion, and our close, close attention to him that night. The trees twisted in various directions, the wind was savage and the great pines cracked and snapped and toppled; one crushed a jeep. We gathered in the dark at the tee, joined our arms in a circle and shouted when a tree cracked in our view; the circle moved as one body for several hours that night.

The trees cracked, their last light burst in the distance. When the winds died and the storm ended we collapsed near the vehicles and slept until dawn. The morning was clear, cold, and bright; the sun touched the earth between the broken pines, and we remembered. The broken, fallen trees surrounded us, hundreds of trees blocked the dirt roads. We made radio contact with our company; we were the last to reach the bivouac area because it took two days to clear the road.

We learned that the eye of a typhoon had passed over the island, the worst storm in more than a generation on Hokkaido. The great wind had crossed the southern islands earlier, moved out to sea, and would have weakened as other storms had done for centuries, but this typhoon turned to the north, then to the west with no warning, and passed over Hokkaido. The typhoon was not predicted, the military weather reports indicated light rain; people were surprised by the wind, but there were some who remembered the signs. Thousands of homes were destroyed, and hundreds of people had died on land, more than a thousand at sea. Coastal towns suffered the most damage.

Lucky must have sensed the sudden turn in atmospheric pressure; he would have sensed it once earlier, under the eye of the storm, when his town was blown to pieces. About the same time the dog had moved from the tent, a ferry turned over in Tsugaru Strait, between Hokkaido and the main island of Honshu. First Cavalry Division soldiers died that night on the train ferry. Our battalion was lucky; we had been ordered to the Imperial National Forest.

Monday, September 27, 1954, the *New York Times* reported that more than a thousand people had drowned when a train ferry capsized in the typhoon, the most violent since 1938. The dead and missing included more than fifty "United States soldiers, dependents, and Army employes. . . . There was only one known soldier survivor."

"The typhoon did widespread damage over the main islands of Japan," wrote Lindesay Parrott. The *Toya Maru*, an open train ferry with a blunt bow departed at dusk from Hakodate, on the island of Hokkaido, bound for Aomori, the main rail line terminal on northern Honshu. "The *Toya Maru* capsized at an emergency anchorage off Nanaihama, west of Hakodate, after a four-hour battle with winds and storm-lashed waves.

"The vessel carried soldiers of the United States First Cavalry Division transferring from Hokkaido to new posts on Honshu. . . . Besides those drowned many were apparently killed when railroad cars on the ferry broke loose and crushed passengers.

"The ferry, one of those that link the Hokkaido and Honshu railroad systems in a seventy-mile trip across the strait, loaded last night with passengers and cars of the express train bound for Ueno Station in Tokyo. As far as could be learned to date, the *Toya Maru* immediately met heavy seas. Spray and solid water, pouring over the bow and through the cutaway after deck and open stern, quickly soaked and incapacitated one of the twin engines.

"Losing power, the *Toya Maru* was carried off her course and swept toward the shore southwest of Hakodate. The crew of the ferry dropped anchor off the Nanaihama break-water, hoping to ride out the storm. . . . The *Toya Maru*, roll-ing and careening in the offshore surf, staggered toward the beach without sufficient power left in the engines to claw out to the open water. The vessel overturned when it hit a reef running out from the Hokkaido shore."

Lindesay Parrott wrote later that National Railways offi-cials, the operators of the ferry between the islands, an-nounced that "there were 171 'confirmed survivors' of the ty-phoon disaster. The overloaded ship had 1,275 passengers, crew members and railway employees aboard. One thousand eighty-six persons were missing or dead at the last count."

Lucky was content to be a member of the First Cavalry Division, but he was wise to move with caution when the bears waited near the treeline at dusk for our leftovers. These black bears were enormous; these were the bears of Emperor Hirohito.

The Imperial National Forest had been sacred, an in-spired and vast natural forest that no sensible person would have entered without permission. Who would have dared plead for concessions from the divine and absolute ruler of the empire? The bears were aware of these divine rights; there were few humans and no hunters in their memories. We were soldiers, the first to violate this divine forest, and we did so by invitation. We were encouraged to be uninhibited, to plunder the trees of the Emperor. Once more, the schemes on high in the command seemed to be chance as the trees were felled. We learned later that we had been the unwitting hired hands to thin the forest; the stumps were counted and a high price was paid to the government of Japan.

Our battalion occupied a square mile of the forest; we were told to choose a site and build whatever we fancied as a home for two months. Some soldiers built log cabins, others shelters from lumber broken and blown loose by the ty-phoon, and the least imaginative lived in trucks and trailers. Some soldiers lived alone, others in families. My house was made with canvas and mosquito nets; the sides rolled up, and at night the sounds of the forest were closer. The bears were not a problem, at first; they moved on a dry creek bed behind my house, but then an officer fired his pistol at the bears in the wet garbage sump. The fool might have wounded the animal. The primal fear of bears, the mania to be a bear, and the repressed desire to hunt bears were precarious emotions in the forest. Most of the soldiers were urban, the children of teddy bears. The company clerk, who had shared my house, moved to the command tent and slept under his desk. The captain was insecure and issued ammunition to the hundred men in the company.

The few soldiers who heard my lectures on bears were not convinced that humans are more vicious; they would not believe that bears do not attack people in their sleep, that bears are not savages or demons, that bears do not rape women and menace children. The very night of my third lecture on the bearty of bears, a huge bear, estimated to be more than a thousand pounds, tore open a tent and, according to the survivors, attacked them in their sleep. Later, it was revealed that the survivors, who were indigenous employees in the mess, had stolen meat, and it was the scent of fresh beef that the bears pursued, not human flesh.

The soldiers were frenzied, and shots were fired that night at shadows and apparitions. Worse than that, bears were reported to be lurking at the side of the trail near several houses, and a drunken posse was out on a hunt. The posse rode in jeeps and terminated the bears with automatic weapons. We learned later that the bears were weathered stumps with wild phosphorescent eyes and noses that simulated snowmen, and teddy bears.

Lucky was a great companion, the company mascot, but he sensed my concern that soon we would leave the forest. The captain even praised the dog, but he warned me that no mongrels would be allowed to travel with us by train to the southern island; the sergeant hated dogs and women, and he cited various regulations. "No ifs, ands, or buts," he sputtered. "That damn dog stays behind where he belongs."

Lucky was a blessed mongrel; indeed, several weeks before we were scheduled to leave, an old man and his granddaughter walked into our company area from the the west. This was very unusual because there were no roads in that direction or civilians in the area. One small village was located about twenty miles to the south, and three families tended the dam nearby, but the old man was not from these communities. He was thin, not a bear, a man but not an Ainu. I was enchanted by the old man and his granddaughter; they must have been on a journey, a haibun journey in the traditional literature of the Japanese.

"Indeed, one of the greatest pleasures of travelling was to find a genius hidden among weeds and bushes," Basho wrote in his travel sketches, "a treasure lost in broken tiles, a mass of gold buried in clay, and when I did find such a person, I always kept a record with the hope that I might be able to show it to my friends."

Lucky was gracious and needed no instruction on survival; he was at the side of that girl the instant she entered the area. Lucky touched her; he sneezed and pushed his nose on her hand. He smiled when she tried to say his name. The old man and his granddaughter were our guests at dinner; we ate outside, standing at high tables. The bears, as usual, waited in the brush at the distant treeline. Lucky had my best portions of beef; he knew it was time to leave. The old man bowed, once, twice, expressed his gratitude, and walked down the trail hand in hand with his granddaughter.

Lucky looked back once to me; of course, he was at the side of the little girl, a mature journey, a natural balance in the late autumn. Lucky was never mine; that mongrel was a soul that posed in the great wind, he waited there to lead me home.

March 1955: When the Mist Clears

━━━━━━━━━━━━━*My* first typewriter, a portable
Remington Quiet-Riter, was on the *Toya Maru* train ferry the
night it overturned in the Tsugaru Strait. I had mailed my
typewriter home to prepare for our move south with the First
Cavalry Division.

Several weeks later the ferry was raised, bodies were removed, and most of the lading was recovered. The military
postal service returned letters and arranged to reimburse the
value of insured parcels. We were summoned to a warehouse
and one by one told to identify and then open our parcels in
the presence of postal investigators and military police. Several soldiers were arrested over the remains, because their
boxes contained weapons and other stolen government property.

I could not remember if there was a wool shirt, or even
more, packed around my typewriter. I pried open the
wooden box and took a deep breath before opening the case;
the investigator hurried me. Relieved, and lightened, there
was nothing stolen. The salt water or some organisms had
eaten holes in the metal cover and rubber parts, but the plastic keys were in perfect condition. My second portable typewriter was purchased with the insurance money, an identical
machine, several months later at my new post near Sendai.

I had experienced a bout of automatic writing, about fifty
pages one night, in the day room at the base near Mount Fuji.
That would have been my first novel, acute descriptions and
wild dialogue between street toughs, hard metaphors and
cushion shots, over a game of pocket billiards, but the manuscript was burned several years later in Minnesota. My aspirations beat my abilities as a writer then; that manuscript and

my first story, "When the Mist Clears," a lamentation and romantic bewilderment, are indications of my earliest ecstatic prose transcriptions on a typewriter.

I was twenty, a director of entertainment in special services, when I wrote my first serious poems and stories, and received my first rejection letters from magazines. "The Balcony" is one of my earliest poems, an earnest description written for Aiko Okada at a resort hotel in Anabara, Japan.

> The balcony,
> Bamboo frame
> And overhanging tin roof,
>
> Where the sun browned leaves
> Of fern and palm, bow
> To the ground on the edge below the rail.
>
> Where the summer sun
> Bakes and bleaches the stone,
> Where the birds land, rest and sing.
>
> Where the moon
> Illuminates happy faces,
> While the night birds sing of love.
>
> The balcony and room behind
> Give rest and happiness,
> That are vivid in many memories.

I had written poetic fragments, dialogue, and travel scenes for several years, but these were my first serious descriptions and stories, too serious. My first autobiographical story was written in the tenth grade, about my experiences in the Minnesota National Guard. The teacher refused to accept my work; she insisted that someone else wrote the story.

I had read novels and stories by James Fenimore Cooper, Jack London, John Steinbeck, Thomas Wolfe, and *Sayonara* by James Michener, but not *Dubliners*, the moist blue eyes over the cinders in "Ivy Day in the Committee Room" by James Joyce. My first serious fictional story is a sentimental closure on the metaphors of the hearth.

WHEN THE MIST CLEARS

The fire in the marble fireplace is crackling and throwing small particles of burning wood grotesquely against the golden fire screen. There really isn't any need for the fire to-night, in the middle of June, except that it fills the room with a fervent stillness. It is doubtful that anyone can explain the incentives of a glowing fire in a fireplace. Not unless they are experiencing an emotional sadness.

He is just sitting there, in deep meditation, staring into the glowing yellow and red coals, examining each burning log looking for an answer, or looking for some personal satisfaction. It seems strange that he should find this answer, or satisfaction, written in a fire. As he keeps staring into the fire, the crackling becomes louder and the burning more intense. The flames seem to crawl slowly from the fireplace and almost fill the entire room with fire. Then he turns suddenly away, trying to escape the frightening mental image of flames. But they are still there. Everywhere he looks he can see irregular streams of red and yellow flames. On the walls, on the ceiling, everywhere. Slowly the flames diminish and then flicker out, leaving him alone, internally cold. In those few minutes he had escaped. Escaped from sorrow, but now conscious, again he must face reality. Why must a thing like this be? There must be some explanation.

A cool evening June breeze fills the room with a sweet fragrance of cherry blossoms from the garden. Entering through the French door and settling in every corner of the room, where it leaves its lingering essence. Where does a breeze like this originate? How far does it travel before it finally sifts through the redolent cherry trees in the garden, and fills the room? The breeze is probably the most mutable creation of nature. Imagine how it can first carry a mist of salt water from the ocean. Carrying it for miles and leave it suddenly on a distant shore. Then pick up an exotic balm of flowers and carry it twice as far. Then become cold and vicious, and suddenly become innocent and fragrant with the blossoming of the trees. So many changes and yet here it is now, gently filling the room with the essence of nature's perfumes. With all this magnificent tranquility and solitude, still he sits in sorrow.

There in the other room is the candlelight table set for two, but he thought to himself, "There will only be me." Sitting alone in all this peacefulness and still disturbed. It is strange, that about you there can be absolute silence and peace and yet there is a disturbance, a mental disturbance. Creating noises, images, and scenes never experienced physically, but emotionally far more confusing.

How can one escape this sadness? I can look into the burning red and yellow fire in the fireplace, until the room becomes an inferno and escape my sorrow momentarily. Or I can stroll through the garden unconsciously, like the warm June breeze. But one can't stare into the fire all day, because the flames will dwindle, flicker, and die, along with one's soul. Nor can one saunter through the garden indefinitely, for soon the gentle breeze shall bring with it snow and ice. There seems to be no definite escape from sorrow. No matter how tragic, it must be faced.

The time is nearing for dinner; soon I shall seat myself again at the candlelight table, as I have been doing for many days, and sip my wine in sorrow, picturing opposite me my loving wife. There she sits modestly eating with me. I can picture her well. So well that I can hear her answering my every thought. A gesture with her fork, a sweet smile and a gentle laugh. We finish and walk to the fireplace. Now I can see her. There she stands daintily by the fire warming her hands and whispering softly across the room, as I pour our wine. Then she turns and calls for me and extends her arms, and as I walk toward her, she smiles. Closer and closer I come to her and with each step, a mist settles between us. I can still hear her through the mist, but when I reach for her, she vanishes, just like before, into the mist.

I must not go on like this. There must be someone, someone to fill this emptiness. Someone to drink with, someone to talk and laugh with, someone to love. This very minute I must face reality. I know there must be someone, someone to be there when the mist clears, there to love me. I will find her, because finally the dream had died; yes, it had perished right there in the fire. It has long burned, but now falls to ash. In that very same fire that I found contentment and an escape from emotions. I needn't escape anymore, because now I can say confidently, "Let the mist clear, let it come home between that pensive dream, but never come between my reverence for her."

June 1955: The Moon over Matsushima

▬▬▬▬▬▬▬▬▬▬▬▬*T*he Camp Schimmelfennig Library was a wasteland, said some of the college-educated soldiers, but it was there, in my own loose time and humor, that I found *The Prophet* by Kahlil Gibran, and *A Stone, A Leaf, A Door* by Thomas Wolfe, two authors whose prose transported me in that barren military library. "A stone, a leaf, an unfound door; of a stone, a leaf, a door," wrote Wolfe, and "of all the forgotten faces." I read his prose poems to the end, with my shoulder to the metal shelves that afternoon and remembered the metaphors. I read *Look Homeward, Angel,* and his other novels, in my first year at New York University.

I have never overcome my wearisome want to raise the word from the page, to sound out the passion and the sacrifices of literature in the voice of the crane. Wolfe roamed an interior landscape and rounded boundaries on a prose run; his language was wild and immense. Gibran told spiritual posers, and turned me inward, but not secretive. "In your longing for your giant self lies your goodness," he wrote. "But in some of you that longing is a torrent rushing with might to the sea, carrying the secrets of the hillsides and the songs of the forests."

Thomas Wolfe came to me in a military library, but he should be read on a train, his enthusiasm for trains was unbounded; his prose is a landscape from a parlor car, an interior rush and double vision on the railroad window. He was too loud, some critics have piped; he shouted so loud he would wear some words out, but listen, he was on a train: "Few buildings are vast enough to hold the sound of time, and now it seemed to him that there was a superb fitness in the fact that the one which held it better than all others should be a railroad station. For here, as nowhere else on earth, men were brought together for a moment at the beginning or end of their innumerable journeys . . . here, in a single instant, one got the entire picture of the human destiny," wrote Wolfe in *A Stone, A Leaf, A Door.* "And everywhere, through the immortal dark, something moving in the night, and something stirring in the hearts of men, and something crying in their wild, unuttered blood, the wild, unuttered tongues of its huge prophecies—so soon the morning, soon the morning: O America."

Aiko Okada was in the audience for the last performance of the satire *If Men Played Cards as Women Do* by George S. Kaufman. We had adapted the play for a military stage. I was one of the players, a pretender at a card game. Aiko was the only Japanese woman there, and she caught my eye near the last scene. I rushed out the side door at the end and invited her to stay for a party. She could not, she insisted, but she did give me her address at work, the Silver Star Bar in Sendai.

I was there the next day, that evening, and the next afternoon, more and more. We were lovers and traveled together to Tokyo, and other cities; to Anabara, Noboribetsu, Matsushima, and other resorts near the ocean, and in the moist mountains. Aiko was six years older and she had studied languages and literature in college; she could read and write English and French. I was twenty, an entertainment director in civilian clothes, and aspired to be a creative writer; these were serious matters.

Matsuo Basho visited Matsushima and wrote in his haibun travel diaries about the moon over the pine islands. We were there three hundred years later and remembered the master haiku poet. Aiko told stories and poems and touched the sand creases near shore; we held the water, raised the moon in our hands, wished in silence to hold that night under the pines. Leashed boats turned on their moorage in the bay. We waited in the fresh shadows and then crossed the wooden bridge back to the mainland and the hotel.

"Much praise had already been lavished upon the wonders of the islands of Matsushima," wrote Basho in *The Narrow Road to the Deep North.* "Yet if further praise is possible, I would like to say that here is the most beautiful spot in the whole country of Japan. . . . The islands are situated in a bay about three miles wide in every direction and open to the sea through a narrow mouth on the southeast side. . . . Islands are piled above islands, and islands are joined to islands, so that they look exactly like parents caressing their children or walking with them arm in arm. The pines are of the freshest green, and their branches are curved in exquisite lines, bent by the wind constantly blowing through them. Indeed, the beauty of the entire scene can only be compared to the most divinely endowed of feminine countenances, for who else could have created such beauty but the great god of nature himself? My pen strove in vain to equal this superb creation of divine artifice."

Aiko told me that her father hated Americans. He was a conservative nationalist who had lost his business at the end of the war; my hand and manner would remind him of surrender. They lived on Kitagojunin Matchi in Sendai behind a high wall and wooden gate. The houses in that area were spacious, and hidden from the silent streets. I walked the last few blocks up the hill because the taxicab driver was hesitant to enter the neighborhood with a foreigner.

Aiko was given permission for the first time to invite me to tea, and that was the only time we were together with her family. She met me at the gate, warm, excited, but we would not touch; the anticipation and discretion turned our conversation to inanities. I removed my shoes at the entrance, and then her father appeared; he bowed, blushed, held his distance, and then closed the paper panels. There was no surrender over tea in the garden, a perfect enclosure.

I mimicked my own manners and mocked the gestures of Americans; my expressions were the cause of much humor in the house. Aiko was more at ease once her mother laughed at me. Her father was courteous to me at the door with his daughter, but no more than once; his cultural honor would not be lost to the humor of a common soldier.

The United Service Organizations produced a variety show that toured several times a year in the Far East. I was responsible for local engagements and performance schedules at several military posts near Sendai in northern Honshu. Twice we loaded the show on helicopters with a piano and other properties to entertain soldiers on maneuvers. Entertainment was a critical business in the military; the post commander, a colonel with a banal sense of humor, was dedicated to a regular schedule of events, and he made available the necessary equipment and transportation. I was thrilled to meet so many talented performers, and to bear the uncommon realities of entertainment, the wild stories, and the irreverent humor about the military.

Once a month we produced our own show for tour; the plays were adapted from Shakespeare, Chekhov, and some modern comedies. For instance, *If Men Played Cards as Women Do* was a very popular satire. *The Cherry Orchard*, on the other hand, was one of our most creative productions, but we never found an enthusiastic audience in the military. The slapstick, sexual innuendos, and humor of variety shows were the most popular, and we had a good time with the audiences.

I was certain that no one had a better military assignment than mine. I was on detached special services, wore civilian clothes, and had a budget to buy properties each month; however, there were certain adventures and risks, such as the wives of the officers. I mean, the wives had invited me to direct their proposed original comedy about family life on a military base. Not a chance, not with the wives of men who could send me back to a combat unit in a second, but my public poses were more strategic. I told the wives that my duties made it impossible for me to assist them in their leisure activities. In a few days the colonel had directed me to produce the play; he promised the resources of his command, which were considerable. The message was clear: the wives would have their play.

My initial hesitation turned to humor; the wives were generous, and their creative presentation of the common burdens of families living on military bases overseas was a great success. The audience, officers and dependents, understood the subtleties and the arcane language; they laughed and applauded at all the right moments. The play was honest, the actors were sincere, and the production was a great pleasure, a proper conclusion to my military career.

Aiko was tired, but she was eager to leave the city and spend the weekend at Matsushima. We arrived in the afternoon, crossed the bridge to the island, and sat on a bench in silence under the pines. The water was weak, the islands were buried in blues, wisps of mist and light on the rise. The past, our time together, rushed to touch each word. I told her about my plans to study television production; my acceptance letter from the Capital Engineering Institute, a four-year college, was at hand to prove my practical intentions. I had decided not to study at Sophia University in Tokyo. She was troubled, but she would not have lived with me in any case. We never made promises, and were not bound to the idea of marriage, but we were trothed by trust and honor. She was distracted and silent that night, most of the weekend; we returned to Sendai late on Sunday.

I returned to the barracks to check my mail and discovered that departure orders had been posted and my name was on the list; the train would leave early the next morning for Tokyo. I packed my duffel bag and worried about Aiko. She was at home, and wanted to leave. I was leaving for home, but there was no home, no home was real to me then; not nostalgia as a home, but home with communal aspirations. That night the excitement of our departure was real, and it seemed to me then that she was on the outside, and she needed my care. I wondered how to tell her, and even considered not telling her anything; just leave and forget the past, but she said she would call me the next day. I could not bear the thought that she would find out about my departure from a third person in the morning.

I arranged for my duffel to be delivered to the train depot and then, about three in the morning, took a taxicab to Kitagojunin Matchi. I pounded on the gate several times and rang the small bell, and then shouted for Aiko. Her father told me to go away and stay away, in Japanese. He must have thought I was drunk. Aiko opened the gate at last. Time would not be silent that night, the last hour was at hand. My departure was at the gate, not the train station, not in public, we were alone; tormented by the last touch, and swollen with tears, the burdens of our rushed memories. We were hushed in the shadows, and then the last touch, the last wave at the corner. I cried and walked for hours to the train depot. I wanted to change my mind, to stay at home in Japan. I had no home; how ironic that there was no home at the end of my last road home.

I watched other soldiers and women embrace at the station; their touch, the words they whispered were familiar. "People were speaking the universal language of departure, that varies not at all the whole world over," wrote Thomas Wolfe in *From Death to Morning*. "And he saw and heard these familiar words and actions. . . . the overwhelming loneliness of familiarity, the sense of the human identity that so strangely unites all the people in the world, and that is rooted in the structure of man's life, far below the tongue he speaks, the race of which he is a member."

The troop ship sailed out of Yokohama and Tokyo Bay on a northern course that August, and a week later docked overnight in the Aleutian Islands at Adak, Alaska. The islands and enormous trees on the Inside Passage were specters, shrouded women in the mist; the fog was thick in the morning and the ship pushed the demons to their shores. We were animals in the sea, and then our silence was broken. My tongue was cold, our shouts over the bow were held in the cold trees, and the sea was cold; on the starboard there were mammals whose blood held the sea, our course between the ice, the women, and the islands. I was lonesome, and the ship was silent and smooth on the water; we could have been lost. The sea would be my blood, my home.

Seattle was clean and clear in the distance; the ship eased to the dock in the afternoon. I suppose we were the last of the new warriors to return, because a military band marched to "The Stars and Stripes Forever" by John Philip Sousa. An enormous banner over the dock read, "Welcome Home Defenders of Freedom." I was embarassed by the dubious praise, and troubled by the word "home." I was even more lonesome and grieved over my decision to leave Japan.

Fort Lawton was my separation center. I was there about two weeks; the elders called it "dead time," but it was more like "slow death." I was assigned to a fence detail; in three days seven soldiers dug holes, buried posts, fastened low wooden rails, and painted the poles green, in that order. The next day we were told to remove the fence, cover the holes, and then, of course, start over again. The sergeant in charge of our detail said he was a decorated combat veteran and he would not be humiliated by "dickheads behind desks." He was right, we agreed.

I was named to head the fence detail the next day, a terrible measure of my tolerance, military absurdities, and the cardinal virtues. I was determined, however, to beat the dickheads at their own game. In record time, we planted and removed the fence the same day. The dickheads could not bear my serious attention to the details and decided to promote me to "supervise a lawn sprinkler" attached to a water hose. A new lieutenant marched me to an empty barracks, ordered me to turn the sprinkler on in the morning and off in the late afternoon.

"What about the rest of the day?" I asked.

"Sleep, read, but stay away from the fence," said the lieutenant. He gave me a key to the barracks, directed me to a bunk, and turned down a mattress. "This is your only assignment, this bunk and the sprinklers."

"Yes, sir." I watched the sprinklers and was on the bunk for about a week, to the end of my military service. Everything made sense, in the manner of the military, but one afternoon the water pressure increased and the sprinkler reached to the street. I was asleep when two officers came into the barracks.

"On your feet, soldier."

"Yes, sir."

"What's your name."

"Private First Class Vizenor, sir."

"What are you doing here?"

"This is my job, sir."

"What job, this is an empty barracks?"

"Watching the sprinkler."

"Are you serious, soldier?"

"Yes, sir, and sleeping until my discharge."

"Watch the sprinkler then."

"Yes, sir." The officers understood in the end because they were waiting to be discharged too; most of the people on the post were counting the days to freedom from the realities of the absurd. My duties as a sprinkler guard allowed me time to be alone, to consider my return, and to remember stories from my military career.

Chitose was closed to soldiers for a time when it was declared a "sex circus," but several of us went into town anyway. Our scheme was foolproof, or almost without a hitch. We signed up for dental examinations, which were done at the post hospital on the other side of town. We bribed the bus driver to stop in town and then to pick us up again at the end of the day. We spent the day at House Tokyo. The bus came back too early one afternoon; we missed it by seconds with our boots in hand. We waited until dark, and then climbed fences near the gasoline storage tanks to avoid the main gate and the military police. The tanks were lighted; my strategy was based on the lights, and a potential explosion was our cover. The Army hired Japanese guards to protect the tanks. I was right; the guards shouted at us to halt several times, loaded and aimed their rifles, but did not shoot because we ran close to the tanks. We made it back to camp and celebrated with sloe gin at the enlisted club.

Once upon a time we were on maneuvers, a simulated war between battalions. The "aggressors" wore helmets with wooden crowns. The soldiers were issued blank ammunition, and our weekend combat was on the road. On the first night several of us maneuvered into town, ate, drank, and stayed overnight in comfortable beds. The next night we circled the combat area and captured the enemy commanders in their sleep; we tied the lieutenants, captains, and majors together with rope and marched them back to our battalion for interrogation. Naturally, they were furious and demanded their release; the game was over, they insisted. We broke their radio codes and issued spurious orders; at last, they agreed to surrender. We were declared the winners of the battle, but never the war.

I was called for prison guard duty at the post near Mount Fuji, a few weeks before my transfer to entertainment. Guards were issued loaded shotguns, several mean prisoners, and duties for the day. The first day we hauled ashes in a dump truck. The prisoners taunted me, tried to fake me out, dumped ashes on my polished boots, and then told me to ride in the back because the prisoners were crowded on the seat with the driver. The prisoners were huge; they menaced me with their muscles, or so it seemed to a welterweight who wrestled in high school. We were told that if a prisoner escaped the guards would serve their sentence in prison. I opened the truck doors, ordered the driver out, cocked my shotgun, pressed the barrel on the neck of the prisoner with the biggest mouth, and said, "Guards don't serve time for dead prisoners." The prisoners rode in back with me, on the ashes. The next two days, the last of my prison duty, I was assigned to guard prisoners in the hospital.

We were detained once in the cold rain on the rifle range because one soldier could not hit the target and qualify with his carbine. He tried, and tried, and missed the circles. We passed the word down the line, and the next time he fired a round at the target, we fired too and blew the center out of his target. He passed and we marched back to the barracks.

The cherry blossoms were in high bloom, and paper lanterns lighted the wooden bridge and the path through the trees to the hotel. Aiko was at peace; we there for the weekend, a beautiful resort near Sendai. Saturday night, a new moon, and we watched the stars shout over the balcony; the most distant stars traced an unseasoned course with my pulse. Aiko held warm cherry petals that she had selected earlier; she placed them on the hard pillows.

I heard familiar voices later, from the lower rooms, and discovered that the sergeants, and other soldiers from my battalion, were at a dinner, and a sex circus performance. Women danced down the low black tables over the food and pushed their cunts into the faces of eager soldiers. Other women were harnessed with dildos and fucked other women over the rice, over the suimono; the soldiers were wild. No one saw me at the back between the panels. I returned to our room and said nothing about the show. Aiko loved me, she touched me with cherry blossoms, her breath was sweet.

I checked on the sprinklers one last time, turned in my hose, and was given an honorable discharge on August 31, 1955, three months short of my three-year enlistment in the Army. Two hours later, the military gave me my first and last airplane ride back to Minneapolis. I visited old friends, but my memories there were too close to remember with humor. Minneapolis said leave, leave, to me, and the city must have said that to my father. He stayed there and was murdered; our mixed blood and memories were held in the same pronouns and stories, but my heart told me to leave once more.

I bought a 1951 Chevrolet coupe and drove to Washington, D.C. There, I registered at the Capital Engineering Institute, rented a private room in an old mansion, and planned my new future as a television broadcast engineer. A few days later, however, my plans had changed once more. I packed the car and drove to New York City to visit my close friends from the Army; they had registered to begin college in a few days and urged me to join then as an undergraduate. I did, and that chance connection was the start of a new career at New York University.

Thomas Wolfe was born in Asheville, North Carolina, but he lived in New York City, and first taught at New York University a decade before my birth. "What is the fury which this youth will feel, which will lash him on against the great earth forever? It is the brain that maddens with its own excess, the heart that breaks from the anguish of its own frustration," wrote Wolfe in *Of Time and the River*. "For what is it that we Americans are seeking always on this earth? Why is it we have crossed the stormy seas so many times alone, lain in a thousand alien rooms at night hearing the sounds of time, dark time, and thought until heart, brain, flesh and spirit were sick and weary with the thought of it; 'Where shall I go now? What shall I do?' "

Gerald Vizenor, Camp Chitose, Hokkaido, Japan, 1953

Gerald Vizenor with tank crew, winter maneuvers, Hokkaido, Japan, 1954

Private Gerald Vizenor with friends, winter maneuvers, First Cavalry Division, Hokkaido, Japan, 1953

Gerald Vizenor in Tokyo, Japan, 1954

Train to Noboribetsu, Hokkaido, Japan, 1953

*TOP Aiko Okada,
Matsushima Island,
Japan, 1955*

*LEFT Aiko Okada
and hotel manager,
Anabara, Japan, 1955*

TOP Gerald Vizenor, Jim Perry, and Bill Nelson, Noboribetsu, Hokkaido, Japan, 1954

RIGHT Gerald Vizenor, Lake Shikosu, Imperial National Forest, Hokkaido, Japan, 1954

Home, Imperial National Forest,
Hokkaido, Japan, 1954

Hokkaido Brown Bear in the Imperial
National Forest.

Children, Noboribetsu, Hokkaido, Japan, 1953

Children, Muroran, Hokkaido, Japan, 1954

Sapporo, Hokkaido, Japan, 1954

Chitose, Hokkaido, Japan, 1953

TOP *Tokyo, Japan, 1953*

LEFT *Tokyo, Japan, 1954*

BOTTOM *Gotemba, Japan, 1955*

Hotel in Noboribetsu, Japan, 1953

Gotemba, Japan, 1955

Japanese War Veterans, Tokyo, Japan, 1954

Imperial Hotel designed by Frank Lloyd Wright, Tokyo, Japan, 1954

Imperial Hotel designed by Frank Lloyd Wright, Tokyo, Japan, 1954

Gerald Vizenor, honorable discharge, 1955

January 1956: King Lear in a Wheelchair

━━━━━━━━━━━━━━━━Orson Welles played King Lear in a wheelchair at the City Center in New York. I was astonished when the star of *Citizen Kane* rolled out on stage to introduce his wounds, and enchanted to be in the audience for such an unusual performance.

Welles had broken bones in one foot, and then in the last scene on the night of the premiere he sprained his right ankle; a second fool in the play pushed the tragic king in his wheelchair. That night, a chance encounter with a brilliant and wounded actor became a metaphor in my stories, and one more good reason to live in New York City.

"During an early performance, Welles fell from a ramp backstage and broke two bones in his left foot," wrote Frank Brady in *Citizen Welles*. "He decided to go on, nevertheless, with the premiere on the scheduled date, January 12. So on opening night, Welles performed *Lear* with cast and cane." Lear with a cane was reasonable, but confined to a wheechair the aged king was postmodern.

Welles, at the conclusion of the premiere, "tripped over a prop at his final exit and sprained his right ankle. He showed up to a packed house on the second night confined to a wheelchair. . . . Then he heard and saw someone using a camera in the first row center: 'Please don't take pictures,' he said with a smile. 'That clicking noise sounds like the breaking of bones.' "

New York University, at Washington Square, accepted my application to be an undergraduate student on the condition that my high school records would be provided at a later date; naturally, my records would never be revealed. I had completed courses recommended for graduation through a correspondence school in the military, and two college courses, but the high school dean refused to honor them for credit.

I had done well in my first semester at New York University, and assumed that at the end of the college year the high school records would be forgotten. Not so, and the rest is an academic catch with a new number: since my admission was conditional, my transcript would not be released until I passed an entrance examination. I had completed two semesters and worried about failing an examination to do what I had already done with success. I passed and then returned to Minneapolis. The University of Minnesota accepted me with advance standing and no one said a word about my high school records again.

Thomas Wolfe, Orson Welles, Louise Bogan, and Eda Lou Walton come together in my remembrance, a coincidence at New York University. Less than four years earlier my imagination and insecurities were cornered by social workers; in my first year of college, these late crossblood burdens were rich conditions in literature, studied as metaphors and cultural themes. Some encounters were comic and ironic; certain adventures were coups and contradictions. My liberation was the military in Japan; my education, chance and coincidence.

Thomas Wolfe taught at New York University; that was an important association for me at the time. Moreover, he had shared a faculty office with Eda Lou Walton and she praised my stories in her writing class. That small cluttered office was enlivened when she told me about her institutional connections with Wolfe.

"You have read Thomas Wolfe?"

"Yes, of course."

"Has he influenced the way you write?"

"Yes, I think so."

"I can see that in your descriptions."

"Yes, thank you, sometimes." She was generous, an eager teacher, and she praised imagination and the power of description, but her comments on grammar, structure, were rough and direct. Thomas Wolfe she said, and it never occurred to me then that she might have been mocking the novelist, his wild influences on me. Even so, her most bitter criticism would never dissuade me from the celebration of chance and coincidence at New York University.

Eda Lou Walton earned her doctorate at the University of California and taught at the University of New Mexico in Albuquerque. She studied tribal cultures and literatures and published two collections of Native American poetry. She encouraged me to study in the Southwest, an unusual tribal connection; had she studied haiku the coincidence might have been a hindrance.

She published *Dawn Boy*, a collection of Blackfoot and Navajo songs, more than sixty years ago in a limited edition. Witter Bynner wrote in the introduction, "Miss Walton, a poet not only bred in Indian terrain but well versed in her art and well attuned in her spirit, has brought into more congenial English than any other interpreter has found, the simplicities, the serenities, the grave and happy mysticism of Indian song." Bynner bears a dose of white man's burden, too much burden.

I discovered her imaginative alterations of tribal stories and songs many years later; now, her romantic transcriptions would catch negative criticism. "I have left out tiresome refrains, repetitive, and parallelistic lines," wrote Walton in the preface to *Dawn Boy*. She was sensitive and direct as a teacher, her students must remember her attention with fondness; however, her ideas about tribal literatures are neither reliable nor stand to reason. "I have, I am sure, been closely true to the essence, the heart and spirit of the Indian poetic conception. I have presented these poems simply and directly, without artificiality of diction, letting the beauty of the idea or symbol stand clear-cut." She was right to be critical of the anthropological interpretations, but she does not seem to be aware of the racialism and invalidations of certain translations. For example, she identified Washington Mathews as "the greatest authority on the Navajo." The Navajo, of course, are their own best authorities on matters of culture, language, healing songs, and spiritual solace. She was never insensitive to the literatures of other cultures; her edition of *This Generation* was one of the few anthologies published forty years ago that included minority authors.

Eda Lou Walton was a most considerate teacher; with pleasure she raised the beams on literature, praised imagination, peeled the seals on precious prose, healed wounds, and she allowed me to shout and brush the wild nation with descriptions in the manner of Thomas Wolfe.

Louise Bogan, poet and critic, taught a course on poetry writing at New York University. I could not register for evening courses, but heard most of her lectures and discussions on poetry; a silence seemed to surround her manner, an impersonal attention to figuration and style. I learned from her to avoid the use of the affix "-ly" that indicates and modifies as a resemblance, and to retreat from sentimentalities in poetry. She never read my poems but she held books of poems with a firm and confident hand.

Elaine Showalter, in her essay "Women Writers between the Wars," wrote that Louise Bogan "chose a severely impersonal poetry," a dissociation of sentimental excesses. "At the same time that Bogan pursued her austere credo of withdrawing 'her own personality from her productions,' she envied male poets their space, ambition, variety, and freedom to express personality."

Eda Lou Walton touched me as a creative writer; she pushed me to create new storms, the words that moved the water. Louise Bogan was distant in the classroom, her practices in literature were acute; she was never harsh, but she was a sharpshooter at the blackboard. These two teachers influenced my earliest expressions as a creative writer. Miscues were natural, and there were misgiven resolutions to abide the canon and institutions, but literature, and my first teachers of literature, rescued me from the nemeses of the social sciences.

The Dell Publishing Company hired me as an assistant to a nervous man who answered book orders and inventories. He would receive by mail or telephone an order for several paperbound copies of Plato, Chaucer, or other more popular books, and it was my responsibility to be sure that the titles were available; the actual stock was in a waterfront warehouse. However, most of my time was given to mitigation and milk runs; he had stomach ulcers and bad manners with women, secretaries who typed the orders for shipment. Some of the women taunted him, only to talk with me to relieve the boredom of their work. Hundreds of women sat at metal desks in an enormous open area; one manager headed two rows of young secretaries. The women dressed bargain basement, but not on fragrance day, one special day each month. The perfume was nauseous; some women wore their treasures, an inherited jewel in a ring or necklace, synthetic hair, talismans, and secret charms to hold the gaze of a man in the movies. The company published several screen magazines, and once a month paraded a male movie star through the offices, down the rows and rows of desks between the women; the stars were featured on the covers of screen magazines, and their appearance in the office must have been tied to a contract. I could imagine my mother there on the aisle, a scent of lilacs in her hair; seventeen, sincere, lonesome, and summoned to a cold tenement with George Raft.

I was astonished, some women screamed, and some climbed on their desks to be seen in their best clothes. I had been a movie usher once and remembered the rush of younger women when Johnnie Ray sang "The Little White Cloud That Cried." The myths of the movie men touch a silent promise, a chance signature, and are sustained by the tours of movie stars once a month between the desks. The myths prevailed, but the services of the women were soon superfluous.

One morning the company cleared a section in the center of the work area; desks were moved closer together. An enclosure with windows was built in the area; the women were incurious and paid no critical attention to the reorganization of the company, but they complained that the movie stars would not be able to move down the narrowed aisles.

I worked there about fifteen hours a week for several months my first semester at New York University. In that time the enclosure became a computer center, a system that would replace most of the typists and secretaries; most of the young women waited on the movies and became redundant to the company. Dell Publishing seemed more concerned and provided more protection for the new machines than for the humans who had done the same work; the machines were cooled and cleaned by the best technicians. Once the women were gone the movie stars were hailed and adored by computers once a month.

I continued my studies and applied for other work that demanded no more than twenty hours a week. I failed as a cutlery salesman; the district manager tried to train me, but my constant criticism of his unscrupulous sales methods ended that dubious career. I worked as a clerk at the information desk at the university for a time, but found a better job at a new car dealership. I was hired as an "expediting manager" to be certain that new cars were delivered to the buyers on time; the title could have been ironic, but the pay was good. The automobile business was feral, wicked, diseased, without honor, and never monotonous. The treasurer of the company admired my honesty, he said from behind his wide desk, and then fired me at the end of four months because of my anger over an unethical new car sale. A retired fireman bought an expensive new sedan; he said it would be his last. The car was scheduled to be serviced when the rear end and one side were crushed by a truck; a mechanic had backed the car out of the garage too fast into traffic. The sales manager had the car repaired and painted overnight, but the frame was out of line. I protested and was fired before the car was delivered to the fireman as new.

That experience, the high cost of tuition at a private university, the harsh traffic, the press of people in the city, and a suicide on the subway, a black man who leapt in front of a fast train, convinced me that when the school year ended it would be time for me to return to Minnesota.

I passed my courses in both semesters, but received low letter grades in two business administration courses: one was earned in accounting, a bill-of-lading problem, and the other was a punitive grade in a management course. I had completed a very good final paper, a time-and-motion study of Chock Full O'Nuts, a restaurant chain. I shared an early draft of my paper with a fellow student who had been out sick; he handed in my work, and the instructor, who had praised my research earlier, punished me for causing the temptation to plagiarism. Competition and economic countenance were the elitist standards he celebrated; my values would never survive the eastern manners of social Darwinians. Two courses in business administration were more than enough for me, forever.

June 1956: Return to Salvation

━━━━━━━━━━━━━━━━━━━━━*The* Salvation Army hired me as a counselor at their summer camp for public welfare mothers and their children. I returned with twenty dollars, no place to live, and discovered my salvation at the Silver Lake Camp near Minneapolis.

Colonel Martin asked me about my religious experiences in the final interview. I told him about my mixedblood families, the fur trade, and the mission of the Roman Catholic Church; however, he understood that most my associations with religion were evangelical. I mentioned the cinder block chapel, my time in fosterage, our religious songs and labors, but not the glorious breasts we waited to see at the construction site. The colonel would hear the truth, my encounters and needs, and there must have been a certain advantage, and some evidence of reformation, in my loose connections to Catholicism.

Colonel Martin and his wife, who held the same rank, were generous and astute observers of human ambition, weakness, and the practical politics of religion; they gave me a home, good conversation, a salary at the camp, and became my family for a time. Their trust and good humor were indeed a salvation on my return from New York University.

Jay Martin, their son, was a college student eager to be involved in business and economics; we held no views or public estimations in common. We argued over ideas and evidence, over water, wind, and weather; but we were, it seemed, more dedicated to counterbalance than domination. We cared for each other, and in this manner, some families are healed with humor and contradictions, and others are overturned by the obvious and the banal. My idealism was contested, my passions remembered, but never with mere toleration; these were unusual experiences in families at the time.

The public welfare children at the camp were wild by day, and their mothers were wild by night. I taught the children about animals, birds, and sacred creation stories; they had their own ideas about flowers and weeds. Some of the mothers pursued their sense of nature at night, in the brush with mosquitoes, and their lovers. Their sense of a vacation was not tied to the same ideas or inhibitions as those of the evangelists who invited them to the camp. The meals were regular and we wondered, given the natural pastures at the camp, how many children were conceived that summer.

Two particular evangelists hover in my memories of that summer camp: one was a short captain with thick black hair on his arms, the second short captain in my military experience, who shouted at night to save the sinners on the humid shore; the second was a celebrated evangelist who was on the road to save souls but who had the most trouble with his own.

The captain shouted for several weeks that humid summer to save the women on welfare, and then he turned his rage on the counselors, on the canvas, on the weeds, the water, the thick air. We could have been saved, from one thing or another, but not by a man in uniform. We resisted and he stared at us over meals, and then we decided to confront him on his own ground, under the circus tent.

I attended the revival with the life guard, a single woman who taught literature in high school; we sat near the back of the tent. The captain roared and raved over our generic sins, and one by one the women leapt to their feet, raised their arms, and shouted back the need for a power greater than the captain, "Jesus, Jesus, hold me Jesus." The women shouted their needs, their witness to his power as a salvationist; one more tarnished soul on the right road to salvation. We waited, and listened; we were the last two sinners seated in the tent. The others had been saved and the end was near at hand. I stared back at the short captain, leaned toward him on the metal chair, and pretended that he held me closer to witness the power of his voice and spirit, on the rim of salvation.

We were the last to stand and he was relieved; he turned in circles, raised his arms, and shouted hallelujah, hallelujah, hallelujah. We smiled and moved to the aisle; the others turned to witness our moves, and he returned our smile. He was certain that we would come forward for his special blessing, to be touched, an inspiration to the women. Instead, we nodded, turned, and walked out of the tent. The women sighed with doubt and wonder that we had resisted his summons to be saved; some of the women reconsidered their witness and salvation that night. The short captain was furious, and shunned me the rest of the summer. However, once he was seated near me at a dinner; he was a sweater, but he sweated more in my presence. He must have seen me as the demon who came to test his faith and dedication under the canvas.

The free-lance evangelist seemed to be more at ease with the women, a manner that did not seem to please his wife; he told stories about the wages of sin with cheap wine, and invited sinners to witness salvation with a clean breath, and some humor, he insisted. That he held to humor and cheap wine belied his courage and correction; his laughter seemed unnatural, and he drank the best liquor.

His face was burdened with wicked secrets and the undercurrent of peevish humor. His wife was too nervous, and overdecorated; she wore too much perfume, and her toenails were painted red and wild under the table. She admired her toes when she crossed, and uncrossed, her legs. Their guest apartment was next to mine; the walls were thin, uninsulated. I overheard them argue, hold their sex with mutual contempt, and dispraise their hosts and the purposes of the camp. They were not at ease with the children, and he could not seem to bear the breath of the poor. The evangelist was weak and hateful, he cursed the poor and welfare women, and he drank whiskey. Two empty bottles were found in the trash and the welfare mothers were shamed for violating the rules against beverage alcohol.

George Bernard Shaw might have measured a suitable comment here: "But there are millions of poor people, abject people, dirty people, ill fed, ill clothed people," said Stephen Undershaft in *Major Barbara*. "They poison us morally and physically: they kill the happiness of society: they force us to do away with our liberties and to organize unnatural cruelties for fear they should rise against us and drag us down into their abyss. Only fools fear crime: we all fear poverty."

Colonel Martin invited me to discuss my concerns about the spurious evangelist. We sat on the screen porch of the main house, with a view of the lake. He tried to hold me to humor and natural descriptions, but my mood was severe and my criticism of hypocrisies had never been loose or gentle. What troubled me the most was that he allowed the welfare mothers to be blamed for his habits. I would sooner be on public welfare, the source of my identities, than in the ruined humor of a wicked evangelist.

"We heard about the alcohol," said Colonel Martin.

"Who told you?"

"No one," he said.

"I don't understand?"

"The whiskey was much too expensive."

"Naturally, but they were still blamed," I said.

"Some of the women drink, but not with such luxury."

"He and his wife bad-mouth the camp."

"Did you hear them?"

"Some," I said, but decided not to continue with my harsh criticism of the evangelist. I should not have been listening, and in any case, chance determined what was overheard. I might have been out that night and heard nothing. I tried another critical method, and mentioned their manners. "They did not seem to like us very much."

"You might be right."

"They criticize the program."

"Some," said Colonel Martin.

"More than a little. They seem rather hateful about the leadership of the camp." I was uncomfortable and this was my last comment on what was heard through the walls of my apartment.

"I don't believe that," insisted Colonel Martin.

"I heard him say as much."

"I don't believe that," he repeated.

"That man is a lonesome lush."

"Not so lonesome."

"Then a lush, at least," I pleaded.

"The private lush?"

"Would you want him to teach your children?"

"He's not a lonesome man."

"It's true," I said.

"No, you're not the hateful leader, are you?"

"You're right as usual," I said and ended the discussion. Colonel Martin measured the best conversations with the converse, the turn in tone and sense. We listened to the water, the animals on shore; there was laughter in the brush over the mound, and mosquitoes bashed the screen on the porch.

The Salvation Army was my salvation that summer, a secular return and deliverance from the burdens of my past. The salvation families were dedicated to communal values and believed that service to people in need was an honor. These salvationists were tribal, and comic in their uniforms. The short captain wanted me that summer, he wanted my soul to decorate his hat, but he was denied a crossblood on the run. No one else pressed me to their religious heat, no one would have dared to tease a trickster or the demons.

October 1957: Death Song to a Red Rodent

The best hunters are never in competition with their environments; tribal hunters are the primal posers in the brush, and tricksters the overtures in their stories. The hunter and the trickster would laud the hunted, pretend, and mock the sacred, but never minister the cold trinities, monomercies, and resurrections.

The mythic and moral heart of the hunter is wasted in competition with other hunters; the instincts of the tribal hunter are measured best when he is not with others in the woods. Together, hunters depend upon each other for their identities; alone, the hunter must trust his own survival instincts with birds and animals, and move with the natural energies of the woodland, trees, and water.

I pretended to be a tribal hunter, but my survival identities were urban. I ate squirrels and other wild game; the animals were never wasted, but my time in the cities did not depend upon the hunt. The death of an animal was remote; the separation, and then a sudden adventure, seldom a sacred chase in wild weather. I hunted ducks, pheasant, and the smaller animals, but never moose, deer, or bear.

I walked into the woods alone, found a place in the sun, and rested against an oak tree. The animals and birds sensed my presence and waited in silence for me to pass. My energies were mechanical from the cities; my breath had been over concrete, and my hands on gun oil. My rifle was cold. The oak leaves rattled on the breeze. The squirrels waited in the distance, a natural escape distance; they sensed my intentions. I had come from the cities to kill them with my rifle, to breathe concrete into their souls, to eat their bitter thighs.

I fell asleep against the tree; later, the environment seemed closer to me, as in a dream. I awakened with a new sense of sound and motion; birds were singing, and squirrels were eating and running between the trees near me. I pretended to run with them: we were the hunted and the hunters.

I raised my rifle, took aim, and fired at a large red squirrel running across an oak bough. He fell to the ground near the trunk of the tree, bounced once, and started to climb the tree again. The bullet had passed through his shoulder and shattered the bone. His right front leg and paw dangled from torn flesh. He dropped to the ground and tried to climb the tree again, and again. I understood his instinct to escape; in a dream we reached up with our right paw, shattered and blood soaked, but it was not there to hold us to the tree.

The squirrel fell down again and watched me with his dark eyes; I watched him and he watched me that autumn. Blood spread down his body. He tried to climb the tree again, and again, to escape from me, to escape from my dream, the city in me; my breath, weapons, cold hands, haunted him at the end.

He had been a wise survivor, a curious red rodent, but then he scolded and dared to come closer to a sleeping hunter. That he dared was the mortal ruin of the squirrel, not his curiosities. He knew when and how to hide from most hunters, their harsh voices were burned in the memories of his animal tribe. I was alone, and said nothing. My presence was masked by sleep; my movements were not the same as those hunters in competition, their shouts, and sudden silence, their marches over the oak leaves. I had never learned the language of the squirrels, or the stories of their brutal death at the hands of urban hunters. That red squirrel dared me to hunt him; his dare was a response to my silence, as he would respond to the songs of a tribal hunter.

The best urban hunters learned never to let a wounded animal suffer, as if the hunter were bound to a moral code of the state ministrants; the animals we wounded must be put out of their miseries, our miseries. The Boy Scouts of America, and waltonians, members of the Izaak Walton League of America, taught me monomercies and the coup de grâce.

"Hunting disturbs moralists because it enjoins men to be joyful in killing," wrote Paul Shepard in *The Tender Carnivore and the Sacred Game*. "Men with only hand weapons do not need to invent stern codes to insure that hunting is a challenge rather than an amusement. The hunter's confrontation of the enigmas of death and animal life inspire attitudes of honor and awe expressed in ceremonial address."

I fired one shot at his head when the squirrel tried to climb the tree again, to put him out of his miseries. The bullet tore the flesh and fur away from the top of his skull. He dropped to the ground and turned on the oak leaves. He looked at me. I watched his dark eyes; he was close to death, he wanted to live. I fired a second time at his head. The bullet tore his lower jaw away, his teeth were exposed. He watched me and then moved in the leaves toward the tree. Blood bubbled from his nostrils when he breathed. I fired twice more, the bullets shattered his forehead and burst through his left eye. He held to the base of the tree, his last paw weakened, and he watched me with one eye. His breath was slower, slower, more blood in his nostrils, in his mouth. In his last eye he wanted to live, to run free, not to dare me, to hide from me. I kneeled beside the squirrel, my face close to his blood-soaked head, my eye close to his eye, and asked him to forgive me. I begged him to forgive me before he died. I looked around at the trees. My breath was sudden, short. I remembered the moment, nothing more; my hands were strange, alone, distant, isolated in the environment.

The blood bubbled from his nose; the bubbles were smaller, smaller, and then disappeared. I moved closer to his eye once more and pleaded in tears, please forgive me. Please live once more. I begged that squirrel to live again, to come alive once more.

He blinked at me. His eye was still alive. Did that blink of his eye mean that he had forgiven me? I moaned close to him in the leaves, please forgive me. At last, my piteous moans were silent. No birds were in the trees; the leaves were silent. The squirrel blinked once more, but he would not breathe. I moved closer to him, stretched out on the ground next to him, and ran my hand down his back. The blood was warm, my hand was warmed with his blood. I cried beside him, and watched him die, his breath was gone; his life passed through me in his last eye. I owe so much to that red squirrel who dared me to hunt him in the oaks, who died in me. I sang a death song, a song in a low voice without words until dark that autumn.

The hunter "returns to the natural state, becomes one with the animal, and is freed from the burden of the existential split," wrote Erich Fromm in *The Anatomy of Human Destructiveness*. "Of at least equal importance for the passionate hunter is an entirely different motivation, that of enjoyment in his skill. It is amazing how many modern authors neglect this element of skill in hunting, and focus their attention on the act of killing. After all, hunting requires a combination of many skills and wide knowledge beyond that of handling a weapon."

I sold my rifle and never hunted to kill animals or birds again. The violent death of a wild animal caused by my weapon was a separation from the natural world, not a reunion. I would defend squirrels and comfort them in death; that would be the natural human response. I would not shoot an animal again unless my life depended on the hunt.

June 1960: Haiku in the Attic

━━━━━━━━━━━━━━━━━ *R*obert Vizenor was three months old when we moved into a narrow attic apartment in Prospect Park near the University of Minnesota. Judith Horns Vizenor had been an elementary school teacher and she would return to graduate school in education. Our apartment was a summer adventure; there was a kitchen area, but the sink was in the bathroom. We bathed and washed dishes in the bathtub. I copied hiragana and wrote haiku on the low slope of the ceiling. Fifty dollars a month included the back porch, a pleasant perch in the maple trees. Robert walked late that summer, in that apartment, for the first time.

I registered in summer school, four more courses to complete my degree, worked in the new anthropology library, and several hours a week attended animals in a special research program at the school of dentistry. More than a dozen dogs had their mandibles broken to observe the various methods of healing. I fed the dogs once a day, and assisted the doctor in surgery. One by one the dogs were sacrificed in the interests of science; my visits to the kennel became last rites on death row at the university.

Professor Edward Copeland opened his course on Japanese literature that summer with haiku in translation. The sense of impermanence, he said, is in the weather, the seasons, and in haiku; at the same time, we are aware of culture and tradition. The trees were in bloom near the windows. I was fortunate to have found a memorable course with an inspired teacher, and blest now to remember several distinguished teachers in four years at two universities.

Copeland nurtured literature, he turned poems over and over with a courteous hand. His voice was clear, the sound of mountain water, never strained; not a mere murmur at a blackboard. He would seldom complain and never consume literature. We met four times a week in the morning; the class was small, about fifteen students. He wore loafers and a sweater, the autumn colors rounded his thin shoulders, and he arrived one minute past the bell at the hour.

Copeland recited and translated one of the greatest haiku poems by Basho: *furuike ya*, the ancient pond; *kawazu to-bikomu*, frog leaps, or jumps; *mizu no oto*, sound of water, or splash. The poem shows the season, and suggests tradition and impermanence in the most subtle images and motions. Copeland paused, a natural silence, as a poem would score, and then he continued his introduction to the course.

Issa, we would understand, was near to nature, an elusive treasure in haiku imagination, and we wondered if our teacher had been the poet in one of his past lives. Copeland, Issa, and Takuboku seemed to be our teachers that summer. Literature, haiku, our seasons at the window were there in the imagination of our existence, and yet, and yet.

Issa celebrated common creatures, the earth as it turns, runs, and blooms, impermanence and human ironies; he was poor, an orphan, and he loved nature. Copeland told a haiku by Issa: world of dew, world of dew and yet, and yet.

Japanese literature became the source of my second liberation; the first was in the military, and then in the summer of my senior year at the University of Minnesota. I studied culture, literature, art, and language with Edward Copeland.

We read introductions by Donald Keene, selections from diaries, and the *Manyoshu*, translations of haiku by R. H. Blyth, and Harold Henderson, and novels by Kawabata Yasunari, and Dazai Osamu. Someone mentioned Lafcadio Hearn.

Copeland was moved by the poems of Takuboku Ishikawa; a limited hand printed edition of *A Handful of Sand* was published, in translation, the year of my birth. Takuboku had traveled to Hokkaido. Later, his mother and wife suffered from tuberculosis; he wrote to a poet, "I have no money to take care of us and no courage to write. Really this has become a worthless world for me." He died at age twenty-seven. Copeland praised his poetry, the power of his dramatic images. I complained that the poet suffered so much to write, "and such a small book for so much hardship and death." My insecurities were on the rise. I worried that my life would be miserable, reduced to a thin volume of poems. My teacher paused, then he said, "Takuboku might have written nothing, how lucky we are that he left these poems." Then he read several poems from *A Handful of Sand*:

My father and mother are aged. . . .
O mosquitoes!
One and all,
Come and bite my skinny legs.

With the joy of meeting
A long lost friend,
I listen to the sound of water.

Coming home from my duties
Late at night,
I hold my child
Who has just died.

When I breathe,
There is a rolling sound in my chest,
A sound more desolate
Than that of a winter blast.

O, the sadness of lifeless sand!
Trickling,
It falls through my fingers
When I take it in my hands.

Copeland handed me a note at the end of the hour in the second week of class. The trees were rich and tender in their greens. The note, folded once with a deckle edge, was written in a gracious hand, "You have been looking out the window during my lectures. What do you see?" I waited, looked once more at the trees outside the window, and answered his note with this summer haiku:

> In search of poems
> How many trees have fallen?
> Sound of the wind.

I read his note several more times and worried because two days had passed; he had not responded. I was vulnerable, my response was personal; would he think his lectures were the sound of wind? Copeland said nothing, and then on the third day he handed me a second note, folded once more on deckle paper; his response was a translation of a haiku by Buson:

> Morning breeze
> Fur
> Seems to blow
> Caterpillar!

I was warmed by his generous response with a poem, and heartened by his praise of imagination and literature. Copeland and Eda Lou Walton came together in my memories of the best teachers. His note and our poems started a friendship; several years later he contributed four of his translations of haiku by Basho, Issa, and Buson, to introduce the seasons in my first important collection of original haiku, *Raising the Moon Vines*. I was a graduate student then, studying Japanese and Chinese history, art, and literature, and library science. *Two Wings the Butterfly*, a paperbound limited edition of my very first original haiku, with ink paintings by

Judith Horns Vizenor, was printed in April 1962 by inmates at the Minnesota State Reformatory.

> Did the old grey stump
> Remember her strength today,
> Raising the moon vines.

> In the dark grass
> Her gentle hands alight,
> Two fireflies.

Peter Stitt published the first review of *Two Wings the Butterfly* on October 15, 1962, in the *Ivory Tower*, a literary magazine at the University of Minnesota. He wrote, "Vizenor has an ability to capture the essence of a natural scene or object and concisely express it in some fine poems." Stitt was critical of the "anecdotes" and "lack of suggestiveness" in some poems. Roland Flint reviewed *Raising the Moon Vines*, and *Seventeen Chirps*, my third collection of haiku, for the *Minneapolis Tribune* on January 24, 1965: "The 'emptiness' in haiku is a positive, not a negative, characteristic; it is a succinctness, a deliberate restraint, an avoidance of clutter," wrote Flint. "It invites the reader to supply what is missing, and Vizenor is particularly good at its use. In one of his poems a child's angry grief is suggested but not quite spelled out:

> Crack, crack
> His hoe against the garden stones
> Mother died.

I sold my meager properties, books, and car at the end of my second year at the University of Minnesota, and sailed on the *Nieuw Amsterdam* to Southampton, England. My closest companion on the ship was a bald retired iron worker. We had both sold most of what we owned to travel, but his idea was comic: he wanted to "cash out" on the road; he planned to travel to his death. Henry was certain that his life would run out sooner than his money. He tried to teach me how to drink aquavit with a flourish, but my breath was lost on the first sip. Henry won the popular vote in the tourist class hat contest, but he was disqualified in the end because of his gender. Women wore the hats in this contest; his was an apple and an arrow. I heard his raucous laughter several weeks later on a train in Switzerland. Henry tried once more to teach me how to down aquavit.

I was broke in five weeks and returned with stories, poems, and eight dollars. I was hired as an orderly at Homewood Hospital located at Penn and Plymouth avenues, a few blocks from my first rented room on Willow Street. The hospital admitted people with various mental problems and neurological disorders. There were wanderers in speech and hand, the wild, the touched, and the shocked, on the aisles, but the real lunatics were the orderlies and medical administrators. One man pretended to be a doctor: he wore a white coat, carried a stethoscope, and examined older women; he delighted in electroshock, and his comments were recorded with humor. One orderly was a certified kleptomaniac; theft was his best discourse. Roger would not feel good until he had stolen something, anything, from anyone. I pointed out, however, that he never stole flowers; he would steal whatever he could get his hands on at a flower shop, but never from nature. He stole from patients, friends, and the staff; the more he stole, the happier, but not with malice.

Roger had studied medicine; that is, he attended classes for more than a year before he was discovered and removed as an imposter. He took me on a wild medical tour of the University of Minnesota Hospital. We started in the locker room, white coats, hammers, but no names; he determined that no names indicated more significance. Roger demonstrated microtomy, and he moved a resident pathologist aside to show me a slice of tissue under a microscope. My tour ended in the operating room; we were dressed in greens and wore masks to observe an emergency appendectomy. The surgeon instructed an intern to make the first incision; there were at least a dozen interns and medical students crowded around the patient. I moved to the outside when the surgeon started to ask questions. Roger answered, he was the most impressive student there; he understood the manners of the game, but not the rules of the game.

Homewood Hospital was a circus; the nurses and orderlies were the trainers, the acrobats, and the patients were the animals, the sick animals. One of the nurses had an eye tic that stopped conversations; she would never answer a telephone because she saw fire shoot from the receiver. She took a patient home with her once, a former priest who was not able to leave a house on his feet because he saw fire on the threshold and believed that he would lose his soul if he crossed. We pretended that they were the perfect couple: he could answer the telephone, and she was secure that he would never leave the house. I delivered a parcel to their house once, and when he opened the door he moved back in fear. I was a demon in the fire.

I worked the late afternoon and evening shift. Most of the patients could not tell one orderly from another; we were the crazier ones in white coats, but some patients were sensitive, and more aware than others. Laura, for instance, was restrained, stranded in a mental hospital with advanced Parkinson's disease. She was strapped into a chair to hold her down in front of a television set with other patients. Laura twitched, and shuddered, her head was a wild pitch on the plastic chair, her neck strained, and clicked on the rebound. Laura moaned as best she could to warn me, and then pissed in the chair. She was humiliated once more as the warm urine ran on the floor. I took her to her room to change her gown. Her face was taunt, and twisted, a Parkinson's mask, but her eyes pleaded with me to honor a simple moment of privacy. I was moved to tears. Laura held her beauty in her eyes; courteous turns and gestures, her warm touch, smiles, were lost in a nervous wilderness. We were both humiliated that she must wear a hospital gown, tied at the back. She had been deserted by her body and her family, but she held her freedom in her eyes. I left her alone behind a screen; later, she appeared in a lovely print dress with the buttons undone at the back; that moment of privacy, that small favor, brought her such joy in a cruel and inhuman mental hospital.

I worked there during the school year and into the summer. There were hours of great humor, compassion, and sadness, but most of the time the hospital administration was harsh, peevish, and tragic. The regular use of electroshock in the hospital troubled me; lonesome women lost their past, their best memories. The dubious causes of their depression were crossed with electric currents to the brain. Muscles leapt, and tightened, bodies pounded on the hard table; in the end these women, who could afford to be treated by men, learned to smile at the psychiatrist and were released to their husbands.

My reasons for leaving the hospital were connected to the use of electroshock and other medical abuses, but the actual decision was based on an unusual comic encounter one night with four male patients at the end of a hall.

Frank lived on the wake of a wild ritual, a circle of generous manners and then persecution and fecal decorations; the rituals were turned in about three weeks. He was on the rise, gracious, and concerned about others that night.

Robot Joe marched; rather, he did a hospital shuffle, from one end of the hall to the other. When he reached the end he moaned and marched in place until he was turned around. Robot Joe was a Thorazine man, an enormous beast; that night he was stopped, and marked time, behind a door at the end of the hall.

Super embodied the cruelest ironies; he had been the director of a mental hospital in North Dakota. He wore a tailored suit, vest, starched shirt, and conservative necktie; he was forever checking his pocket watch to be sure that his institution was run on time. He had fired me, and others, hundreds of times; every time we took his temperature, turned his pillow, or talked with him about the weather, we were fired for insubordination. Super fired me that night.

Heart Throb was a little man with nervous manners who simulated heart attacks three or four times a day. My first night as an orderly the nurses abandoned me in his room, with no information, when he had one of his heart attacks. Heart Throb convinced me the first time. I climbed onto his bed, pressed, and pounded his heart. "Stay alive, you bastard, you're not dying on my first night," I shouted over his moist red chest. He was terrified and never staged one of his heart attacks near me. He would rush out of his room nude, into the hall, and pretend short breath and chest pains.

Robot Joe was turned around and on his march back that night when Heart Throb opened his door, dropped nude to the cold floor, and moaned about chest pains. Robot Joe stopped at the door and moaned over Heart Throb. Frank heard the commotion and leaped out of his room to see what was the matter; his hairy ass stuck out of his hospital gown. He stood over Heart Throb and told Robot Joe how terrible it was that no one helped the patients in the hospital. Robot Joe seemed to moan his agreement, or at least Frank seemed to understand. I waited in the toilet at the end of the hall, watched myself in the mirror, and listened at a distance.

Super lived across from Heart Throb; he pushed his door open and investigated the cause of the disturbance in the hall. He was a born leader and took command of the situation. Frank asked him where he got the nice suit, and then agreed that hospital administrators should wear suits on duty. Heart Throb turned over, moaned louder, and held his chest; the more he was noticed the more he moaned. Super ordered Frank to read the pulse of the sick man on the floor, and he told Robot Joe to stand guard at the door. "You will be needed later," said Super. Robot Joe moaned and smiled; he seemed to understand.

"Show me, show me the pulse," said Frank.

"There, on his wrist," said Super. He wondered out loud about an orderly who could not read a pulse. Frank was nervous at first, not a good sign on his ritual circle, but when he heard that he was an orderly he proved that the times do make the man, even in mental hospitals.

"He's got a good one," said Frank.

"Damn nurses, you can't find one when you want one," said Super. He opened his gold pocket watch and read the time, "nine seventeen" one summer night in a mental hospital.

"What's the problem?"

"Who are you?" asked Super.

"I'm your nurse," I said and touched Heart Throb on the cold shoulder with the toe of my shoe. There was terror in eyes when he saw me. No time to continue his heart attack.

"You're fired," shouted Super.

"Who, me?" I shrugged my shoulders and pretended to be concerned. Heart Throb was heartened by my dismissal and returned to his simulation on the cold hard terrazzo.

"Pick up your pay on the way out," said Super.

"Vacation time too?"

"You're fired," repeated Super.

"Wait a minute," said Frank. He was troubled, wild creases distorted his face and expressions. "You shouldn't fire us, we were just helping out." Frank pounded one bare foot on the floor, smack, smack, smack. He turned his identities to the side of the victim.

Heart Throb could not sustain his simulation under nurses who were to be fired by the director of the hospital, so he stood up and took part in the argument, still holding his damaged heart. "Frank's right," he announced. Later, he said Super was right, and Robot Joe was right, but he never included me in his tribute.

"I quit," I shouted.

"You can't quit," said Super.

"Why not?"

"Because you're fired," said Frank.

"No shit," I said.

"Yes, no shit," said Frank. His face loosened at the mere
sound of the word. He delighted, at the bottom of his ritual
circle, in the decoration of his room with shit; walls, windows, bed, chairs, and dishes, covered with his shit.

Super held his chin, raised his voice, and lectured us on
the proper attitudes toward patients in his hospital. Frank
agreed, but his mind was focused on shit, and he pranced in
the circle; the urge was upon him to decorate his room that
night. Robot Joe moaned; he even seemed amused for the
first time. I closed the door but he would not move, he remained in the circle. Heart Throb said the director of the hospital was right, even "very right" that night. He described a
heart attack and complained about the medical care in the
hospital. They were right, very right, and it was time for me
to leave before the charge nurse ordered me to clean more
shit from the walls.

"The contemporary world makes schizophrenia possible,
not because its events render it inhuman and abstract, but because our culture reads the world in such a way that man
himself cannot recognize himself him in it," wrote Michel
Foucault in *Mental Illness and Psychology*. "Only the real conflict of the conditions of existence may serve as a structural
model for the paradoxes of the schizophrenic world."

I lived in Pioneer Hall my first quarter at the University of
Minnesota. The next quarter I was hired as a residential counselor at the Ramsey County Home School for Boys, better
known as Totem Town. Thomas Houle had been hired a few
months earlier and we became close friends. There was as
much humor as stress, as much pleasure as horror, and there
was more than enough to loathe in an institution that promised to hold, nurture, educate, and reform boys who were
wild and lost, even those who had committed the crimes of
adults.

Stress is unforgiven, remembered on the run; the pleasures were common, generous emotions and honorable resolutions to troubles between some boys, their parents and
teachers. The horrors haunt my memories. For instance, the

boy who tortured and hanged domestic cats, chickens and then, years later, was convicted of the torture, mutilation, and murder of a woman. The easier memories and the best remembrance are the ironies, and the humor of human imperfections. One master social worker decided to manipulate an obvious condition of adolescence, masturbation. Most of these boys did not have their masturbation papers.

Uncle, as he was known at Totem Town, organized small groups of boys, talked about sex, and sexual fantasies, and then he had a good group masturbation session. The older boys roasted the group masturbation and named them "Uncle Jacks," or the "Night Junkles," and the "Masterbeaters." Uncle was rather naive, to say the least; he was a lovable innocent, but the boys responded to peer pressure and were no longer interested in group beats. This was read as "maturation over masturbation."

Uncle was persuaded by the older boys, once they learned how to use his romantic notions, to hold an overnight camp in the woods behind Totem Town. The institution was located in rural Saint Paul. Uncle, in turn, persuaded the director to support the overnight. I opposed the inevitable with humor and my best wishes. The older boys insisted that some younger boys come along, a good plan. The campers cooked hot dogs over an open fire, and sang camp songs. Uncle waited until dark and then told stories to the younger boys around the fire; soon they were fast asleep. Meanwhile, the older boys had arranged for their friends to meet them at the nearest gravel road. More than a dozen boys roared around the cities that night with perfect alibis. They drank, fucked, stole cars, robbed stores, threatened people, and were back in their sleeping bags before dawn. Uncle counted his boys, and his blessings as a social worker; he was so pleased to report later that day to the county sheriff that his boys were fast alseep under his protection. Uncle was loose; he seldom brushed his teeth, and he had no shame to remember.

I lived in an industrial medical clinic during my third year at the university. I cleaned the clinic, stoked the coal furnace, shoveled snow in winter, and maintained the radiators for a monthly salary and an apartment in the basement of the converted mansion. The doctors were too serious to laugh; they examined and treated employees under contract with local business and corporations. However, there were rich ironies and humors in their practice. One doctor could not stand the sight of blood, and when there was an emergency he would call in the X ray technician, who was eager to play doctor. Once the doctor was alone and he called me to his office to assist him in treating a woman with a simple cut on her finger. The doctor invited her into his office, declared a minor wound, and ordered me to treat it with prepared bandages; he claimed an emergency at the hospital and drove away in his Mercedes-Benz convertible.

The medical clinic contracted to have the floors cleaned and polished once a week by professionals. I met the cleaners once or twice on weekends; the man who owned the company seemed familiar. We shared the weather several times and then, at last, he asked me my name. His mouth opened but he was silent for several minutes.

"Please, don't leave," he said. There were tears in his eyes, but he assured me that everything was fine. He was very nervous and excited. "Please, I'll be back in a minute."

He returned with his daughter, who was about my age. They both touched me and then told me stories about my father Clement Vizenor. They said we looked very much alike, and noted that my father was about my age when he was murdered. This man was a painting contractor twenty years earlier and he had hired my father and my uncles as painters.

"I promised your father we would take care of you if anything ever happened to him, and it did," he said. "But when he was murdered we couldn't find you anywhere." They were tired to remember the death of my father, but that moment, a chance encounter at a medical clinic, was a pleasant resolution to an old promise. They were strangers to me; our memories were bound by the death of my father.

"You and my daughter should have grown up together," he said.

"Looks like we did all right anyway." We touched and promised to plan a proper family visit. They never called me; I never called them. We never got together as they had promised.

April 1966: The New Fur Traders

Naanabozho, the compassionate tribal trickster of the Anishinaabe, approached an evil wiigiwaam and raised a thick mat of scalps to enter. Inside, the evil gambler cursed the wind and weather; he seemed almost round, a curious being in the shadows.

The trickster thought he could not be a very good gambler. The evil gambler raised his wicked hands, as if he could read the mind of the trickster, and said, "So, Naanabozho, you too have come to try your luck. And you think I am not a very good gambler." He grinned and chuckled, and made a horrible sound, scorn and ridicule mingled in the wiigiwaam. He reached for his war club and continued, "All those hands you see hanging around the wiigiwaam are the hands of your relatives who came here to gamble. They thought as you are thinking, they played and lost their lives in the game.

"I seek no one to come and gamble with me but those who would gamble their lives. Remember, I demand that those who gamble with me and lose, give me their lives. I keep the scalps, the ears, and the hands of the losers, the rest of the body I give to my friends the wiindigoo, the flesh eaters, and the spirits I consign to the world of darkness. I have spoken, and now we will play the game."

Naanabozho laughed when the evil gambler concluded his speech. The trickster worried about the wiindigoo, the evil spirits and flesh eaters, but he was not afraid of the gambler or his game. The gambler was surprised that the trickster was not scared, and that made him uneasy.

The evil gambler moved the pagessewin, the traditional dish game of the Anishinaabe, to the center of the wiigiwaam and invited the trickster to gamble his life on the game.

"Now, here are four figures, the four ages of man, which I will shake in the dish four times. If they assume a standing position each time, then I am the winner, and you lose your life. Should they fall, then I am the loser."

Naanabozho laughed once more; he pretended not to be worried about the wages of the game. "Very well," said the trickster, "I will play, but it is customary for the party who is challenged to play any game to have the last play." The evil gambler consented to allow the trickster the last four throws of the figures in the dish. The evil gambler started his four throws; he struck the dish on the ground, a sharp blow. The figures, the four ages of man, were standing in the dish. This was repeated three times, and each time the figures were standing in the dish. One chance in the game remained, and the destiny of the trickster and tribal people depended on that last chance.

Naanabozho was not worried, and when the evil gambler prepared to make the final shake of the figures, the trickster drew closer to the gambler and when the dish came down on the ground he made a whistle on the wind, the sound of a surprise, and the four figures fell in the dish. Then the tribal trickster seized the dish, as the evil gambler had agreed, and prepared to start his four throws of the game. "It is now my turn, should I win, then you must die." That game, the four ages of man, continues to be played with evil gamblers in the cities.

Beverly Oien was blonde, bourgeois, and burdened with the romantic notions of civilization and savagism; she was named director of the American Indian Employment and Guidance Center, associated then with the Waite Neighborhood House in Minneapolis. I was hired as an advocate to serve the Indian communities near Franklin Avenue; and, at the same time, continued my studies in the first semester at the William Mitchell College of Law.

Laurel Hole In The Day was waiting for me; she opened her mouth to speak, but her dream would not come out that spring morning. She stood in silence at the back of the kitchen of the Waite Neighborhood House. Tears ran down her cheeks, blotted her print dress.

"Would you like some coffee?" I tried to ease her burdens in a public place. Laurel nodded, and I passed her a cup and poured the coffee. I asked her if she wanted to talk about something that had happened to her family. Laurel nodded a second time. "Too serious to tell me now?" Laurel nodded a third time.

Laurel was married and the mother of nine children. The youngest, an infant daughter, was scheduled for surgery to repair a cleft palate. The eldest, a daughter who was sixteen, was in charge of the other children back on the reservation.

The Hole In The Days, related to the distinguished tribal leader with the same dream name, were practical people with a rich sense of humor to endure their hardships in the world. Their home on the reservation was a paper covered cabin, perched high on concrete blocks. Two automobiles were abandoned behind the cabin: one, with a broken windshield, became a house for two mongrels; the second, a station wagon, was used for storage and a secret place for the boys. The cabin was heated with a wood stove. The windows, covered with sheets of plastic, rattled in the winter wind. Inside, the small rooms were warm and smelled of birch and cedar smoke. The public health nurse on the reservation arranged for the parents to live in the city one week while their daughter recovered in the hospital.

Laurel sipped her coffee in silence. She seemed more at ease, but she could not tell me her dream to leave the reservation, move to the city, and live in an apartment with her husband and children. I placed two sheets of blank paper on the table and asked her to note what she wanted. "Your dreams on one sheet, and on the second the problems you must overcome to get close to the dream." She nodded a fourth time.

The dreams: we want to live with our children in the city together. We need a place to live and my husband wants to woik so to pay the rent on time. This is all we want.

The problems: my daughter is getting better. She is very sick and she will be able to talk when she grows up because of the operation. Peter is with her now. We do not have money and no work so we could not pay the rent right away. Peter has a bad back from the woods. I hope you can help us, we got to go back next week.

Laurel returned the sheets of paper to me. The words were written in a clear and readable hand. She had been educated at a federal boarding school where the teachers had demanded precision, correct grammar and spelling. I nodded and told her to come back to see me in three days with her husband; we would try to find them work and an apartment. I found them both jobs at at a small firm; they could work together for a few weeks and save money. The company manufactured plastic caps for glue bottles. The owner, who was sensitive to the real problems of tribal people, agreed that the couple would plan their hours, but he would not provide a cash advance.

I located an apartment with two bedrooms in the urban reservation near Franklin Avenue. The owner agreed to a short lease and free rent for two weeks on the condition that the tenants paint the apartment at their own expense, and repair the windows and locks.

Laurel returned with her husband and spoke in a whisper; they held back their happiness over the apartment and the jobs, but she cried and said she was so happy to live close to people she knew from boarding school and from the reservation. I nodded.

Laurel and Peter worked on the assembly line that night and moved into their apartment the next morning. Friends of mine and staff members from the Waite Neighborhood House had painted the apartment while the couple was at work. Their infant daughter recovered, the other eight children came down from the reservation, and the Hole In The Days were together in the city for the first time.

In a few months there were new problems. Other tribal people stole their food and used their telephone for long distance. Laurel was worried about her children in the neighborhood; she wanted to move away. "We work hard for nothing," she pleaded. "When we come home the back door is broken down, even with our oldest children here, and people take our food and everything."

I located a small house in a better neighborhood on the north side of the city. The rent was less than the apartment on the urban reservation, and the house was larger, with closets in each bedroom, windows, and doors that locked. The Hole In The Days moved, but soon they were lonesome and missed the casual humor on the urban reservation. The white people in the new neighborhood stared at them; they were separated and the children had no friends. Laurel and Peter returned at night to drink with old friends in tribal bars on Franklin Avenue. Peter drank too much, missed too much work, and was fired; two weeks later he was gone with the car.

Laurel applied for welfare assistance. Several months later, in the spring, when the juncos returned, she moved with her children back to their cabin on the reservation. She found her husband there, alone in the woods. She set aside her dream to live in the cities.

I had written several magazine articles critical of the government and institutions that served tribal people on the urban reservation. The games were similar to those on the reservation in the past, between the federal agents and my families; my games were with the new urban fur traders. I organized demonstrations and several radical movements that year to draw attention to racism and the failures of the Bureau of Indian Affairs. The fur trade metaphor was an obvious humor at the time; Roy Bjorkman, a prominent furrier, had a burden to bear as a white man on the board of directors of the American Indian Employment and Guidance Center. He once said, "Tell me, where were you Indians when we needed you? Now you're coming out of the woodwork."

The fundamental encounters were racial and rhetorical, and at that time writers and speakers had a considerable advantage in the game. "How was it possible in the real world," I asked the directors, "a blonde with no experience is the passive director of a center that has promised to serve tribal people?" What does "guidance" mean in the name of your corporation? That the board of directors was white, dominant, and masculine was an indication that these patricians were misguided explorers, conspirators with a monotheistic determination to hold tribal people hostage in definitions of failure, or both. The members of the board were indeed colonial explorers. They were prominent citizens, doctors, lawyers, judges, and newspaper executives, but they had lost their common sense and human compassion; they responded to most tribal people as they would to children. These white men were possessive, and they would consume tribal cultures; they were the wise white rulers of the tribes, and their values became the measures of truth in the historical records of human encounters. They resented my mixed blood, my public intrusion into their private racial missions. I would overturn their dominance, their imposed histories.

Bower Hawthorne, executive editor of the *Minneapolis Tribune*, and the judges, lawyers, and other professionals on the board, were not pleased to read my name on the published agenda of their regular meeting; they would have no choice but to tolerate my crossblood notions with an audience. I accused them of racism, to warm them up to the real issues, and demanded that they resign and turn over the board to tribal people. I wondered later, when they hired me as director of the center, what if they had resigned, closed their leather bound notes, smiled, and departed with the best of manners? The issues and the games would be the same.

That white board moaned, groaned, and threatened, but in the end I used their tactics and forced them out of their colonial service. I studied the bylaws of the board and demanded special meetings of the board with short notices. Few of the white members attended. I then moved that those members who missed one meeting be removed from the board. I had my way; the motion passed, and in three months time we had a new board. I had scheduled enough meetings to remove the dominant fur traders, but not without recriminations. An appreciation dinner would have been wiser, but not honorable. They threatened me with a lawsuit. "Our pleasure," was my response; the public attention would have advanced our audience and cause. The board was new, but the racial games have not ended.

The Waite Neighborhood House receptionist told me that Gus Hall was outside and would like to see me about the planned demonstration at the area office of the Bureau of Indian Affairs.

"Gus Hall?"

"Yes," she answered.

"Are you certain?"

"That's his name, he's outside."

"Gus Hall is the General Secretary of the Communist Party in America, and that means trouble, television and newspapers, too much attention for the wrong reasons," I said.

"Who cares?"

"Senator Hubert Humphrey."

"Naturally."

"Tell him to wait a few minutes for me," I told the receptionist. I was concerned and needed more time to consider the consequences of a sensational Communist at our protest demonstration. I would report that he was invited because he was critical of central bureaucracies. However, the board of directors would never understand.

I had organized the first urban protest movement against the Bureau of Indian Affairs in Minneapolis. George Mitchell and Mary Thunder assisted me and persuaded others to participate, and to understand that protests were not criminal, but tribal and a constitutional right. Dennis Banks, who wore a summer suit and necktie then, would not support the protest or our movement. He said, "Demonstrations are not the Indian way."

Later that morning there were nineteen tribal people, most of them children, in the garage behind Waite Neighborhood House. They waited for transportation to the first urban demonstration. We were very nervous, and we worried about being humiliated in public.

"Mister Gus Hall, this is a pleasure," I said and touched his shoulder. "We will be leaving for the area office in a few minutes and we would be pleased to have you march with us this afternoon."

Hall wore a brown tweed suit coat, standard spectacles, and smoked a pipe; his fingers were stained from the smoke. He looked down when he listened, sometimes he concentrated on his shoes, moved a stone, or traced a crack with the toe of his shoe. His gestures were gentle, his pipe smoke was thick and foul.

Archie Goldman, the warm and nervous director of the Waite Neighborhood House, came around the corner of the building and recognized Douglas Hall, the labor and civil rights lawyer. I thought Douglas Hall was Gus Hall.

Douglas Hall marched in the demonstration that afternoon; he carried a sign that demanded rights on the urban reservation. Later, he was an active member on the board of directors, and he served other organizations and movements as a partisan and legal adviser. We became close friends, even closer when we worked together two years later to overturn the death sentence imposed on Thomas White Hawk in South Dakota.

Glenn Landbloom, the area director of the Bureau of Indian Affairs, invited the demonstrators outside his building to come in and talk. "My door is always open," he said, but we ignored his invitation. "We came here to change policies, not to cultivate conversations," I told the director. The tribes had given too much time to conversations and treaties that were seldom honored. Landbloom ordered that the window blinds be drawn so the employees would not be distracted by the demonstration and demands printed on picket signs.

My demands were not unusual or unnatural; the demonstrations were unusual, and with that we started a movement that won public support and brought substantive changes in services to tribal people. The need for services to people on the urban reservation, one of the largest uncertain reservations in the state, had been established with honest emotions at the demonstrations, but my demand that a portion of federal funds allocated to the tribes be redirected to urban centers was not a popular notion on the reservations. Elected reservation leaders had their own problems and would not support urban diversions.

I wrote to Robert Bennett, who was then the commissioner of Indian Affairs, about these conditions, and the problems of tribal people being denied services in urban areas. "Hundreds of tribal people in this and other urban tribal communities are being denied hospital services because they are identified with reservations." I told him that hospital administrators send people back to the reservation for medical care; even emergency care is denied in certain urban hospitals because it was assumed that tribal people were protected by the federal government. "Indians transfer their intent of residence, and we cannot treat them here," said the administrator at the Minneapolis General Hospital.

"I have your letter relating to the picketing of the Area Office of the Bureau of Indian Affairs in Minneapolis as a protest of the discontent by Indian people with the bureau's inability to work on urban Indian problems," responded Robert Bennett.

"I am sure that you and many other Indian people feel that you should not be dependent upon the Bureau of Indian Affairs for services, particularly when you have established residence in cities. . . . I know that you would not want the Bureau of Indian Affairs to follow Indian people wherever they may go in this country but that you would rather share in the community life wherever you establish your home.

"The ability of the Bureau of Indian Affairs to provide services to Indians who have established residence away from the reservation is a matter of law as well as policy in that funds appropriated by Congress are for particular services, primarily for those on or near Indian reservations."

Bennett was a patron of bureaucracies and their catches, and he had been misinformed by the hardline assimilationists on the matter of treaties, law, service policies, and the intent of funding by the United States Congress. Minnesota representative Donald Fraser reported that no such exclusive reservation intention had been tied to funds appropriated for the Bureau of Indian Affairs. We had won one game, and the rules were changed.

Senator Walter Mondale responded to our demands and we won one more game; his intervention resulted in a small grant from the Bureau of Indian Affairs to run the American Indian Employment Center for about six months. The evil gamblers in the government revealed a catch that followed the positive press release. We must report and show "proper" receipts each month; only then would funds be paid, and that would take two months, but the catch would not hold us down to the peevish control of the Bureau of Indian Affairs.

I was named the first director that autumn and we opened in a house borrowed from the Northside Citizens Community Center at 1718 Third Street North. We started with a director, a secretary, one desk, but no telephones, and no heat in the building. There were four visitors that clear and cold morning. The first was a tribal man with one leg and a cane who was drunk and chased me around the desk. We had never met, but he accused me of raising the hopes of Indians. He tired on the fourth round, smiled at the end, and hobbled out in silence. His captious introduction became a tribal governor in my remembrance and stories.

A few minutes later a couple drove up in an old Checker automobile; they were casual, and he told stories about some urban fur traders he had known. He asked me if we had money to run the center, for salaries, and telephones. I told him about the conditions of the funding. Then she said, "How much do you need to run the center for a month?" My pause was a restrained pose: "two thousand dollars." She wrote a personal check to me for that amount with no conditions. Louise McCannel was the name on the check. Malcolm wondered if the building was heated, "or did they leave that to the fur traders too." They wished us the best of luck, made no passive liberal promises, and drove away in their durable Checker.

The fourth visitor that morning parked his station wagon in front of the center. He wore a dark business suit and a camel hair overcoat. Carol Hill, the first secretary, said he looked important. "More money," I said in humor. The man opened the door, looked around, and seemed pleased; the rooms were bare. He asked me about the finances of the center, complained about the conditions imposed by the Bureau of Indian Affairs, and said he wanted to pay the salaries for the first month.

"How much?" he asked with his checkbook in hand.

"Who are you?"

"Ronald Libertus," he said. He was shy about personal recognition and directed my attention back to the cost of salaries. "I would like to pay the salaries for the first month."

"Four hundred dollars," I said.

"That's not much," he said and opened his checkbook. I explained that my salary had not been determined, and in any case would not be included in the budget for the first month or two, until the center was established. He listened, handed me a personal check, and said he was late for a meeting. Libertus was a mixedblood from the Leech Lake Reservation; at that time he worked in management at Minneapolis Honeywell Corporation. One month later he accepted a nomination to serve on the board of directors of the center, and then we elected him treasurer. These most uncertain ambitions and personal assurances brought new friends closer together for the best reasons.

I continued as a writer that year, established the center, sponsored a tribal candidate alderman in the city elections, continued my work as an advocate in tribal communities, and was named the first chairman of the Indian American Task Force by Minneapolis mayor Arthur Naftalin. We began a series of meetings with public officials; the most serious problems were with the police and hospital administrators.

I had studied two years in graduate school at the University of Minnesota. My resolutions to complete my thesis for the master's degree and study law at the same time were undone in a few months at the center. My activities as a writer and advocate were more critical at that time than passive citations on a thesis. I withdrew at the end of the semester from the William Mitchell College of Law.

In three months we had a cash flow at the center, several more advocates were hired, and my salary was set at nine thousand dollars a year. We moved to the heart of the urban reservation, corner offices at 1632 Chicago Avenue; several months later, when interstate construction divided the community, we moved to Franklin Avenue.

Our six-month report indicated that we had served over five hundred tribal people, most of whom were referred to good jobs. About a hundred applicants were not hired; at the end of nine months about fifty people were still employed. The applicants were mixedblood and more than half were single, and had been in the city less than six months. About a hundred tribal people were graduates of high school and under thirty years of age. Most of the applicants were Anishinaabe from reservations in Minnesota. Despite our obvious success as advocates in urban tribal communities, five times more placements than the Bureau of Indian Affairs, the area director wrote that our grant would not be continued, "as our staff has been supplemented and will be able to give the services specified in the contract during this period." We whistled on the wind, and the evil bureaucrats were maddened because we would not die; we won one more game and the center was funded by private foundations and community agencies. I resigned to be a member of the board, once the budget had been secured, and to pursue my vision as a writer.

Late that summer, near the end of my responsibilities as director of the American Indian Employment Center, an unforgettable couple wandered into the office at closing time. The two sat in overstuffed chairs near my desk. The man, a mixedblood with bright blue eyes, had a primal sense of personal and cultural doom. The woman wore an oversized shirt, stained with vomit. She was drunk, ancient from abuse, and when she moved her lips to speak the dark creases on her face sagged under an awesome cultural burden. The stench of her slow breath and the vomit on her clothes saturated the moist air in the small office.

The man blamed racism and the dominant culture for his problems, alcoholism, and poverty, but I was not in a mood at the end of the week to listen to racial raves about white demons blanking out the beautiful red sunsets forever, so I told him in a bitter voice that some shaman would take his tribal blood back one night and solve his problems.

"You need white people, more than they need you now, to blame for your problems," I said, but not with conviction. "You need them to keep you the way you are so you can moan in self-pity."

The drunken tribal woman raised her head and looked around the room. She smiled as best she could, and then she stood near my desk; she motioned with her chin and lips in the tribal manner. "Stand now," she said. "The flag is coming through the door." She pointed to the traditional tribal ceremonial staff of eagle feathers, and sang a tribal song in a strong voice, then an honoring song, over the frightful protests of her mixedblood man. Tears trailed down the creases on her cheeks. She was sober in her songs, her dark eyes were clear, and then she reached out to me with her small hands; she said in a gentle voice, "It feels so good to just talk again." She sang in the oral tradition, the tribal staff was there. We touched hands; she was warm and sober.

N. Scott Momaday, the tribal novelist, said at the First Convocation of American Indian Scholars that telling stories is "imaginative and creative in nature. It is an act by which man strives to realize his capacity for wonder, meaning and delight.

"It is also a process in which man invests and preserves himself in the context of ideas. Man tells stories in order to understand his experience, whatever it may be. The possibilities of storytelling are precisely those of understanding the human experience."

That tribal woman in the shirt stained with vomit imagined the stories she told; she sang in a good time, a visual time of wonder and memories, about her experiences in the new urban world, and her collective memories from the tribal past. She moved me in her stories, and we remember her creation on the urban reservation.

June 1968: The Second Coming

~~~~~~~~~~~~~~~~~~~~~ *F*rank Premack, the curious city editor at the *Minneapolis Tribune*, warned me that the second coming of Jesus Christ was worth no more than a page and a half of typed, double-spaced copy. "So, let that be your guide in writing news stories."

I was tired, under the heat of my emotions and the seal of newspaper time several months later. Frank Premack held me to that pious measure when he edited my front page story about the funeral of Dane Michael White in Sisseton, South Dakota.

November 20, 1968: Catholic funeral services for Dane White were held here Wednesday in English and in the Dakota language at Saint Catherine's Indian Mission Church. Following the service, attended by seventy-five people, all but six of whom were Dakota Indians, Dane was buried here in Saint Peter's Catholic Cemetery.

Born in Sisseton thirteen years ago, he took his own life Sunday in the Wilkin County Jail, Breckenridge, Minnesota, where he had been held since October 7, awaiting a juvenile court hearing.

The Reverend William Keohane conducted the service. Two hymns were sung in the Dakota language. "Dane is here, in the background of the banquet table. Lord, remember Dane in your Kingdom," Father Keohane said in prayer, pointing to the large painting of the Last Supper behind the altar of the small Indian church.

Six of Dane's school friends carried his gray metal coffin from the church. Fifteen cars formed the procession to the cemetery on the edge of town. Following the service at the grave, the six young Indian pallbearers removed their honoring ribbons and placed them on the coffin. A cold Dakota wind blew across the slope of Saint Peter's cemetery. The six pallbearers were the last to leave the grave.

A trickster signature, chance, and the racial sauce of nature, culture, blood, and politics, earned the best scores in the game over my sudden career as a journalist. Bower Hawthorne, the autogenous executive editor of the *Minneapolis Tribune*, endured my indictment that he and other editors and publishers of newspapers were racists; in spite of these wild episodes at a conference, he invited me, in his modulated manner, to become an editorial columnist. Joe Rigert was a celebrated editorial writer, but my admiration of him would not make me a columnist. I told Hawthorne to wait on the new position, and start me out at the bottom as a news reporter; and he did, for an annual salary of eleven thousand dollars, but he must have bewailed his evident intention to hold my temper over the heads of editors at the newspaper. Later, he would praise my abilities as a writer, but never my critical attention to his editorial policies.

Gwyn Jones-Davis might have loosened the trickster manner in my stories that afternoon; she was invited with me to lecture on race and the media at the annual association of newspaper editors and publishers, held in the journalism auditorium at the University of Minnesota.

Jones-Davis raved over the racial detractions and abuses of the media, the racist attitudes of journalists, and photographers, and the death of ideas in editorials. "Our children are bombed and burned and you fuckers beat off over a comma," she shouted at the editors. She was rich and moderate at that conference, compared to other lectures and sessions she had conducted. The writers and editors at the Minneapolis Star and Tribune Company, for instance, were told to attend her lecture in the company auditorium; that session would be one that most of them never forgot.

Gwyn, the program director at The Way Community Center, cursed and scolded people in the aisles as they searched for the right seat; she was so wild and rude, so abusive and crude in her denunciations that at least half of the audience turned and ran out the back door. She moved closer to those who remained, and in a warm and courteous tone of voice she said, "Those of you who are offended by the word fuck will never understand what I have to say about poverty, racism, and violence." She was a generous teacher, and she was right. Martin Luther King, Jr., was assassinated on April 4, 1968, by James Earl Ray, in Memphis, Tennessee.

My presentation to the editors and publishers that afternoon was a seven point indictment, the historical inventions and political invalidations of tribal cultures right down to the advertisements and editorial columns of the best newspapers. I cited diseases, treaties, and five concrete racist violations of human rights in stories and advertisements published in recent issues of the *Minneapolis Tribune*. I named and accused certain writers, editors, and publishers of racial violence, acute misrepresentation of tribal cultures, and unconscionable public humiliations in news stories and editorials. I cited the headlines, the pages, the dates, and demanded that "the editors be tried for crimes against humanity." I never mentioned the racist stories about the death of my father.

Bower Hawthorne approached me at the end of the conference; he wanted to continue the discussion in his office. I retreated from his liberal pose, but several weeks later he invited me to write for the newspaper. At first my interest wavered, but my savings had been spent on travel to investigate the capital punishment case of Thomas White Hawk in South Dakota. I was broke and needed a job. The city editor had read my articles in the *Twin Citian*, a local magazine edited by Roger Swardson, and was eager to hire me as a general assignment reporter.

Frank Premack assigned me to a desk and typewriter in the enormous newsroom on Monday, June 3, 1968. He told me to listen for a day or two, then mock some writer, any writer that impressed me, "and then get to work writing stories for this paper." I was amused that no one in the company asked me about typing or driving, the two most important qualifications for a reporter. I could do both, of course, but pretended otherwise for two days to press the humor of the editors.

Dick Youngblood, a nervous assistant city editor, told me to write a practice story about the weather. I practiced in my own cursive hand and dropped the story on his desk with instructions to save a carbon copy for me when it was typed.

"We type our own stories around here," said Youngblood.

"That's news to me."

"You can type, right?"

"No, not me."

"With two fingers?"

"No, never was good at typing."

"How the hell did you get here then?"

"Normal course of events."

"Jesus Christ, this is a first," said Youngblood.

"By the way, how do you get around?"

"You don't drive either?"

"No one asked about typing and driving."

"Premack, what is this shit?"

"Never mind Youngblood, we'll find him a secretary to type his stories if he ever writes one." Premack roared from his desk; his wild voice could reach the most private corners of the newsroom, even the toilets. Frank was his own opera; once, he stood on top of his desk in the newsroom and with an eager audience cut one of my stories in half. His smile was sinister, and he shouted, "You think I'm going to run the top half with your name, not so, the bottom goes to press, and remember, the second coming is worth a page."

"You said a page and a half," I protested.

"I was wrong, once." Premack was mad, in the best sense, and his wild and clever scenes in the newsroom were memorable word wars, but at the same time he towed a hard line on solid, accurate news stories. My seven page story on corrections and the state parole board was not published in halves; he sent the bottom, and the rest to be composed later.

Thursday, June 6, 1968, Senator Robert Kennedy died of gunshot wounds in Los Angeles; Sirhan Sirhan was indicted the next day for murder. James Earl Ray was arrested two days later in London. Premack told me to write a feature news story that we were *not*, in essence, a violent nation. Three days as a staff writer and my first assignment, a feature news story that would controvert the public notions on violence.

My first story as a *Minneapolis Tribune* staff writer appeared in the feature section, front page, on Sunday, June 9, 1968. I interviewed Luther Gerlach, a professor of anthropology. He said that violence grows not only from the sense of powerlessness but out of an emerging need to achieve that power.

Acts of assassination in the United States cannot support the emotional contention that American society is inherently violent, a University of Minnesota anthropologist declared last week. But while the assassination of a public figure may not prove that ours is a violent society, the potential for violence nevertheless is built into the traditional structures of our society.

In America, he said, minority citizens are systematically excluded from the dominant society—socially, economically, politically. Thus, "black people and Indians are without power or significance as human beings."

"The problem is how to deal with the reality that violence produces power," Gerlach said. "We cannot simply classify the movement, the quest for power, as a collection of civil disorders and law-enforcement problems." In a society where power is mutually shared by all segments, the need for violence is not found, he emphasized.

"We are involved in a revolution," he said, and it cannot be "bought off" with federal grants and welfare payments "simply to expunge guilt feelings as a substitute for action." He called for the immediate use of "intermediary forces" of committed volunteers who can act as buffers between the dominant and alienated segments of the society.

Many people would like the police to act as what Gerlarch referred to as the "leopard skin chief" of Africa, a mediator respected by both parties in a quarrel. He maintains the balance of power between the segments. The police cannot function in this role, he said, because "the police, and the Army, have always been identified with weapons—they are regarded as the oppressive agent of the dominant society. There was more, and my story stimulated an active discussion in editorial letters; one week on the job and my first story was a front page story in the feature section.

Professor Elden Johnson should have been indicted for directing the desecration of tribal graves, and tried in a bone court, where the sacred remains of humans have the right to be protected from archaeologists and the University of Minnesota. Instead, college students received credit for tribal desecration. Fourteen archaeology students on a summer session dig at the prehistoric Kathio Indian village eight miles north of Onamia, Minnesota, lived in less space than did the people they were digging up, I reported on September 29, 1968. "The students, six men and eight women, who are known at the Mille Lacs Indian Reservation as the 'grave diggers,' are registered in a six-credit, five-week course in the methods of archaeology through the University of Minnesota." That story was the foundation of my critical essay on the institutional collection of bones, and my proposal to establish a federal bone court to hear the natural rights of buried human bones; tribal bones have the right to be represented in bone court.

I attended regular church services that autumn to report on the honorable attempts of a group of Catholic dissidents to create a dialogue of the gospel about race, poverty, and the war. The group was serious and secretive, and they respected me as a journalist; they would reveal the time and location of the church about an hour before the target mass. I wrote several stories, two ran on the front page, and these stories caused more rancor than any other issue in my career as a journalist. People warned me on the telephone, and there were angry letters; someone in composition altered stories, and it seemed that certain paragraphs were transposed, and names changed in the earlier editions. Stories at that time were set in hot metal on a Linotype machine. Gerald Vixen became my name in one proof sheet edition of a story on the church dissidents. That religion, sewers, and gun control drew the most public heat was a truism in the newsroom. My stories were about religion, never sewers.

Everett Vizenor, my uncle, was a member of Our Lady of Victory Catholic Church; he was concerned that if the dissidents attended mass, there might be trouble, and he was right. He said, "They are such good people, with a decent message." Many police officers were members of that parish in north Minneapolis. I was there for mass with the dissidents on Sunday, November 17, 1968.

Three members of a group attempting a dialogue during mass were physically removed from Our Lady of Victory Catholic Church when they criticized the omission of the sermon. And a father followed his daughter to the church and slapped her in public for associating with the dissident Catholics he accused of being "Communists" and "outlaws."

The fourth attempt by the group to create a "meaningful dialogue" in conservative Minneapolis parishes was foiled when the celebrant omitted the sermon and conducted the entire mass in Latin. Between the entrance hymn and the offertory hymn, the Reverend Joseph Musch kept the morning congregation of about seven hundred standing more than ten minutes while he intoned the traditional mass in Latin.

Members of the congregation seemed restless as they stood for more than ten minutes, but only those of the dissident group planning to provoke a dialogue during the sermon appeared surprised when the sermon was omitted.

I spoke to Father Musch before the mass but he was not interested in any discussion of the dissidents, even though most of them were members of his parish. He warned me that "no newspapermen are allowed. It is my option who attends the mass. I might have to sue you." I attended the mass, watched several young people thrown to the concrete in the parking lot for nothing more than their love of the church. I was moved by their spirit, courage, and dedication.

I had written in an earlier story, The three successive attempts by a group of dissident Twin Cities Catholics to create a dialogue of the gospel during mass has changed little more than the conversation in the parish parking lots. Undaunted by criticism from liberal and conservative priests and laymen, the group of about thirty Catholics plans to carry on its efforts to change the Catholic Church.

While most of the members of the group were first drawn together in antiwar and draft resistance movements, they have not brought up these issues in the three parishes they have visited. The group seems to be moved by simple emotional issues of community love and humanity, rather than by the design of individual leaders.

Critics have said that two former priests, Joseph Selvaggio and James McDonell, are leading the group, but only three members of the group actually have spoken out during masses they have attended. The two former priests have participated silently.

The group has not shown hostility or discourtesy toward any individuals in the parishes they have visited. While they have been accused of being "unchristian," they consider the hostility they have encountered to be "unchristian." One member of the group, who did not want to be identified again because she said she has received threatening telephone calls, said she was "frightened by the ugliness of their voices."

Former Alabama governor George Wallace was scheduled to speak at the Minneapolis Auditorium on July 3, 1968; more than four thousand people waited to hear the presidential candidate. I was there in the press section as a writer and photographer, but not assigned to cover the event.

Meanwhile, about fifty demonstrators came down to the platform from various sections of the auditorium and started to square dance; the allemandes and honors were sincere, but the dance was ironic. Most of the dancers were black citizens out to tease a southern racist. At the same time a white country band began to play "Happy Days Are Here Again." The band members were decorated with thousands of spangles.

Matthew Eubanks, a dedicated civil rights organizer, was arrested with John Cann and charged with breach of the peace in connection with the riot provoked by a security guard with the presidential campaign, and then by the police. The guard drew a revolver; minutes later dozens of police circled the square dancers, pushed them out of the auditorium, and sprayed them with Chemical Mace.

I stood on a platform close to the dancers and photographed the violence, a series of negatives that became evidence at the trial of Eubanks and Cann. One of my photographs was published in the *Minneapolis Tribune* on July 4, 1968, showing Eubanks being held back by friends at the demonstration. I was subpoenaed twice to identify my photographs and to describe my view that night. Douglas Hall, the defense lawyer, argued that the police caused the violence, not the dancers and demonstrators.

Bernie Shellum, political reporter for the *Minneapolis Tribune*, wrote the front page story: "Negro and white protesters scuffled with security men for George C. Wallace, and others in the hall, Wednesday night, delaying the presidential candidate's Minneapolis speech one hour and thirty-five minutes."

Shellum focused more attention on race and time lost than on the actual demonstration; most presidential candidates are late, the band was there to entertain the audience, most of whom were supporters, for that very reason. "A Negro jumped to the platform and attempted to address the audience," wrote Shellum. "Another Negro became involved in a tug-of-war with a security man who fell from the platform. Drawing his gun from a shoulder holster as he fell, the security man, still unidentified, is alleged to have struck a Negro." The first word in his story is "Negro," a racial burden and separation that harks back to the minstrel shows.

The dancers and demonstrators were removed by police, and there was no evident reason that George Wallace could not have given his entire speech that night. Instead, he mounted the platform and said, "These are the folks that America is sick and tired of." Later, at a hotel press conference he said, "I can assure you that if I'm elected president, I'll show you how to keep law and order."

I was a member of the board of directors of the Minnesota Civil Liberties Union at the time, and the only board member who witnessed the dance, demonstration, and violence in the auditorium that night; the board discussion was bitter, emotional, and motivated by the politics of race and rights of speech. Evidence aside, the board voted to release a statement that George Wallace's right to speak had been "abridged."

I resigned from the board of directors to protest the statement that the dance and demonstration had anything to do with "abridging the freedom of speech" of George Wallace. The First Amendment rights abridged that night were those of the dancers. Wallace and his security guards might have posed a demonstration, invited racial violence, and police intervention, to gain more favorable attention from an otherwise critical northern and liberal media.

In an unsigned editorial the *Minneapolis Tribune* argued: "Perhaps one measure of Wallace's commitment to law and order was seen in 1963 in his resistance to desegregation of local schools in Alabama. . . . Wallace sought to prevent desegregation of schools in Birmingham, Tuskegee, Mobile, and Huntsville by use of executive orders, dispatches of state police and the like." Wallace defied federal laws and blocked the doorway and the registration of black students at the University of Alabama. "Some respect for law and order by a man who wants to be president."

Senator Eugene McCarthy told the nation that the Central Intelligence Agency had established covert domestic operations in thirteen cities, a violation of their charter. I reasoned, with that invitation, that Minneapolis would be one of those cities and set out as a reporter to locate one of the most puissant secret agencies in the world. I used standard methods and common practices of investigation, except in one instance, to find the spies who were gathering covert information on dissidence and demonstrations in the area.

Sam Romer, a wise political reporter who had retired several years before my time at the *Minneapolis Tribune*, gave me a secret telephone number that had been given to him, he said, when he returned from an assignment in Cuba. The number was a covert intelligence contact. A woman answered, but she would not give me any information past the number. I then called the listed number for the local personnel office of the Central Intelligence Agency. The same woman answered both numbers, but she would not reveal the location of the office. A friend traced the secret number to a name that paid for the telephone service; he was a lawyer, but there was no address and his name was not listed in the telephone directory. His name, however, was published in a standard directory of lawyers; indeed, he was a member of a firm in Minneapolis, a friend of Hubert Humphrey's, and the short biography revealed that he had been an intelligence officer during the Second World War. The dubious law firm was located in the Midland Bank Building in downtown Minneapolis.

The names of several lawyers were listed on the door, but the office was small, with one receptionist. I entered the office and asked for my man, the apparent domestic agent, by name. She said he was not available for cases at that time. I explained that a friend had recommended him, that only he could help me with my problem. She was suspicious, naturally, and even more so when I moved to the side of her desk, to observe the numbers listed on the telephone console. There, in black and white, were the two numbers, one secret, and the other listed as the Central Intelligence Agency. I watched the office from a distance that afternoon and no one entered; at the end of the day the receptionist was the only one to leave. I found the maintenance crew in the basement and asked them if the federal government paid the rent for any of the offices in the building. Yes, the government paid the rent for the lawyer with the secret telephone number. I wrote the story for the *Minneapolis Tribune,* named secret names, and proved that domestic covert operations were located in the fair liberal city of Minneapolis. That morning two agents visited the executive editor; he stood by my story. The Central Intelligence Agency moved from the Midland Bank Building a few days later. I used the same methods to locate their new office on a military base at the airport. Five years later President Gerald Ford appointed a commission to investigate the illegal domestic activities of the Central Intelligence Agency.

I worked on a special report, Indian Education in Minnesota, with Catherine Watson and photographer Skip Heine; the stories were published in two sections of the Sunday *Picture Magazine* in March 1969. We traveled for a week and visited schools on the White Earth, Leech Lake, and Red Lake reservations. Jerome Buckanaga, the principle of the elementary school at Pine Point, released students early to attend the funeral of Violet Ora Butcher, who had committed suicide at age fifteen. Friends on the reservation said she was depressed and troubled in the high school.

Native American Indian students were bused from the White Earth Reservation to the consolidated high school in Park Rapids, a small white town, where tribal and rural students were the outsiders. No more than one out of ten reservation students ever graduated from Park Rapids. There were ambitious and generous teachers there, but colonial pedagogics, and the dominant social unions in the town contributed to the horrors of modern consumer education. The most sensible response, in my view, was to leave high school; that could be a sign of good mental health, tribal or white, in Park Rapids. The consolidated school was a new aluminum and urethane cenotaph to the human spirit, no soul behind the sealed windows, no solace on the carpets. The cheer leaders were praised too close to deliverance in a racist town.

Walker, Minnesota, became my home when the school board hired me to direct a federal desegregation program for one year at the high school in Park Rapids. I had taken leave from the *Minneapolis Tribune*, taught for one year at Lake Forest College, and then returned to northern Minnesota. The landscape was wild and handsome, the winters were beauteous and harsh, and the thunderstorms were demonic.

The problem was the high school, the slipstream of material culture, not the reservation; of course, most teachers, and the town parents, saw the issue as racial, even as genetic. Indians, in the racist patois of the high school, were inferior and would never master a rational education; this, the wicked whites reasoned, was in tribal genes. I would prove otherwise with rational evidence, that most of the brighter reservation students were the casualties of modern education, but racialism would not be overturned at Park Rapids. I studied the reservation students who should have graduated in a three-year period; their academic records were available at Pine Point and at Park Rapids.

Why would these students choose to leave? The tribal students who never completed high school earned above average grades in elementary school on the reservation, and they scored one year above average, as a group, on the standardized national achievement tests. Their high grades and better-than-average scores raised questions about the assumptions that reservation children suffered a cultural bias on tests. However, these same students received the lowest grades, and below average national test scores when they were bused from the reservation to the white high school in Park Rapids. This information was dismissed by most of the white high school teachers; they *reasoned* that the older white teachers on the reservation "loved Indian children too much and gave them higher grades than they deserved." The love of tribal children became a racial transvaluation to most of the town teachers.

Park Rapids was about thirty minutes by car from the reservation in fair weather, but the distance in spirit was too great to understand in town, in a seminar with teachers; that racial distance becomes the dreadful burden of tribal children.

The Pine Point school board and the board at the high school had never met to discuss the spiritual distance between reservation and town, between tribe and racialism. I scheduled a meeting between the boards late in the summer on the reservation at Pine Point. The white board and the superintendent were on time and sat on one side of an extended conference table. The tribal board members came in later and sat near the back of the classroom. Policies, programs, dates and numbers were mentioned, a rather slow and remote discussion. Then the weather turned wild, a trickster signature; demons howled in the huge ventilators, and a red pine was blown down near the school. We moved to the basement when the storm worsened and the thunder crashed, and crowded into a reconditioned coal bin. There, shoulder to shoulder, the board members, most of whom were the age of my father and uncles, told stories about the past in town and on the reservation, stories about families, natural disasters, the depression, but there were no stories about shared adventures since the Second World War. The end of the war seemed to be the new start of racialism, the promises of materialism, and the cultural measures of consumer education. The storm ended, the stories ended, and we returned to the distance between the tribe and the town around the conference table.

Vice President Hubert Humphrey accepted an invitation to join the faculties at Macalester College, and at the University of Minnesota, a month after he lost the presidential election to Richard Nixon. I reported on the election and his endowed professorship for the *Minneapolis Tribune*.

Humphrey reminisced to an audience of about six hundred in the Janet Wallace Fine Art Center at Macalester College. "I was on this campus twenty-five years ago and I've had, you might say, a rather extended sabbatical, and I want to thank you for your patience." He said his basic research on political institutions had been completed: "The American people took care of that, although just barely." Humphrey had lost to Nixon in one of the closest presidential elections, by less than a million votes. George Wallace won about thirteen percent of the popular vote, and carried five southern states. Humphrey lost the election, in a sense, to Wallace.

Arthur Fleming, president of Macalester College, pointed out that when Humphrey lost his first bid for mayor of Minneapolis, he came to teach at Macalester, and the next time he ran for mayor he was elected; the audience cheered the parallelism. Humphrey returned to the United States Senate two years later, but he was never a presidential candidate again.

The day after he lost the election I followed him down the basement stairs where six-year-old Jill Solomonson took her grandfather by the hand and led him to the corner of the amusement room. Humphrey, with his three grandchildren at his side, read outloud the message printed on the blackboard:

> A vote for Humphrey
> Is a vote for me.
>
> Love
> Jill, Amy and Vicky.
>
> Do not vote for Nixon.
> Boo!

I reported on the front page of the *Minneapolis Tribune*, November 8, 1968, that the grandfather who almost became the next president of the United States turned toward Vicky, who was having an early birthday party, and said, still smiling, "I tell you, don't we have fun." Humphrey held back his tears; he smiled, hugged his grandchildren, and then he was served pretend tea at a play table in the basement.

I was on the Red Lake Reservation two weeks later when Frank Premack told me by telephone to be at the burial of Dane White the next morning. I drove most of the night and arrived in time to attend funeral services at Saint Catherine's Indian Mission Church. I stayed in Sisseton, South Dakota, the rest of the week, and wrote several front page stories.

Dane Michael White could have been placed in the Pierre Indian Boarding School in a few days after a juvenile court hearing, but he hanged himself with his own belt from a shower curtain rod in the Wilkin County Jail, Breckenridge, Minnesota, on Sunday afternoon, November 17, 1968. He had been held in jail for six weeks awaiting a hearing and placement; he was thirteen years old and had been held behind bars, isolated as a criminal. Dane was visited only twice in that time: once by his father, and once by his stepmother. The Wilkin County Coroner reported that that cause of death was "strangulation, due to hanging, self inflicted."

Dane had been apprehended early in September in a stolen car with his older brother and two other boys; he was released then to the custody of his father, Cyrus White. But Dane ran away from his home in Browns Valley, Minnesota, several times to live with his maternal grandmother across the border in South Dakota. White said he asked the sheriff to jail his son because he would not stay home and attend school.

Marian Starr, his grandmother, who lives in Long Hollow, about seven miles west of Sisseton, said Dane was very happy when he stayed with her. She did not want Dane to leave, she said, but the sheriff came and took Dane away.

Dane was five when his parents, Cyrus and Burdell White, separated after seven years of marriage and five children. Cyrus, who was born near Enemy Swim Lake, north of Waubay, South Dakota, was granted custody of the children and moved to Montana, where he worked as an auto mechanic. Burdell, who was born in Sisseton, moved to Chicago, Illinois, where she married a construction worker.

Cyrus returned to Sisseton when Dane was twelve, a year before his death. Then he was hired as a mechanic in Browns Valley, twelve miles east of Sisseton. Three months before Dane hanged himself his father married Maxine Salvage, a divorcée with five children. When Dane and his brother Timothy, who was two years older, ran away from home, there were eleven children in the family: ten children

Gerald Vizenor boarding ship at Southampton, England, 1959

Gerald Vizenor with his son Robert Vizenor, Minneapolis, 1961

Gerald Vizenor, publication of Raising the Moon Vines, *1964*

Robert Vizenor, Clear Lake, Minnesota, 1964

Gerald Vizenor, graduate student, Minneapolis, 1962

Gerald Vizenor with his son at the grave marker of Basile Hudon dit Beaulieu, Madeline Island, Wisconsin, 1962

Gerald Vizenor, Walker, Minnesota, 1970

Gerald Vizenor, protest at Bemidji State University, Minnesota, 1972

Gerald Vizenor, protest at Bemidji State University, Minnesota, 1972

Thomas White Hawk, Federal Court, Sioux Falls, South Dakota, 1967

Gerald Vizenor with his son Robert Vizenor, Oxford, England, 1991

Gerald Vizenor with his wife Laura Hall, Bonn, Germany, 1991

Gerald Vizenor with his wife Laura Hall, Savran Books, Minneapolis, 1981

'Violence' View Challenged

By GERALD VIZENOR

Minneapolis Tribune
Staff Writer

Acts of assassination in the United States cannot support the emotional contention that A m e r ican society is i n h erently v i o l ent, a U n i versity of M i n n e sota anthropologist declared l a s t week.

Gerlach

But while the assassination of a public figure may not prove that ours is a violent society, Prof. Luther P. Gerlach argued, the potential for violence nevertheless is built i n t o the traditional structures of our society.

Gerlach, 38, who lives in Blaine, speaks Swahili and holds a Ph.D. degree from L o n d o n University with certificates in Islamic and African law.

SETTLED in the booklined, basement s t u d y of his split-level h o m e, he t a l k e d in an interview about social change, black power, and his theory of how a "segmented society" nourishes the potential for violence in our country.

In America, he said, minority citizens are systematically excluded from the dominant society — socially, economically, politically.

Thus, "black people and Indians are without power or significance as h u m a n beings," Gerlach said.

VIOLENCE g r o w s not only from the s e n s e of powerlessness, Gerlach explained, but out of an emerging need to achieve that power.

And finally c o realizatior cently

other raises livestock, the third produces vegetables —there is interdependence and independence, no one society dominates.

IN A SOCIETY w h e r e power is mutually shared by all segments, the need for violence is not found, he emphasized.

Gerlach is not traditional in his scholarly d e t a c h ment. He is intensely concerned that America is not committed to a balance of power within the segmented p o w e r within the s e g mented society.

The typical reaction to the demands of minority people, Gerlach f e e l s, is suppression — the cry for stringent law enforcement.

The "problem" in t h i s country is white, not black, G e r l a c h contends. The

same d o m i n a n t power which created the "problem" is the same p o w e r which c o u l d be used to eliminate the "problem," he says.

The black-power movement cannot be compared with the similar demands for equality by European minorities in this country, he said.

They were able to maintain their language, pride and cultural identity, Gerlach explained, while at the same time they were building political and social power in the cities.

"Finally they could form power blocs and people could melt in the melting pot.

"THE PROBLEM in the black segment of the society is that they must build everything from noth-

ing. Everything is coming at once—language, culture, hair style, African dress.

"That's w h a t b l a c k power is all about," he said.

One of the most important aspects of the black-power movement, Gerlach said, is that it is a movement to change the Negro community.

"This is often overlooked. People just don't understand what is at stake. The black revolution is worldwide, and white people are in the minority."

Gerlach is determined that the American society must "maximize the equal distribution of justice, dignity and economic opportunity, and the access to

Gerlach
Continued on Page 7C

Gerlach

Continued from Page One
power and leadership."

"WE ARE involved in a revolution," he said, and it cannot be "bought off" with federal grants and welfare payments "simply to expunge guilt feelings as a substitute for action."

He called for the immediate use of "intermediary forces"—committed volunteers—who can act as buffers between the dominant and alienated segments of the society.

The black patrol in north Minneapolis or the Urban Coalition might be the ginning of the

First story as a journalist for the Minneapolis Tribune, June 9, 1968

Kin, Friends Attend
Rites for Young Indian

By GERALD VIZENOR
Minneapolis Tribune Staff Writer

SISSETON, S.D.—Catholic funeral services for Dane White were held here Wednesday ln English and in the Dakota language at St. Catherine's Indian Mission Church.

Dane

Following the service, attended by 75 people, all but six of whom were Dakota Indians, Dane was buried here in St. Peter's Catholic Cemetery.

Born in Sisseton 13 years ago, he took his own life Sunday in the Wilkin County Jail, Breckenridge, Minn., where he had been held since Oct. 7 awaiting a juvenile court hearing.

The services and burial for the young Dakota Indian were attended by his father, Cyrus White, Browns Valley, Minn.; his mother, Mrs. Burdell Armell, Chicago, Ill.; his maternal and paternal grandparents; his older brother, Timothy, 15; three younger sisters, Jodi, 12, Joan, 11, and Mary, 9, and many of his school friends.

The Rev. William Keohane conducted the service. Two hymns were sung in the Dakota language.

"Dane is here, in the background of the banquet table. Lord, remember Dane in your Kingdom," Father Keohane said in prayer, pointing to the large painting of the Last Supper behind the altar of the small Indian church.

Six of Dane's school friends carried his gray metal coffin from the church. Fifteen cars formed the procession to the cemetery on the edge of town.

Following the service at the grave, the six young Indian pallbearers removed their honoring ribbons and placed them on the coffin.

A cold Dakota wind blew across the slope of St. Peter's cemetery. The six pallbearers were the last to leave the grave.

No. 217

Expires December 31, 1975

Gerald Vizenor

Press
Minneapolis Tribune

Press Pass, Minneapolis Tribune

Minneapolis Tribune, front page, November 21, 1968

Mondale Cites Indian Suicide Rate and Assails Education

By GERALD VIZENOR
Minneapolis Tribune Staff Writer

Senator Walter F. Mondale said Monday that recent reports indicate that the suicide rate among young Indians is the highest in the nation.

The senator commented yesterday on the suicide of Dane White, 13, who hanged himself 10 days ago in the Breckenridge, Minn. **Mondale** jail where he had been held six weeks awaiting a juvenile-court hearing.

"The tragic death of this helpless child is part of the shocking national trend of suicides among young Indians.

"IT STEMS from the educational system which destroys the Indian's respect for himself and his culture," Mondale said in a telephone interview.

Mondale, D-Minn., is the acting chairman of the subcommittee on Indian education of the Committee on Labor and Public Welfare.

Prominent psychiatrists and psychologists, including Karl Menninger from the Menninger Clinic in Topeka, Kans., testified before the committee last month on the mental-health conditions of young Indians on reservations and in Bureau of Indian Affairs (BIA) boarding schools.

Mondale attributed the suicide of Dane and other young Indians to an "identity crisis" resulting from educational experiences "depicting the Indian as a pagan savage.

"THE PROBLEMS are particularly pronounced in boarding schools where children are separated from parents and community and sometimes discouraged from even visiting their parents.

"Indians find themselves alienated from their own culture," Mondale said yesterday.

Arrangements had been made through the BIA Agency in Sisseton, S.D., to place Dane, 13, in the Pierre, S.D., Indian Boarding School.

The principal of the school, James Vance, said last week that although all of his teachers are white, most of his staff at the school, including teacher aides, are Indians. Vance pointed to a new program at the school emphasizing the Indian culture in the classroom.

MONDALE SAID one witness testified at the hearing that in one jail near a Navaho reservation, "In a single year three Indian youths hanged themselves from the same water pipe in the same cell."

"Robert Kennedy had spent some time with one of the youths who hanged himself," Mondale recalled. "I was told that the experience had a lasting impact on Sen. Kennedy."

Kennedy had set up the subcommittee on Indian education. When Kennedy was assassinated last June, Mondale became acting chairman of the committee.

Mondale said the federal educational system destroys Indian self respect in several ways: "By showing no respect for Indian language and culture, which is often taught by people who are anti-Indian, and by the use of teaching methods which fail to deal with the human and psychological needs of the Indian child."

WHEN MONDALE asked the BIA how many psychiatrists and psychologists they employed in their school system, he said "they could identify only three psychologists and no psychiatrists in the entire system."

Dane had never been approached by the BIA while he was in jail. Nor had he seen a psychologist or psychiatrist. His father and his court - appointed attorney, Donald Pedersen, had made the arrangements with the BIA to place Dane at the Pierre boarding school.

Mondale said subcommittee hearings will be resumed next month in Washington, D.C.

Minneapolis Tribune, November 26, 1968

Ojibway, Christian Funeral Rites Conducted for State Indian, 124

By GERALD VIZENOR
Minneapolis Tribune Staff Writer

WARROAD, Minn. — John Ka Ka Geesick, who practiced Indian herbal medicine until his death Friday at the age of 124, was given both Ojibway and Christian burial here Tuesday.

Ka Ka Geesick ran a trap line along the shores of Lake of the Woods until four years ago, and was a member of the Midewiwin — the Ojibway grand medicine society.

Following the Medewiwin service in his native language attended by family and Indian friends, and the traditional Christian service, Ka Ka Geesick was buried next to his brother, Chief Na May Puk in the Indian Highland Park Cemetery.

MANY Warroad businesses were closed yesterday afternoon for the services in the high school auditorium, a tribute to the Indian who said he was 16 years old when Abraham Lincoln became president.

About 300 persons, half of whom were Indian, attended the Christian services conducted by the Rev. Leonard Lindholm, minister of the Evangelical Covenant Church in Warroad.

The pallbearers included: Richard Roberts, mayor of Warroad, and two former mayors of the village.

Ka Ka Geesick, who entered the Warroad Nursing Home four years ago, is survived by a daughter, Mary Angus, Warroad; three grandchildren, 14 great-grandchildren and 6 great-great-grandchildren.

Daniel Raincloud, the Midewiwin medicine man from the nearby Red Lake Reservation, conducted the Ojibway service in the auditorium while the minister and those attending the Christian services waited outside.

RAINCLOUD SANG two Ojibway honoring songs over a small bundle of food and a package of cigarettes. He accompanied himself with a small rattle.

Raincloud then placed a pair of red cotton gloves in the coffin to accompany Ka Ka Geesick to the grave.

Ka Ka Geesick probably was born at Buffalo Point in Canada on the shores of Lake of the Woods. He was given a land patent in 1905 signed by President Theodore Roosevelt.

Until four years ago, Ka Ka Geesick lived in a small house on the 102 - acre land grant on Muskeg Bay, in Warroad.

THE UNCERTAINTY of Ka Ka Geesick's birth was resolved' in 1964 when the Warroad village council passed a resolution establishing his date of birth as May 16, 1844.

On the same day the council decreed that the name of Muskeg Bay should be changed to Ka Ka Geesick Bay two years after the death of the Indian medicine man.

Tom Lightning, now 94 and recognized as the oldest Indian in Warroad, said of Ka Ka Geesick that "he was an old man when I was a little boy in the village."

Ka Ka Geesick was dressed in a blue suit, white shirt and blue stripped tie. But he was remembered by residents of Warroad as always wearing mocassins, a buckskin jacket and in the winter, a muskrat hat.

■

JOHN KA KA GEESICK
He died at 124

Funeral for John Ka Ka Geesick, December 11, 1968, Minneapolis Tribune

from previous marriages, and a son born to Maxine and
Cyrus. The Whites lived in a comfortable home; they owned
two cars and new furniture, and could not understand why
Dane and Timothy ran away. The Whites were good people,
clean, disciplined, and they worked hard to be responsible
members of the community. I was there and pretended to run
away, across the border to be with my friends and the animals in the house.

Dane and his brother ran away to live with their grandmother in Long Hollow. I was at home near the kerosene
space heater; she could have been my grandmother. The li-
noleum was worn to the black and cracked at the thresholds;
there were no pretenses. The weathered house was next to an
abandoned church; there were several cats and dogs in the
yard. "Dane liked it out here," said Marian Starr. "He was a
happy-go-lucky kid, always laughing and joking around with
the other boys." I imagined them there, with me on the run.

Timothy moved to Chicago to live with his mother. He
returned to the funeral in Sisseton. At a gathering after the
funeral, Timothy told the family that "Dane was unhappy
and didn't want to go home." That afternoon at Long Hollow, Timothy took his gun and went hunting in the valley,
behind his grandmother's house.

Bower Hawthorne, the executive editor who had hired
me at the *Minneapolis Tribune*, ordered me to his office. He
was close to rage: "What you have done is shit, the same as
shitting in the living room." He had just read a copy of my
civil rights complaint against my employer, the Minneapolis
Star and Tribune Company.

I had recorded my concern about racist advertising in the
company newpapers, and had complained many times to
various editors about the derogatory images and messages.
Hawthorne heard me and promised the problem would be
corrected. I warned him one last time and then filed a specific
complaint against my employer, and Fairmont Foods Company. My complaint was filed September 26, 1968, with the
Minneapolis Department of Civil Rights. The advertisement

named in the complaint depicted a simulated Indian with a package of "Indian Corn Chips" in one hand. These phrases were used in the advertisement published in the *Minneapolis Star*: "Introducing the fast-vanishing American . . . American because they brighten up any munch or lunch in a star-spangled manner. Heap yummy . . . Honest Injun . . . Indian War Marks."

Hawthorne was even more worried when he learned that my plans included a television press conference later in the afternoon to release the contents of my complaint. His neck and ears were red and swollen.

"What will it take?" asked Hawthorne.

"To do what?"

"Withdraw the complaint."

"What you promised last month, establish a review committee with the power to correct derogatory advertising, and show me in writing the new policies and members before three this afternoon."

Hawthorne retreated to his office in silence; he seemed to be worried more about my complaint on television than about racist advertising. He was aware that Sage Cowles was a member of the Minneapolis Commission on Human Relations; she was married to John Cowles, Jr., president of the Minneapolis Star and Tribune Company. Cowles was my employer and he was named in the complaint.

"Your ass is on the line," said Frank Premack.

"Naturally."

"Can't do anything for you this time."

"Not even a page and a half?"

"Not a chance, you won't be coming back," he said.

"Hawthorne probably doesn't know that my complaint is a hard bluff, because stereotypes in the media are not considered violations of the Minneapolis Ordinance on Civil Rights."

Bower Hawthorne agreed to my demands in less than three hours. As promised, my complaint was withdrawn. I canceled the television press conference, and waited to be fired in a few weeks. Very few derogatory advertisements have appeared in the two newspapers since then. Hawthorne retired as he had planned. Charles Bailey became the executive editor of the *Minneapolis Tribune*. My leave was approved to teach college for one year. I continued for several years to write stories as a contributing editorial writer.

May 1970: Water Striders at Lake Forest

～～～～～～～～～～ Professor George Mills hired me to teach at Lake Forest College in Illinois and inaugurated my career as a college teacher in the most unusual manner: haiku poems, not a doctorate, earned the highest honors.

Mills was chairman of the social sciences department; he had studied to be an anthropologist, but he earned his doctorate and turned to art and literature. Jerry Gerasimo taught in the department and introduced me and my haiku curriculum vitae.

Doctor Gerasimo was on sabbatical leave in Minneapolis. We met at a conference on American Indian Education. He was a stranger and curbed me at the entrance to the hotel; my escape from the colonists became a chance encounter that led me back to college as a teacher.

Gerasimo had a renaissance saunter, a clean smile, clean boots, and he wore a watch cap; he was Greek, but he could have been a tribal trickster in my stories. We argued about education, movies, and the social sciences for one hour and seventeen minutes, and then we introduced our surnames. Later, we told stories about our rencounter, and we continue to revise the point of view, and the trickster signatures.

George Mills and his wife had invited me to dinner at their house for the final decision on my appointment. The meal was delicious, but my mind was on the chairman and how he would respond to me. His wild brows leapt to names and metaphors, his lower lip turned down on common verbs in the past tense; there were birch, madrones, and winter animals in him that night, but what did he mean by the doctored courses on academic diseases? He had peeled the academic veneer from his primal bones, but this was my chance to teach for the money. What did he mean, the social sciences hold their breath under water, cold, cold methods, and cockamamie moods, and never reveal their data as brain dead? I knew what he meant, but how could he hire me to do the same? The more he drank the more he raved, a wild, rich, humor in the bluster, and the more we ended the courses he would have me teach.

"What would you have me teach then?"

"What would you teach, then?"

"Literature in the social sciences?"

"Fuck the social sciences," he roared. Mills beat the end of the table, his eyes were wild, dangerous. The silver bounced on the plates; his heart bounced, he roared and beat the social sciences more, and more, and the telephone sounded in the distance.

"Give me an idea."

"Haiku, haiku," he said and leaned closer to me at the table.

"That's great, but what about the social sciences."

"Fuck the social sciences, any bastard can teach and be dead, but you can teach haiku in the social sciences, that's why you're here, you can write haiku, that's what's great about this." He stared in silence at the end of the table, the wine was over, his breath was slower, and then he whispered a haiku by Basho: *That frog, the old pond, great sound of water.*

"Did haiku get me the job?"

"Indeed, your haiku."

"The whim, the world of dew and yet, and yet." I told him one of my haiku: *Calm in the storm, master Basho soaks his feet, water striders.* The telephone sounded closer. Gerasimo must have called twice to see if there would be haiku and a reception to celebrate my appointment as a lecturer.

I was a lecturer for three quarters, and decided at the last minute not to sign a second contract. The use of narcotics on campus was a serious problem; when I asked the president what he planned to do about the drug problem, he said, "What drug problem?" I was discouraged, and eager to leave;

then he explained, "I mean, what drug problem, faculty or student?" He was right, and my mood turned back to Minnesota. I had been hired to direct a federal desegregation program in the Park Rapids School District near the White Earth Reservation. I returned to teaching one year later and directed the Native American Studies Program at Bemidji State University; the campus was on a lake and near three reservations in northern Minnesota. I won a fellowship, the following year, for graduate study at Harvard University, and then returned to the *Minneapolis Tribune* as an editorial writer.

The Ethnic Studies Department at Berkeley first hired me to teach Native American literatures in the winter quarter of 1976. For several years I taught two quarters a year at the University of Minnesota, and winter quarters at Berkeley. For a short time, between Berkeley and Minnesota, I was a visiting professor at Tianjin University in the People's Republic of China. Russell Thornton invited me to teach in the American Indian Studies Department, and Dean Fred Lukermann supported my tenure and promotion to professor at Minnesota.

James Youngblood Henderson invited me to lecture for a week in February 1975 on economic development at the University of California. We met at Harvard University; he was a law student then, and I was there on a graduate fellowship. Professor Terry Wilson, who was coordinator of Native American Studies and later chairman of the Ethnic Studies Department, created a permanent tenured position for me at Berkeley.

Bemidji State University owned several houses at the end of a parking area; the buildings were scheduled for demolition, and my first proposal to save one of the houses for a tribal center was denied. Meanwhile, I learned that the vice president who turned me down had created a secret slush fund, cash profits from the bookstore. My second proposal to save the house was more direct, with a reference to state auditors. The vice president did not test my honor; he agreed to turn the house over to me and provided some funds for utilities and support programs. I established a corporation, named the Oshki Anishinabe Family Center, the new tribal people, to celebrate the idea of tribal families and communities. Earl Nyholm, Charles Aubid, and other healers and singers dedicated the house in a special tribal ceremony on October 19, 1972.

Robert Decker, president of Bemidji State University, was pleased with the programs at the new family center, but he resisted my proposal for money to acquire more books and films on Native American Indians for the university library, and he would not waive a dormitory requirement for first year Indian students.

Diane Brown, a first year student, complained that she was the only Indian student in her dormitory. The other students were not unkind, but they demanded too much; daily she was tested with information and asked questions about Indians, and students expected her to help them with their course papers on numerous tribal cultures. Diane, with my support, asked the president to waive the dormitory residence requirement. Most of the other Indian students lived at home on reservations near the campus. She was denied a waiver; we appealed, and she was denied a second time.

I organized a protest and led an occupation of President Decker's office; more than fifty students, and other tribal people from the community, were there that morning for the confrontation. The local newspaper ran a story on the reasons for the planned occupation. President Decker called me that night; we discussed the demands and reached an agreement on all but one, the dormitory requirement. He pointed out that the state university board set the rules on dormitories to be sure the bonds were paid on time, but he would support our petition for certain exceptions. That morning in his occupied office he would resist at first, then we would negotiate, and at last he would support our demands in public, as we had rehearsed.

The Minnesota Chippewa Tribe held a power dinner that winter at Bemidji State University to honor Senator Hubert Humphrey, Senator Walter Mondale, and others, for their dedication to tribal education and economic development programs on reservations. State senators and representatives, tribal, and local political leaders were at the dinner.

Roger Jourdain, president of the Red Lake Reservation, was there too; his presence starts the best stories. Jourdain seems to hold the evil gambler on a lunge line, and no one returns to the threshold with better humor; tribal politics has never been a pleasure on reservations, but this man overturns adversities, and once boasted that he had a hot line to the vice president of the United States.

Senator Mondale opened his lecture with notes of appreciation; he held up my new book, *The Everlasting Sky: New Voices from the People Named the Chippewa*, which had just been published, and praised me for the book, and for my magazine article, which he had read into the *Congressional Record*, about our trip two years earlier to federal boarding schools on the Navajo Nation.

That praise was the seed that bloomed wild that night in the mind of Jourdain. He read my book and was not pleased with the attention given to his rivals William Lawrence and Leon Cook. They had opposed him in tribal elections and lost, but they had new ideas for economic development: more independent services, such as gasoline stations and coin operated laundries, and fewer businesses dominated by tribal governments.

"Jourdain has power and he knows how to use it to stay in power," I wrote in *The Everlasting Sky*. "In no uncertain terms he fights to win and he holds the record on the reservation for naming the most white people honorary Indians. . . . He speaks the Anishinaabe language and gets the federal money he wants when he wants it."

Jourdain moved closer to the microphone and paid his dues to those who had supported his proposals. He was on the podium to introduce his friend Senator Humphrey, but he saw me at the fourth table and lost his concentration, and then his temper. Jourdain blathered and hissed, pointed, and waved at me; he was too close to the microphone and the curses were lost in harsh breath. Mondale, at last, moved to the podium to save the introduction of the man who came closer than anyone to being elected president of the United States. Humphrey raised the best humor, as usual, and celebrated the great work of the tribes in the Democratic Party.

The trickster must have brought us together in that space between the double doors. Jourdain cursed me, and once outside we shouted at each other. The last hurrahs, and there we were out on the cold night with nothing good to say about each other. Humphrey, Mondale, and the others waited inside for our storm to pass. Jourdain punched me on the chest with his stout finger and shouted at me, his face shivered; the force of his finger drove me backward around a large concrete planter in front of the double doors. He tired, and then it was my turn to curse and punch, but my finger was lost on his loose chest so I used my fist. We moved around the planter in that manner, back and forth, several times; weakened at last, we made our final insults with humor, and turned to leave in different directions. Humphrey's aide rushed after me and said he had never understood until that night how difficult was tribal politics. "That's nothing," I told him. "We were at our usual winter talk and walk on economic development." That was my last winter in Bemidji.

The American Indian Studies Department in the Social Sciences Tower at the University of Minnesota was a comic opera that turned a tired metaphor and gave tribal politics a new name: Chippewa Balkanization. Three past chairs wandered the corridors with extreme care; no past chair wanted to meet the other. I named our department the chair of tears; once or twice there were survivors, but tribal humor was too low to remember with much humor. There were wicked winds, and no trickster signatures on the rise; even the potted birch trees were dead.

I proposed that the department be sold to the highest bidder and then turned over to the last name on a list of candidates for a new chair, because the best and the brightest had not survived the hatred, racial politics, and crossblood ideologies. One chair represented the values of certain tribal communities, but was not the choice of traditional academics. Another chair was the choice of the academics, but not the students. The last chair had the degrees, he was the choice of students, but not tribal politicians, and more, to no wise end. The department died with the birch trees.

One of my favorite scenes in the comic opera was the last search for a tribal historian. There were three finalists, a mixedblood historian with a doctorate, and two white historians with doctorates, one a woman. The tribal historian was the shoo-in, but he lost his way at a final interview. The students were not interested in the last two white candidates on the list, but they were persuaded to give at least one a chance in an interview. The white man was an outstanding historian, moved by good sense and humor, honest and considerate, and he was the choice of the historians. The students resisted his tweed coat, but he made it past that bias and was on his way to student support; however, the end came with a familiar face. An Indian student who had borrowed money, told lies, and left town a year earlier, returned at that precise moment, praised the candidate, and ended the search. That must have been a trickster signature to save that candidate from the politics of the department. The students accepted the white woman and she was hired as an assistant professor.

Native American Studies is part of the Ethnic Studies Department at the University of California, Berkeley. The departmental offices are located in Dwinelle Hall. My office on the third floor was shared over the years with James Youngblood Henderson, Wendy Rose, Terry Wilson, Karen Biestmen, and Paula Gunn Allen. We had a view of the plaza, and at lunch time we could hear various lectures and performances. The polka dot man may appear in more tourist photographs than any other person on campus; he once carried a water hose and wore clothes with painted polka dots. He declared the plaza his sacred landscape. At Berkeley, the comic opera, those wicked scenes and wild curtains, for the most part, were on the plaza or the avenue outside the department.

"Gerald Vizenor, a visiting professor in the Ethnic Studies Department, has made an official proposal to rename the north part of Dwinelle Hall as Ishi Hall," the *Daily Californian* reported on October 15, 1985.

"According to Vizenor, visiting from the University of Minnesota, Ishi's contributions to the university have been overlooked. While UC Berkeley has honored Alfred Kroeber by naming Kroeber Hall after him, it has granted no distinction to Ishi. . . .

"Vizenor, who is a member of the Minnesota Chippewa tribe, said he has enthusiastic support for his proposal within the Ethnic Studies Department, and he plans to pursue the issue statewide and nationally. 'I hope that every Indian organization in the state will support it,' he said."

My invitation to support the proposal to change the name of the north part of Dwinelle Hall to Ishi Hall included a special naming ceremony to be held on March 16, 1986, seventy years after the death of Ishi; however, my proposal has not yet made it through the Space Assignment and Capital Improvements Group at Berkeley.

Ishi, one of the last survivors of his tribe, was found near a mining town on the Feather River in late August 1911. The Yahi Indian was released from jail to Alfred Kroeber and housed in the Museum of Anthropology.

"Sitting beside him that day in 1913 while Ishi worked, Kroeber thought of Ishi's first coming to the museum, of their growing friendship," wrote Theodora Kroeber. "He recalled that after a few days Ishi was at work making Yana objects for the museum so that outside worlds would know something of his own Yana world; how almost at once he began the fashioning of a new life pattern suited to himself and his new friends and surroundings."

Ishi died on March 16, 1916. When Kroeber learned of his death, and the interest in an extensive autopsy, he wrote, "If there is any talk of the interests of science, say for me that science can go to hell. We propose to stand by our friends." Ishi was cremated according to the customs of his tribe.

Ishi "looked upon us as sophisticated children—smart, but not wise," wrote Saxton Pope, a medical doctor who attended Ishi and studied bows and arrows with him. "We knew many things, and much that is false. He knew nature, which is always true. . . . His soul was that of a child, his mind that of a philosopher."

Ishi was the "most patient man I ever knew," said Alfred Kroeber. "I mean, he had mastered the philosophy of patience." Kroeber Hall is named in honor of Alfred Kroeber; now, the University of California must honor the patience of Ishi.

"In spite of Kroeber's deep sympathy for Ishi," wrote Roy Wagner in *The Invention of Culture*, "one cannot help feeling that he was the ideal museum specimen, one that did the anthropologist's job for him by producing and reconstituting its own culture. . . . Ishi accomplished the metaphorization of life into culture that defines much of anthropological understanding."

Ishi was liberated from the museum in my stories. The praise of historians and the manners of the elite became a trickster signature in my book *The Trickster of Liberty*. Ishi was released from the burdens of culture and became a real person at graduation ceremonies in the redwood grove at the University of California, Berkeley.

Alfred Kroeber, the anthropologist, who was more historian than cold scientist, Thomas Waterman, and Edward Sapir, the linguists, and Phoebe Apperson Hearst, regent of the University of California, Robert Sproul, and Benjamin Ide Wheeler, past presidents of Berkeley, were there in the redwoods with the tribes and tricksters to honor Doctor Ishi at graduation ceremonies.

Regent Phoebe Apperson Hearst came down to the microphone from the right rim of the amphitheater to decorate Ishi with a sash and to present his honorary doctorate; he was a "patient man" and "his mind was that of a philosopher."

Indeed, he was a natural philosopher. "Doctor Ishi Ishi," she said, a surname as a double given in translation, "you are an esteemed intuitive scholar. We have conferred and agreed that you deserve an honorary doctorate as much as the men who have studied you, who have learned so much from you, for they have been so honored in their research and knowledge of your culture. They learned what they know from you, so it stands to reason then, that you should have the doctorate. Without you, there would be no knowledge of you, and the anthropologists would have no cultures, and no degrees." She was nervous over the prepared speech, and hesitated at the trickster signatures. Ishi turned to the audience and waited to be honored with other tribes at the graduation ceremonies.

"Doctor Kroeber Kroeber," continued Regent Hearst, "has recorded the first words that you learned in English when you arrived at the museum, and we are pleased on this auspicious occasion to imitate what you said then, and so, in your patois, is 'evelybody hoppy?' "

Pierre Cardin inaugurated Maxim's de Beijing on October 1, 1983, the thirty-fourth anniversary of the founding of the People's Republic of China. I was there under the armorial emblems for the opening that would be named the site of another revolution in China. The doormen in pillbox hats, the hatcheck girls bound in red and black uniforms, and the waiters must save their annual salaries to pay for one meal in the restaurant.

Zhou Enlai would never have bid a couturier to celebrate his rich restaurant on the anniversary of the nation. China was discovered and the past overturned by Matteo Ricci, Mao Zedong, Pierre Cardin, and twice on television, I wrote in my novel *Griever: An American Monkey King in China*.

"China was discovered twice on television and now the nation lives in three centuries at the same time," said a man on a bicycle with a diplomatic license. We waited at the curb outside the restaurant to see who would enter. Maxim's de Beijing became the third forbidden city in China. The Imperial Palace, of course, the forbidden franchise of Maxim's de Beijing, and the residences of the government leaders.

I was there with my wife, Laura Hall; we were English teachers for several months at Tianjin University. Laura taught graduate students; my students were third and fourth year undergraduates who had never been allowed to browse in the university library. Small revolutions are the most troublesome.

We worked hard, twice the lecture hours of most teachers, and the students were eager and honorable. We accepted our responsibilities with humor, but then we discovered at a festival that there were more than a hundred Chinese teachers of English in our department. We had never seen these teachers before, and wondered if they were ever in the classroom. China has many, many catches to understand her practices. These teachers never taught, we were told, because the only real incentive, when the salaries are the same, is to teach less and less. These teachers were at the top of the scale; they never taught.

Wang Sheng, the foreign affairs officer responsible for the teachers, said, in response to our concern, "We did not want to disappoint Americans, because we know how hard you like to work."

The Beijing branch of Maxim's is a replica of the famous Parisian restaurant now owned by fashion designer Pierre Cardin, wrote Orville Schell in *To Get Rich Is Glorious*. "If I can put a Maxim's in Peking, I can put a Maxim's on the moon," he boasted to his guests at the inaugural banquet. "Close your eyes and you are in Paris. It is Paris right down to the smallest detail. . . . China is changing. My idea would have been unthinkable a few years ago. In ten years this country will be like Japan."

March 1973: Avengers at Wounded Knee

Rodger Kemp was a dedicated teacher at the Pine Point School on the White Earth Reservation when the American Indian Movement was on the radical rise in the cities.

Kemp was summoned late one night by a local reservation radical who had been inspired by the media presentation of urban tribal militants. He pounded on the aluminum door of the house trailer and shouted, "Rog, open up, it's me."

"What's up?"

"I need a jump start," said the radical.

"Car's dead again?"

"Yeah, fuckin' white man's car."

"Come on in."

"Fuckin' battery's dead." he said.

"Sounds familiar, I better get dressed for this." Rodger had earned the reputation of being the most comfortable, reliable, compassionate friend and teacher on the reservation. He listened, he taught children to imagine the world, he humored, he tutored, nurtured identities, coached, wrote proposals, loaned too much money, and jump started cars late at night with a wise sense of humor. I was there for the weekend, my house was under repair and renovation, and I listened to nurture my crossblood identities.

Rodger sat in the living room and laced his boots with deliberate care; the ersatz radical, a military veteran who could not find a good job on the reservation, paced back and forth near the door. He was high wired, and the aluminum trailer shuddered under his hard tread, tread, tread.

"Hurry up Rog."

"Right, one more boot."

"Someday I'm gonna drive to Park Rapids and shoot the fucking white bastards on the streets, and start the real revolution." The radical tried to provoke the calm teacher who laced his right boot. His mind was sudden, wild hits at violent scenes.

"Someday soon?"

"We're goin' in with rifles."

"By car?"

"Yeah, why?"

"Listen, could you do me a favor?"

"Sure Rog, what?"

"Could you get yourself a new battery before you start the revolution." Rodger smiled and waited at the door. The radical missed the humor, the trickster signature; he had assumed too much from the white teachers on the reservation.

Kemp connected his battery cables to the car and the radical roared down the reservation road in the dark with no praise; from a revolution in a trailer to racial insolence and loneliness on the road.

The American Indian Movement overturned the burdens of colonial education, and burned manners at the best institutions. Rather, the media borne tribal simulations, and transvaluations, raised the romantic notions of a material and spiritual revolution in America. Media simulations and ersatz leaders have no real constituencies; the media men, and there were men under the media masks, had learned to rave in television scenes. Some of these men were paroled felons, seldom bound to praise and pleasure; some were wicked, and sold hallucinogens to tribal children. Some of these men were moved by personal power; literature and communal dreams were rare in their travels.

The media radicals encountered the material, not a liberation of the mind, or a revolution in literature. Most of the radicals were petulant about imagination and ideas, and were critical of tribal studies in colleges and universities. However, some of the radicals were eager to learn an older language of identities.

At that time most people understood the tribal name Chippewa, as in the Minnesota Chippewa Tribe, or in the assertion of an innocent child, "I'm very proud to be a Chippewa Indian." Chippewa was the colonial name imposed on a woodland tribal culture.

"The Anishinaabe are the people of the woodland in the language of those who have been known for more than a century in the dominant society as the Chippewa and Ojibway." My essay on the tribal name was published in the winter of 1971 in the *Indian Historian*, edited by Jeannette Henry. I proposed that we "relume the tribal identities of the woodland people by changing the tribal name back to the Anishinaabe." William Warren, the mixedblood historian, wrote in his *History of the Ojibway Nation* that the invented names of the tribe do "not date far back. As a race or distinct people they denominated themselves Anishinaabeg," the plural of Anishinaabe. Frances Densmore pointed out that the name "Chippewa is comparatively modern and is the only name under which the tribe has been designated by the government in treaties and other negotiations, but it has never been adopted by the older members of the tribe."

American Indian Movement leaders declared to the media that their members would return to the reservation to fight for treaty rights. They drove north from the cities by the hundreds armed with new pistols and rifles.

Russell Means, Dennis Banks, and thirteen other armed leaders filed into the tribal Headstart classroom on the Leech Lake Reservation and sat down on wee chairs. They sat in comic poses, their knees tucked under their chins, dressed in diverse combinations of cowboy clothes, simulated, and traditional tribal vestments from the turn of the century. Dennis Banks, who was a charismatic wanderer then, wore his mountain man costume with a fur collar. Most of the leaders of the militant movement were from urban centers.

Simon Howard, then elected president of the Minnesota Chippewa Tribe, entered the classroom, eased down to a wee chair, and twirled his thumbs beneath his stout stomach. The leaders argued with each other about their places in the chain of command, who would sit beside whom at the scheduled television press conferences. Howard wore a thin nylon bowling jacket and a pork pie hat with a floral print in contrast to the media renascence of simulated vestments worn by the militants.

Howard was born on the reservation and his constituencies had been earned there. He was at the meeting as an elected tribal official to keep peace between white people and the militants. The militants were there for an armed confrontation with white people on the opening day of fishing. I was there as a press officer for the tribal government to modulate threats and rumors at scheduled press conferences. Walker was my home, and my work was understood on the Leech Lake Reservation. The militants were never at peace, the press conferences were mordant, and white people were terrified, but Howard managed with humor and astute observations to avoid a confrontation. Local units of the Minnesota National Guard had been placed on alert, and there were hundreds of state police and federal agents in motels around the reservation.

"All right boys, quiet down now and take your seats again," said Howard in the classroom. The tribal leader and the militants agreed to meet twice a day with each other and then with the press. "Now, I don't know everyone here, so let's go around the room and introduce ourselves." Howard looked around the room at the faces, but one by one the militants turned away. "Let's start with you over there. Stand right up, tell us who you are, and where you're from."

The man stood beside the wee chair; he dragged his feet forward and swung his rifle from side to side, a shy student with a weapon. "My name is Delano Western, and I'm from Kansas," he said. His voice trembled. Western leaned forward and looked down at the floor; he touched a spot on the carpet with the toe of his boot. He was dressed in a black hat with a wide brim and an imitation silver headband, dark green sunglasses with large round lenses, a sweatshirt with

"Indian Power" printed on the front, two bandoliers of heavy ammunition, none of which matched the bore of his rifle, a black motorcycle jacket with military colonel wings on the epaulets. "Red Power" and "Custer Had It Coming" patches were on his jacket. A military bayonet was strapped to his body next to his revolver.

"We came here to die," said Western. He raised his voice and repeated his death wish once more. He and about six hundred militants had come to the town of Cass Lake on the Leech Lake Reservation to fight for tribal rights to hunt and fish on treaty land, rights that had already been argued by reservation lawyers in federal court and decided in favor of the tribe. How ironic that the militants were camped on treaty land given over to a church group by the federal government, land that should have been returned to the tribe.

The militants demanded money from public officials in Cass Lake; when the town refused to pay, the leaders held a press conference at a rifle range to scare the public. Means, the media man, smiled for television cameras, and fired his pistol or "white-people shooter" at cans. Banks, dressed in a black velvet shirt with ribbon appliqué, prepared for target practice; he stood in front of a collection of commodity food cans, or what he named "white fishermen," and attempted to fast draw his sawed-off shotgun. The peculiar weapon stuck on the rope holster attached to his belt. Banks stood up and tried again, but it still stuck. Frustrated, he untied the rope and walked away angry and embarrassed; he never carried his shotgun pistol again. Banks, a new shooter from the city, would never place in the fast-draw contests.

The church camp was used in the summer and loudspeakers sounded from every cabin, on every tree: "We came here to die, to defend our red brothers and sisters from those white racist fishermen. Dinner will be served in one hour, and there will be a dance contest tonight. We need volunteers to help out in the kitchen, and some brothers and sisters who know how to hunt deer . . . make that just the brothers for now."

The media reported that deer were being slaughtered by militants on the reservation in violation of state laws. In fact, the brothers out hunting for two days missed every deer they shot at. One deer, the one pictured on television being dressed by militants at the church camp, had been killed in an accident with an automobile. The dead deer was delivered to the camp by the local game warden, who knew the militants needed food. While the militants were out "shining" deer one night, they fired seven rounds at the big round brown eyes of a cow. The militants missed and the owner of the cow fired back; the militant hunters scrambled a fast retreat to the church camp, declaring that they were under attack by white racist fishermen.

"We must go on living on this reservation after you leave," Howard told the militants at their last meeting. Kent Tupper, who represented the Leech Lake Reservation in federal court, told the militants several times during the week that the rights of tribal people must be won according to the law and not by violence.

I was convinced that the weather was the concord at the end of camp for the American Indian Movement on the Leech Lake Reservation. The cold rain distracted the urban militants who were armed for the first time with new weapons. Highway Patrolman Myles Olson said that "two days of rain was worth two slop buckets of Mace."

Dennis Banks was dressed in secular vestments two years later in federal court; he was on trial for alleged violations of laws in connection with the occupation of Wounded Knee on the Pine Ridge Reservation in South Dakota.

Banks told the federal jurors that he was called to a meeting on Monday, February 27, 1973, at Calico Hall on the Pine Ridge Reservation. "I attended this meeting, and the evidence will show that those who were in attendance at that meeting were Oglala Sioux chiefs, traditional headmen, medicine men and councilmen. . . . I heard an Oglala Sioux woman, two women, address their chiefs and headmen in their own language. . . . The plea that they made to the

American Indian Movement." Banks had not attended the meeting.

I was at that historic meeting at Calico Hall two days before the American Indian Movement occupied the village at Wounded Knee. The small cabin on the reservation was crowded with more than a hundred tribal people from several tribes, from cities and reservations. I was obsessed with a sense of spiritual warmth, and moved by the communal anticipation of the tribal people there; then, several drums sounded, slow beats, and then harder, spiritual harmonies, and we were transmuted by the power of the drums, the sound of the drums, the drums, the drums.

My heart responded to the drums, my chest became the drum, and my body was about to leave me in that cabin on the reservation. I pressed to the outside, pressed shoulders, and thighs, closer and closer to chests, our breath the tribal drums, the drums, through the crowd to the door. Outside, the stars were silent, the air was clear, cold, and on the natural rise. I was liberated on the air, in the night sky, and said my name out loud, once, twice; the time my breath returned, the time my body and awareness returned to me. I had been close to my own truth, the absolute truth of spiritual conversion that night; a few more minutes, hours, and my name might have been lost to the tribe behind a bunker at Wounded Knee. I might have raised my rifle to that airplane over the village in the morning; instead, my pen was raised to terminal creeds.

Then, ultimate realities, the scent of fried chicken that cold night. The only other journalist there, representing network television, had opened a box of fried chicken. He tried to hide in the back seat of his car, but in the end he shared conversation and one wing with me. I returned to the cabin with the night in me, and my mixedblood name. I listened to the voices, the racial politics, the ironies, and the lies, and tried to turn the sound of the drums in my heart into a dream song, into literature. I would not become a mixedblood true believer.

Dennis Banks was not seen at Calico Hall, where five traditional leaders gathered to consider a scheme to seize Wounded Knee. Banks was at Cherry Creek on the Cheyenne River Reservation with a television reporter; the media man was chauffeured to Wounded Knee by the reporter, but she departed when federal marshalls surrounded the area.

Russell Means was perched on a high platform behind a table at one end of Calico Hall. Lower, in front of him, the five traditional, or hereditary, leaders were seated in a row on benches. Means, who did not speak a tribal language then, spoke to the leaders through Leonard Crow Dog, a spiritual leader and translator. The traditional leaders listened to radical entreaties in translation and then retired to the basement to consider the plan to capture Wounded Knee. They conferred for two hours, and then postponed their decision until a second meeting could be held with elected reservation officials. Means was not pleased with their indecision, as he had expected the support of the hereditary leaders; he told them not to overlook his response to their needs on the reservation. We have been invited here, but remember, he admonished the leaders through the translator, we can leave to help people in other places.

March 1, 1973, Wounded Knee, South Dakota: "Members of the American Indian Movement held ten people hostage Wednesday at this Pine Ridge Reservation town where more than 200 Indians were massacred by Cavalry troops in 1890. The hostages were being held after a takeover Tuesday night by about 200 AIM supporters." That first paragraph to a story on the front page of the *Minneapolis Tribune*, under my name, was written by a reporter for United Press International. The rest of the story was mine, but the editors had decided to enliven the the first paragraph with hostages.

My first paragraph indicated that there were no hostages; the owner of the store and the priest at Wounded Knee told me by telephone that there were no hostages. Leaders of the American Indian Movement were never charged with kidnapping or any other crime associated with the taking of hostages. I was close to the village, but the reporter for United Press International never moved from his motel room. He ordered a single-engine plane to circle Wounded Knee and filed his simulated story with an aerial photograph of the church, militants, and raised weapons. I was furious that sensational wire service lies had been attached to my news story. My vow never again to write for the newspaper lasted about two weeks. I was director of Indian Studies, an instructor at Bemidji State University, and a contributing editorial writer at that time.

"Killing Indians was once sanctioned by the military of this nation. Who can forget the slaughter of tribal people at Mystic River and Sand Creek and Wounded Knee in South Dakota," I wrote in a six part editorial series published in the *Minneapolis Tribune* in March 1973.

"We had sufficient light from the word of God for our proceedings," said John Underhill at Mystic River. "The only good Indians I ever saw were dead," said General Philip Sheridan at Fort Cob. "I have come to kill Indians, and believe it is right and honorable to use any means under God's heaven to kill Indians," said Colonel John Chivington at Sand Creek.

Killing Indians in South Dakota today is not sanctioned, but it is seldom viewed as murder. For example, Darld Schmitz admitted stabbing Wesley Bad Heart Bull in front of a cowboy bar at Buffalo Gap. Bad Heart Bull is dead. Schmitz is free.

The American Indian Movement could not survive as a revolutionary tribal caravan without the affinity of lawyers, and the press, and the sympathy of the church.

National television crews followed the revolutionary group to Custer, South Dakota, and were on hand to cover the burning of the county courthouse.

Thirty-eight people were arrested on charges of riot and arson. Ramon Roubideaux, a successful criminal attorney and member of the Rosebud Sioux Tribe, agreed to represent those arrested.

About a hundred young adventurers moved uninvited into a dormitory at the Mother Butler Center in Rapid City. The center is owned by the Catholic Church.

Without the press the death of Wesley Bad Heart Bull and the fires at Custer would have been less dramatic; without an attorney many people might still be in jail awaiting trial; and without the church there would be few places to stay. Most tribal people in Rapid City were not interested in taking a militant home for the night.

Many white residents of Rapid City responded to the presence of the young adventurers with a lump in the throat, a grimace on the face, and one hand on a gun. The city had not yet recovered from a terrible flood, and the arrival of the American Indian Movement was very bad timing.

But a few sensitive white people took the presence of young militants as a challenge to right a few wrongs. Most government officials were open for negotiations.

"I think you have a good message for this country," said Mayor Donald Barnett. The mayor seemed to be impressed by the intense dedication of the leaders of the American Indian Movement until he received the criminal files on the militants and discovered they were armed and staying in motels without paying the bills.

"Are these men serious civil rights workers, or are they a bunch of bandits?" Barnett asked during an interview. "People working for civil rights do not carry guns. I have seen the records on these men, and you can't sit and negotiate with a man who has a gun."

Comparing militant tribal leaders to the black civil rights movement, Barnett said: "Martin Luther King was a man of peace. He was never armed." Two dozen members of the American Indian Movement stayed in a downtown motel in Rapid City for two weeks. They were evicted by the police and left a bill of about $2,500 unpaid. No one was arrested, but police confiscated many weapons, including firearms.

"Now, I am no melodramatic martyr," the mayor said, "nor the great white hope, but I believe in communications and working things out through negotiations. . . . I could have done two things: violate their constitutional rights and jail every one of the militants, or try to negotiate."

And the mayor did his best to negotiate. He called and attended meeting after meeting. City officials were open and anxious to negotiate changes, but militant leaders changed the course of the arguments and demands from day to day in an effort to maintain a position of confrontation and confusion. The mayor and city council members moved to adopt a new ordinance establishing a racial conciliation board with investigative powers.

"We were making progress on the resolution," the mayor said, "when at a meeting of council members and militant leaders Vernon Bellecourt changed the demands and told white people to get out of the Black Hills. . . . He was serious!

"Sure, I told him. . . . I looked at my watch. Let me see, I said, give me about two hours to pack some things up before I leave," the mayor recalled. "But they left, in anger. How can you talk to someone who responds like that? The war is over, and it happened everywhere in history. We won and you lost. There is no changing that and we are not leaving." But the symbolic war is real to the believers, and tribal people will not accept the loss.

There were many reports of shoplifting in supermarkets by young followers of the American Indian Movement. They were living at the Mother Butler Center with no money and no food. Rapid City merchants seemed to agree that it would cost less to put up with shoplifting than to make a legal complaint and suffer possible property damage.

Two weeks later the American Indian Movement moved to the Pine Ridge Reservation and then captured the village at Wounded Knee. At the same time the new racial conciliation board was negotiating in Rapid City, Dennis Banks was riding a horse, posing for photographers at Wounded Knee. Banks and Vernon Bellecourt are woodland tribal mixed-bloods and members of reservations in Minnesota.

I was registered in the same motel as members of the American Indian Movement. I was awakened by the police the night the militants were evicted; my identification as a reporter saved me from the humiliation of being ousted, but at the same time it set me apart from tribal people in the motel. That was not a ripe moment for trickster signatures. The next morning several militant leaders complained that several lids of marijuana, and other hallucinogens, had been hidden and left behind in motel rooms when they were evicted.

The American Indian Movement put my name on their enemies list; four tribal goons, two of whom had once been friends of mine, were told to make life miserable for me at an education conference at the University of Minnesota at Duluth. The goons arrived at the back of the auditorium in the middle of my lecture and blocked the exits. I raised a radical pose and turned over the microphone to the goon who could not resist a chance to rave at an audience.

The confusion at the conference, my wild lunch invitation to the goons, and the unsolicited protection of the tribal students at the university, gave me time to leave down the back stairs and beat a retreat out of the city. When I got back home in Bemidji there were urgent telephone messages; my friends warned me that money had been paid by certain militant leaders to bash me around for the *Minneapolis Tribune* editorial series. The American Indian Movement leaders became the new tribal totalitarians and the least tolerant of dissidence.

Kent Tupper, the tribal attorney, advised me to seek a permit to bear a handgun. I resisted at first, but he persuaded me to at least have a gun in the house. I purchased a revolver and registered it with the county sheriff. Tupper pointed out that my resistance to a handgun was romantic, that my values were bound to an older ethic of street fights; the rules were better understood then, the weapons were fists and mouths, and there were negotiations and resolutions. "There is no reasoning with people who might be drug crazed," he said. A badly wired head is not a negotiable instrument, he pointed out. "You could be dead and right, and he'd be alive and wrong with a court appointed attorney, or you could be alive with a troubled conscience."

Clyde Bellecourt, one of the movers of the American Indian Movement in Minneapolis, appeared as a speaker two months later at Bemidji State University. I decided to be out of town when he was there. He was critical, as usual, of tribal studies programs, and he named me in particular. "Most Indian studies classes and courses throughout the United States are not controlled by the Indian students themselves," said Bellecourt. He was there for Indian Week, and his comments were reported in the local newspaper.

Bellecourt said that my views were not "the Indian view" and that my education was a cultural separation. "The way he writes I can sense he is not the man for the job here." He was disappointed that I was not present. "We didn't come here to condemn him, we came to bring unity."

Bellecourt asserted that some students told him that "they have no control or they are in an advisory capacity. When they do make a decision they usually don't get what they want anyway." He said: "Having rock and roll bands and baseball, that's not Indian to us. We feel that only through identity with our cultural background, that's the only thing we have to keep us, save us." Diane Brown, a student organizer of Indian Week, pointed out that Bellecourt had not been invited to the activities on campus.

CHAPTER TWENTY-SEVEN

January 1980: The Russians and Jack London

The University of California at Berkeley is a wild adventure, but not the untamed wilderness, the beaten seacoast, or the natural environment in the literature of Jack London; even so, that campus was my call of the wild in the mind, an interior landscape.

My memories were relumed there, and past experiences were united by chance; the academic poses, the manners of literature, imagination, and crossblood identities were trickster signatures; comic, to be sure, and much closer to communities than institutional tragedies. The acacia and magnolias were in bloom, the jays pounded the ancient redwoods, the polka dot man carried a hose to the campus, the urban tribes romanced their reservations, and the bears were at the treelines in winter.

> Winter rain
> Magnolias lose their past,
> Faces overnight.

> March moon
> Shimmers down the sidewalk,
> Snail crossing.

> Bold nasturtiums
> Dress the barbed wire fences,
> Down to the wild sea.

Two Russian scholars came to Berkeley on a literature

tour and we celebrated the birthday of Jack London at the First and Last Chance Saloon, a decadent log cabin, at Jack London Square in Oakland.

Dimitri Urnov, a champion of American literature and several authors, and Alexander Vaschenko, the master of Native American Indian literatures in the Soviet Union, were both associated with the Gorky Institute of World Literature in Moscow. They were moved by the list of the log cabin said to have been a favored saloon of Jack London's.

The First and Last Chance Saloon was crowded that night with eight people on high stools at the bar; we settled at the last table in the back. The bartender heard an accent and called out, "Where you boys from?"

"Russia," shouted Urnov. His bass voice stopped conversations. The patrons at the bar turned and stared in silence. The Soviet military had invaded Afghanistan a few weeks earlier, and the silence at the bar was a strategic resistance. I had not spoken, and shared the silence, the power of their gaze. Then, the patrons turned to smiles, shrugged their shoulders, and the potential for a personal war had ended at the bar. Russia is literature, and totalitarian power is the Soviet Union. Urnov knew his literature that night at the First and Last Chance Saloon.

The Soviet troops in Afghanistan resembled the invasion eleven years earlier of Czechoslovakia. "The Americans were outraged by the invasion of Afghanistan," wrote Robert Daniels in *Russia: The Roots of Confrontation*, "and frustrated at their inability to counter Soviet gains in the third world."

Soon there were three stools open and we moved to the bar. Urnov said he wanted to drink what Jack London drank on his birthday. The high praise and romance of literature were lost on the bartender; he looked around to be sure no one of importance to his reputation was near to hear, and said, "Martinis, that's what Jack London drank, dry martinis." He waited for our order and pretended to be in touch with the spirit of Jack London.

Urnov and Vaschenko consumed five martinis to my one, and that concerned them. I mentioned the problem of alcohol and driving, to ease their social consideration, but they were not convinced and urged me to drink more, and more. I turned to the politics of alcohol to balance my slow martini manners, and warned that the local police were more severe than the secret police in the Soviet Union.

"Mister Vizenor, you make a joke," said Vaschenko.

"The police lose no love on literature."

"So, neither do the secret police," said Urnov.

"The police would not care that we drank martinis to celebrate the birthday of Jack London." The political contradictions of our salute were trickster signatures; Jack London was a bourgeois socialist and his translated novels were popular in the same country that censured Boris Pasternak and expelled Alexander Solzhenitsyn from the Writers' Union and the Soviet Union.

I should have mentioned *John Barleycorn* by Jack London: "A newsboy on the streets, a sailor, a miner, a wanderer in far lands, always where men come together to exchange ideas, to laugh and boast and dare, to relax, to forget the dull toil of tiresome nights and days, always they come together over alcohol. The saloon was the place of congregation. Men gather to it as primitive men gathered about the fire of the squatting-place or the fire at the mouth of the cave."

Later, we attended a reception to honor the memories of the socialist author in a conference center at Jack London Square. Urnov wondered what novels would be considered that night. "What novels do you think are the most important?" he asked a Catholic priest.

"What novels are those," responded the priest. He wore a clerical collar, bore plastic beads, and he might have been toned with chemicals. The priest smiled and bounced his head in universal agreement.

"Jack London," said Urnov.

"I really don't know, to tell the truth, sir."

"How often do you do this?" I asked the priest.

Gerald Vizenor with Robert Redford and Charlie Hill, Sundance Film Institute, 1983

Gerald Vizenor with Sydney Pollack and Richard Weise, Sundance Film Institute, 1983

TOP *Gerald Vizenor with Waldo Salt, Sundance Film Institute, 1983*
BOTTOM *Gerald Vizenor with Rick Weise, director of* Harold of Orange, *Sundance Film Institute, 1983*

TOP Luci Tapahonso, Andrew Holleran, Gerald Vizenor, John Williams, University of Erlangen, Germany, 1992

BOTTOM Gerald Vizenor with his wife Laura Hall, Dodoma, Tanzania, 1985

Ugamaa Village, Tanzania, Africa, 1986

Gerald Vizenor, Pueblo Bonito, Chaco Canyon, New Mexico, 1986

Gerald Vizenor, San Gregorio Beach, California, 1997

Gerald Vizenor, Wong Tai Sin Temple, Hong Kong, 1993

Gerald Vizenor with Karl Kroeber, "Who Owns the Body?" conference, Berkeley, 2000.

Gerald Vizenor with his wife Laura Hall, Berkeley, Campus, 1995

Gerald Vizenor with his wife Laura Hall, Berkeley, 1999

Gerald Vizenor with A. Robert Lee, editor of Loosening the Seams: Interpretations of Gerald Vizenor, *Berkeley, 1998*

Gerald Vizenor, Provost, Kresge College, University of California, Santa Cruz, 1988

"You mean dinner?"

"Jack London."

"Once a year, on his birthday," said the priest.

"How old is London?"

"God knows, must be a century, I should think." The priest tilted his head and waited once more for a response. He must have practiced the slant of his head in the mirror, and in that manner to hear confessions. These annual social adventures were not in the name of literature, but the mean praise of an author; cults and bourgeois associations were real, not fictions, or the remembrance of literature.

"Would we be rude to leave?" asked Urnov. He was moved by the men of literature, their memories, the earth, and natural landscapes; he was bored by narrow manners, burdened by the mere recitation of names, and that from the mouth of a priest in plastic.

"The priests on reservations were much better drinkers, and had much better stories," I told the Russians on the way to the car. "John Clement, my great uncle, told me about the priest who drank himself to the grave on the reservation, and that was true, when the priest was out cold my uncle and his friends lowered the old rigid priest into a new grave." The Russians laughed and laughed; they thought that was the end of the story. "Then they waited around the grave, and early in the morning the priest stuck his bald head out of the hole and said, 'Jesus, this is resurrection morn and I'm the first to rise.' " The Russians laughed a second time, but their sense of an ending, and the humor of the story, came before the resurrection.

I told them two more stories about Father Sinner, a real priest who surmounted his name, and Father Mother, a reservation-born mixedblood priest who became his name, a source of hologender nurturance. The Russians were amused, but not much with priests and gender humor.

The Claremont Resort Hotel was once a pathetic tour de force in plastic lamination with a spectacular view of San

Francisco Bay. We were seated near a clean window in the lounge; the rush of lights shimmered on the Bay Bridge.

"Are you from Germany?" asked the waitress.

"No, thank you," said Vaschenko.

"These gentlemen are from the Soviet Union." The Russians were not pleased; twice they had been mistaken for Germans. Earlier at the Christian Brothers winery a woman pried into our conversation at the tasting bar and insisted that we were Germans. Urnov protested, she insisted, and he turned his back.

"Sorry," said the waitress. "My folks are from Czechoslovakia and they don't have much good to say about the Russians." She wanted to hold her ground in the lounge to protect her parents and country.

"The Soviet Union, not the Russians."

"Yes, the Russians," she said.

"The Russians are here in literature, not uniforms." Urnov turned in his chair. Vaschenko was more polite; he smiled at the waitress, thin but courteous.

"Something more to worry about," she said. "What's your order."

"Sherry, you're very kind," said Vaschenko.

"Sinclair Lewis was from Sauk Centre, Minnesota, and he wrote about the narrow notions of human encounters on the main streets of small towns." My mention of *Main Street* was an introduction to a story about New Prague, Minnesota, a small town with a wider political vision of the world. I told the Russians about my front page story in the *Minneapolis Tribune* on the Czechoslovakians in New Prague, and their responses to the Soviet invasion of old Prague.

New Prague, August 24, 1968: Mrs. George Layne thinks Alexander Dubcek, first secretary of the Communist Party in Czechoslovakia, has been killed by the Russians. "That's the way they do things," she said. "He gave the Czechoslovakian people their rights and let mothers stay home with their children."

Layne was born in New Prague seventy years ago. Her parents were born in Tabor, Czechoslovakia. Last month she returned from her first visit to the home of her parents. "Being under the Russians, most of the people said they had nothing to show for it. They have no cars or telephones and the people have to live in apartments not of their choice," she said. Layne, a registered pharmacist, was traveling with a group from New Prague. They are second and third generation Czechs, and many still speak Bohemian.

Mayor Alfred Slavik, whose grandfather was born in Czechoslovakia, said: "Some of our people have a natural soft spot in their hearts for the Czech people, but we have been Americanized.

"We might have been more aroused about the invasion if we had just come off the boat, but things have changed and America is our nation today. We believe that we are all born with certain rights. You don't have to be Czech to believe in freedom."

Ralph Slavik, owner of the town Dairy Queen store, shared the same feelings as his brother the mayor, but he added that the United States should become directly involved.

"All the small countries around Czechoslovakia want independence, but look what happens when one country speaks up," said Ralph Slavik. "We should push all the Communists back into Russia and put a fence around them and let other people live the way they want to."

Mayor Slavik believes that the United States should not be involved directly. He said the occupation of Czechoslovakia is a world problem which should be resolved in the United Nations. "Our involvement would only indicate that we should free all other suppressed nations in the world," he said. "We cannot possibly assume that total responsibility."

Urnov listened to my stories and then he turned the discussion back to the literature of Jack London. "He loved the land, the adventures in nature," said Urnov.

"London said the city was a 'man eater' and pretended for a time to be a socialist, but he was a writer with enormous wealth, and Wolf House was no mean measure of individualism." I pretended to argue. "He spoke out against the exploitation of workers in factories, on the waterfront, in the cities, but he would have invited the bourgeois world to dinner in his new ostentatious house at Beauty Ranch." Wolf House burned down the night before they were to move in.

"But I measure manhood less by political aggregations than by individuals," wrote Jack London in *The People of the Abyss*. "Society grows, while political machines rack to pieces and become 'scrap.' " The Russians lived their politics with the weather, sausages, and vodka lines; all the more reason to celebrate individual adventures in literature.

The Russians asked me to drive by the Soviet Embassy on Green Street in San Francisco; we were on our way to the Jack London State Historic Park in Glen Ellen, California. They argued about who would take their mail into the building; they did not want to hear about the invasion in Afghanistan. "How many people do you think are following us around," I said and watched the cars turn in the rearview mirror. I imagined that several agents were trying to figure out the motivation of a mixedblood writer and teacher driving two Gorky Institute scholars to Jack London Park in a blue Chevrolet Nova registered in Minnesota.

Leonid Brezhnev, General Secretary of the Communist Party in the Soviet Union, assumed the natural right to intervene in other states when socialism was threatened; he ordered the invasion of Czechoslovakia and Afghanistan. Relations between the United States and the Soviet Union had deteriorated; political paranoia ran high, and the unnatural power of the secret police caused people to fear even their relatives. I was certain we were watched, probably by agents from both countries. The drive to Jack London Park was a natural test of their surveillance. Traffic was slowed on the highway by a winter storm; we were drenched in waves of hard cold rain as we marched in the madrones and redwood trees, paused at the author's grave, and toured the ruins of Wolf House. Beauty Ranch was ours to imagine that afternoon.

Urnov was touched and romantic about Jack London; he wanted to be at the literal chair of creation, the places where the author wrote his novels. Jack and Charmian lived in a small ranch house, and it was there in the cold winter rain that three crows landed on posts close to the house. Vaschenko saw the crows as a tribal signature.

The House of Happy Walls, built by Charmian after the death of Jack London, was open, but the original ranch house was closed to tourists. The Russians were determined, and we circled the fence to the house; there, at last, the room the author used as a library, the room where he created some of his characters and adventures. Urnov wanted to be alone; he leaned on the window screen in silence. He meditated under a small umbrella that covered no more than his head; he stared inside at a desk and chair. The rain had soaked his suit coat, the wool had shrunk, and the arms were shortened. London and Urnov loved horses, great houses, the individual on romantic landscapes.

Vaschenko waited under a tree close to the house; and close to him three crows swooped down and landed on posts. The crows danced on the posts, in the rain, in silence, black on the rise in the pasture mist.

"The crows, they watch us," said Vaschenko.

"They watch the man at the window."

"Three friends, three crows, are we tricksters?"

"The crows must wonder."

"Wonder what?" asked Vaschenko.

"Who are these mad humans in the cold rain?"

"Jack London, he sent the crows."

"Urnov, three clown crows have come for you."

"Thank you for bringing me here," said Urnov. His voice bounced when he turned from the house; the crows bounced on the posts. "I can write an introduction to his novels with a sense of the real place, the room, the house, the earth, and now these crows."

June 1986: Santa Fe Skinwalkers

━━━━━━━━━━━━━━━━━━━Clyde Kluckhohn owned a
house on Camino Rancheros in Santa Fe, New Mexico, that
was haunted once by skinwalkers. There were skinwalkers in
my dreams there, enormous beasts from the world of the
dead that roamed on the old Armenta Spanish Land Grant.

That land grant was subdivided and became the properties of Amelia and Martha White, the eccentric sisters who
buried their animals under the fruit trees and touched human
bones at their wild parties; later, their land became private
residences, and the School of American Research.

Kluckhohn courted lost harmonies, and told stories
about witchcraft, tortured souls, and death; he turned over
stories, and posed in the rituals of lost souls to enhance his
career as an anthropologist. The skinwalkers are the lonesome, tortured, and abused dead; skinwalkers trace the earth
as humans and animals. There were stories about skinwalkers over the altars at parties, near the graves of animals at the
School of American Research.

Stan Steiner, the author of *The New Indians* and other
books about tribal cultures, invited me to stay overnight in
that house on Camino Rancheros; he owned it then, a splen-
did modern adobe structure with black ceramic tiles, rough
vigas, a secluded library, and ramada. The guest room was
near the entrance on the east side. The room was small and
held no more than a single bed and a night table; the wide
windows opened on the portico and the Sangre de Cristo
Mountains.

The harmonies in that house had been beaten by anthropologists, and wasted by those who possessed stories about
witches and the dead at their parties. The guest room was

cold; coyotes shouted in the mountains, and there were other animals in the distance. Then, about two in the morning, an enormous humanoid creature, coarse and black, with narrow shoulders, came through the door to smother me in my dream. My fright became a roar, and my rituals of protection from the dead were roars; my resound warned the world that night. I was awakened by my own thunder; the skinwalkers were gone, but the sense of death pared the light at the corners; my breath was too warm, and sudden in the shadows. I opened the windows, and listened to the mountains, and waited there until morning.

Steiner ground the coffee and told me stories about wild dreams and the fear of death. I was healed, in a sense, and there were no reasons to warn him about my dream. He must have heard my primal roar and eased my concern with his stories. Later, he said it was better not to reveal the skinwalker stories to his family. I would have left that day, never to stay overnight again in that house, but his stories restored my balance. Then, the skinwalkers returned on the second night, in that same room, in the same dream, and my roar raised me from the bed to the window. I was awakened in my roar at the metal screens.

Skinwalkers were in that house and death had touched me in that room, death came into my dreams there on Camino Rancheros. I dressed, packed my shoulder bag, and waited outside with the mongrels until first light. Steiner drove me that morning to the airport in Albuquerque.

I had stayed overnight, a year earlier, in the library with my son Robert. We camped on the floor in sleeping bags; at our side, a reservation mongrel named Jim. The library had a separate entrance from the house, and seemed to be protected with a rich dust from the mountains. The dried leaves on the ramada thrashed on the wind that summer night. There were no skinwalkers, no sense of death in the library.

The skinwalkers held my dreams in the guest room; death was in that room, bones had been there, animal stories, something touched by death had been stored in that room, or someone was tortured by witches, or died in that room. The skinwalkers hounded their remains at that house, over the whorls and medicine bundles at the museums, and down the wash of that land grant to the School of American Research.

I returned to the woodland and rented a studio apartment in Saint Paul. My plans were to complete research on a novel in a few weeks and then move back to northern Minnesota. I seemed to be bewildered in that apartment, burdened with decisions and distracted by sounds. Then, on my first night there, the same humanoid beast awakened me at the windows. My roar was so wild that several people had gathered in the alley in search of a victim, an accident, or a crime. I watched from the window on the first floor as strangers searched for me; but the skinwalker had vanished.

The next morning I asked the caretaker of the building to repeat the history of the apartment. A man had died in the room two weeks earlier; she said nothing because she did not want me to be worried. She had heard a roar that night. I told her it was me, that traces of death were in my dreams, and on my path; she refunded my money on the apartment.

I contacted a real estate agent in Pequot Lakes, Minnesota, to show me cabins for sale on the lakes in the area. There were several listed: the first was a narrow house with a suspicious smell. The agent said a woman had died in her sleep earlier in the summer. Then, the third cabin she showed me was touched with a death light. I might have died over the threshold in the light of that cabin. The real estate agent was not troubled by death, but she held me to the presence of death, and told me that a widower had gone crazy that winter in the cabin, and died sitting in a chair at the bay window. She said, "He was in that window for two weeks, or more."

I pleaded, "No more cabins of the lonesome dead." She laughed and showed me several houses in town, and condominiums in resort areas; they were too expensive. I settled for a ranch house, with an attached garage, near the highway in Jenkins, Minnesota. The house had been used as an antique store for several years. The owners had moved to a lake cabin;

the house was not haunted by skinwalkers or the lonesome souls of the dead. I planted a garden, vegetables, and flowers; ran on rural roads at dusk, lived alone, and started to write my novel, *Darkness in Saint Louis Bearheart*.

I passed a wild pink house on my runs at dusk; a man sat in a metal molded chair and waved to me on the way out and back. This went on for several weeks and then he waved me over to his house. He was alone; when his wife died he sold the farm and moved to town. Jenkins had a population of a few hundred, a few because the town included many homes that were buried in the woods. The pink paint he bought at a sale in Brainerd, or was it Bemidji?

"Would you like to see my house?"

"Yes, of course." He marched me through from the front to the back door, pointed out the new refrigerator and freezer, and mentioned "cribs" behind two closed doors near the back. He seemed to sneer and mock the words he thought were used in the city.

We turned left at the back of the house and entered the garage through a side door. Machines were mounted on the benches; generators, carburetors, pistons, bearings, hundreds of automobile parts made mechanical mountains. The hard earth was soaked with motor oil, and the garage smelled of grease and wheel dust.

The man carried his sneer to the garage; he would march, then halt and stare out the windows. He was thin, clean, and sudden, but not an animal, and wore blue work clothes. I was not at peace with his manners; he could be a madman, worried that a stranger was near his machines.

"Would you like to see the back room?" He moved to a door at the end of the garage and turned the handle. I remember the length of the garage, but had no idea there was a room at the end. The simple pleasures of that town had ended at the moment.

"You, first." I watched his hands and held my escape distance. His manners were sinister, indeed, but he had no weapons and there was color in his face. He avoided my eyes and pushed open the door. The secret room had been carpeted in red; then, the reason he had invited me to the house. Standing in the middle of the room, with one arm raised, a simulated blonde, a manikin with no clothes.

I turned, backed out of the room, and marched out of the garage to the driveway. I thanked him for the tour, but never mentioned his nude manikin, for fear that he would be jealous, and seek revenge; a cuckolded manikin dresser.

I continued to run past his pink house at dusk; we would praise the weather, nothing more on the move. Several times on weekends there were dozens of cars and pickup trucks parked in his yard, but not one person in sight. I was certain the visitors were crowded around the blonde, rural men, perverse widowers with a room of their own.

His world was not mine, and that rhetorical distance held until early one morning he was standing in the kitchen of my house. I told him to leave, and he sneered; that afternoon the dead bolts were installed on both doors. Who was this man with the simulated blonde? He would never be a skinwalker, but could he be a trickster signature?

Kent and Joan Tupper, close friends from Walker, Minnesota, drove down for dinner. I told them the stories about the man and his blonde manikin, his sneer and presence, the hot pink house, the many cars in the yard, and my concerns that he wanted something from me.

"Will you ever get away from blondes?" asked Joan.

"Get a dummy, he wants to double date," said Kent.

"That's great, we could go to a drive-in together."

"Cheap dates," said Joan.

"Indian politics could be worse," said Kent.

"Very funny, but this is serious." They would not tolerate my concern over the matter of a blonde manikin. Joan said my stories were funny, but that was the end of her consideration. "You don't expect me to believe there is a real man with a blonde dummy, do you?" She said that and the man drove into the yard. "Here he is, the man in his own story." The man called to me to come to his pickup; he had a chair for me, he said, and lowered a broken kitchen chair to view. I laughed and refused the chair. He sneered, as usual, and then told me to wait on the porch with Kent and Joan. I was worried when he leaned into the pickup truck.

"Why wait?"

"I got a present for you."

"No, forget it."

"Wait, this is for you," he said and handed me a shoe box. His smile held a distance, but not an innocence; there were no familiar trees or animals in his sudden gestures.

"Well, open your present," said Joan.

"You open it."

"Not on your life," she said.

"You open it then," I said to the man.

"For your parties," the man said and opened the box. Inside, a hideous plastic animal mask wrapped in white tissue paper. His smile became a sneer, and then he turned to leave. I closed the shoe box and threw it into the back of the pickup truck.

Kent was a lawyer and handled the purchase of the house; later that month he discovered in the title a protective covenant on the property that would restrict the use of the house to the sale of antiques. The skinwalkers returned to the southwest, but there were other reasons to leave the town of Jenkins. The purchase agreement was canceled because of the covenant on the house. I moved back to Saint Paul and rented a room in a mansion at 366 Summit Avenue. The mansion had been the home of Rachel Hill Boeckmann, daughter of James Jerome Hill, and her husband. John Rupp had purchased the mansion from the Catholic Church. My suite of rooms had once been occupied by a retired archbishop; my dreams were wild and carnal there. *Darkness in Saint Louis Bearheart* was completed in that mansion.

Ten years later the School of American Research awarded me a resident scholar grant to write in Sante Fe. The grant provided a stipend and a furnished house for a year at the school. I wrote *The Trickster of Liberty* there, and three essays:

"Minnesota Chippewa: Woodland Treaties and Tribal Bingo" and "Bone Courts: The Rights and Narrative Representation of Tribal Bones," were published in the *American Indian Quarterly*. The third essay, "Trickster Discourse: Comic Holotropes and Language Games," was included in the book I edited for the University of New Mexico Press, *Narrative Chance: Postmodern Discourse on Native American Indian Literatures*.

Douglas Schwartz, the president of the school, measured his manners with banal nouns, and denatured occurrences in common conversations; for instance, he would pause outside with a practiced beam, comment on the weather, and then end each conversation with a coup d'oeil, "I never tire of the mountains." His putative reputation as a scholar was too mean to honor, and his favors were too conspicuous. His consociates either towed his crown or died at the mock adobe gate. The other resident scholars were concerned about their careers, recommendations from the crown; even our humor was tested when the crown held a wedding at the school and a thousand white flowers bloomed. I was the only writer, an outsider at the school; the other resident scholars were anthropologists and archaeologists.

President Schwartz was told that there was a racist covenant on the land owned by the School of American Research, but he would not remove the covenant. I discussed the racist contradictions with him twice in his office; he turned a practiced beam and never tired of the mountains. The school, I pointed out, stated a commitment in a brochure, "to a greater understanding of the diverse peoples of the world." The racist covenant filed on October 9, 1934, provides that "no conveyance shall be made or granted of said premises, or any part thereof, to any person or persons of African or Oriental descent."

The covenant, signed by Amelia White and Martha White, applied to properties located in a subdivision. The White sisters had formed the DeVargas Development Company to purchase part of the old Armenta Spanish Land

Grant; later, the sisters contributed numerous lots in their subdivision to the School of American Research.

The *New York Times* reported that Amelia was the daughter of Horace White, editor of the *Chicago Tribune* and later the *New York Evening Post*. "She was a graduate of Bryn Mawr College and served in World War I as a nursing assistant with the Belgian forces in France, for which she received a commendation. . . . She was also a prominent breeder of Afghan hounds and Irish wolfhounds. In World War II she headed the New Mexico 'Dogs for Defense,' collaborating with the Army's war dog program." The dogs are buried with markers at the School of American Research.

The skinwalkers haunt the graves of the animals and the stories that surround Navajo medicine bundles, masks, fetishes, sacred vestments, and ceremonial material held in museums. The school has been concerned, for public relations reasons, about repatriation of sacred material, and the use of the American Indian Religious Freedom Act. Schwartz was told in a letter that "we should sit down and talk about how we would handle a request from an individual group. Not every Pueblo is interested in religious material, and none would show up *demanding* anything. From what I know of the whole question of repatriating Native American objects, the confrontations only come if institutions are secretive, uncooperative, patronizing, or make unilateral decisions to act or not to act. . . . It is essential that the entire process be carried out discreetly and in a low-key manner which would not draw publicity." Those too close to stolen masks, sacred bundles, and tribal bones would hear skinwalkers in their dreams.

The School of American Research heard my proposal to establish a bone court, where the rights of bones would be represented. The response from other resident scholars, archaeologists, and anthropologists was tolerant; the idea invited some humor as critical abatement, but there was never a mature discourse.

Ishi, the last survivor of his tribe, died in 1916 in a museum at the University of California. Alfred Kroeber was in

New York at the time and wrote to the curator of the museum, "If there is any talk about the interests of science, say for me that science can go to hell. . . . We have hundreds of Indian skeletons that nobody ever comes to study. The prime interest in this case would be of a morbid romantic nature."

Kroeber protected the remains of his tribal friend, and, in his letter to the curator, anticipated by two generations the debate over the disinterment of aboriginal bones and the reburial of tribal remains. Three hundred thousand tribal bones have been taken from their graves to museums and laboratories, asserted a tribal advocate: "If this would happen in any other segment of society there would be outrage. . . . Whether they were buried last year or thousands of years ago, they have the right to the sanctity of the grave."

This is a discourse on the prima facie rights of human remains, sovereign tribal bones, to be their own narrators, and a proposal to establish a bone court. This new forum would have federal judicial power to hear and decide disputes over burial sites, research on bones, reburial, and to protect the rights of tribal bones to be represented in court.

The rights of bones are neither absolute nor abolished at death; bone rights are abstract, secular, and understood in narrative and constitutional legal theories. The rights of bones to be represented in federal court are substantive; these rights are based on the premise that human rights continue after death.

Most human remains were buried with ceremonial heed, an implied communal continuation of human rights; death, cremation, subaerial exposure, earth burial, and other interments are proper courses, not the termination of human rights. The rights we hold over our bodies and organs at death are the same rights we must hold over our bones and ashes. Brain death, or heart death, is not a constitutional divestment; death is not the absolute termination of human rights. In the bone court the last rites are never the last words.

The Santa Fe editor of the *Albuquerque Journal* was sincere, but he would not investigate the racist covenant or land transactions of the School of American Research. However, he did publish on August 2, 1986, portions of my letter to Douglas Schwartz, but not with information from public land records. At last, my concern about racist covenants was raised in a *New York Times* story about Justice William Rehnquist. My letter pointed out the contradictions, not the enforcement, of a racist covenant on land the school owns. Schwartz listens to his lawyers and never tires of the mountains.

I wrote: "The mission of your institution, and because it is supported by public grants, private contributions, and an endowment, should not bear racist covenants. The removal of the covenant would be an operative measure of your racial and cultural sensitivities."

The *Albuquerque Journal* reported that a lawyer for the school said "the challenge was trivial and they would have no . formal response." The president of the school said there was no reason to get rid of the covenant or its racial language. "My time could be spent more effectively promoting the goals of the school. I've got a lot of distinguished lawyers and judges on my board, and I'm sure they would feel that way as well."

Lawyer Booker Kelly said: "When you buy land, it's like buying original sin. Doug Schwartz did purchase a couple of the lots but these restrictions on race would never be recognized if anyone tried to enforce them. They aren't enforceable, have never been enforced and no one expects them ever to be enforced. They are null and void. This reminds me of the controversy awhile back over the word 'Savages' on the obelisk on the Plaza" in Santa Fe.

The president and his lawyer avoided the purpose of my letter, that the covenant was insensitive, bad mannered, and racist, and the covenant included the land that had become the School of American Research.

I wrote to Douglas Schwartz on June 30, 1986: The public land records reveal that you received five acres from the school; the Warranty Deed dated March 26, 1984, was signed by Frank Bond, past chairman of the Board of Managers of the School of American Research.

The minutes of the executive committee meeting held September 19, 1967, indicate that the School of American Research had title to forty acres in Arroyo Hondo, "seventy acres off Bishop's Lodge Road," and several other lots in Santa Fe County. Fourteen years ago, under one trust agreement, the White sisters granted the school eight lots on Garcia Street. You, as president, received two of these lots; five others have been sold. I was also interested to learn from the land records that Hom-Co, a New Mexico corporation, according to the Warranty Deed dated July 16, 1973, received more than sixty-eight acres from the School of American Research.

Moreover, the widow Estelle Twitchell granted the school her property on Grant Avenue in Sante Fe. The Warranty Deed dated November 1, 1972, records that Fedco, a partnership, received this property from the school. The partnership consisted of A. K. Montgomery, William R. Federici, Frank Andrews, Fred C. Hannahs, Richard S. Morris, Sumner G. Buell, Seth D. Montgomery, and Frank Andrews III.

"Do you know who these people are?" asked an assistant in the office of the New Mexico Attorney General. I wanted information about land transactions in the state, the ethics of land given to public institutions and then sold or transferred to private owners.

"No, are they in the Kiva Club?"

"These names are prominent citizens, lawyers, and judges, some of the most powerful people in the state," said the assistant. He was cautious, to say the least, but raised a question about corporations not listed in the state that were involved in land transactions.

Residences on Camino Rancheros and the School of American Research were part of the old Armenta Spanish Land Grant. The subdivision of that land excluded "persons of African or Oriental descent." The houses, land stories, and museums with stolen bones, and lost harmonies, are haunted by skinwalkers.

Clyde Kluckhohn introduced witchcraft and other malevolent activities in his celebrated book *Navaho Witchcraft*. Later, Kluckhohn and Dorothea Leighton wrote in *The Navaho* that witchcraft satisfies hate and social balance at the same time, but then their humanistic notions turn to racialism. "Among other things, witchcraft is the Navahos' substitute for the race prejudice of white society in the United States. The People blame their troubles upon 'witches' instead of upon 'Jews' or 'niggers.' In place of selecting its scapegoats by skin color or by religious tradition, Navaho culture selects certain individuals who are supposed to work evil by secret supernatural techniques."

September 1989: Honor Your Partner

━━━━━━━━━━Gerald Vizenor implies that autobiographies are imaginative histories; a remembrance past the
barriers, and wild pastimes over the pronouns, he said in
"Crows Written on the Poplars: Autocritical Autobiographies," an essay published in *I Tell You Now*, edited by Brian
Swann and Arnold Krupat.

Past the barriers his remembrance is neither sentimental
nor ideological; he is a crossblood descendant of the crane
and loosens the seams in the coarse shrouds of imposed identities. Institutional time, he contends, belies our personal
memories, imagination, and consciousness. The last railroad
schedules, movies, oceans, crows in the poplars and lonesome music, touch our histories in the snow and thunder of
language games. The evil gamblers would take our lives
should we lose the stories.

"Each autobiographical utterance embalms the author in
his own prose, marking his passage into a form that both sur-
renders him to death and yet preserves his name, acts, and
words," wrote Avrom Fleishman in *Figures of Autobiography*.

Language is a listener, imagination a mythic listener, a
presence, being in a sound, and a word; noise, ownership,
and delusions remain, as we are reduced in remembrance to
scenes on color television in the back seat of a white limou-
sine.

"Myth makes truth, in historical as well as in literary autobiography," wrote Fleishman, and the patterns of "exile and
return, of alienation and repossession" are connections with
the past, the voices of the crane in the tribal past. Myth makes
love, noise, war, blue chicken, and crossbloods too. The
crossblood, or mixedblood, is a new metaphor, a transi-

tive contradancer between communal tribal cultures and those material and urban pretensions that counter conservative traditions. The crossblood wavers in myths and autobiographies; we move between reservations and cities, the stories of the crane with a trickster signature.

"When we settle into the theater of autobiography," wrote Paul John Eakin in *Fictions in Autobiography*, "what we are ready to believe . . . is that the play we witness is a historical one, a largely faithful and unmediated reconstruction of events that took place long ago, whereas in reality the play is that of the autobiographical act itself, in which the materials of the past are shaped by memory and imagination to serve the needs of present consciousness." Once more we meet at the seams, my mixedblood pronouns and imagination, in an autumn thunderstorm.

"A good hunter is never competitive," I wrote in an autobiographical story published in *Growing Up in Minnesota: Ten Writers Remember Their Childhoods*. "The instincts of a survival hunter are measured best when he is alone in the woods."

Survival is imagination, a verbal noun, a wild transitive word in my mixedblood autobiographies; genealogies, the measured lines in our time, and place, are never the same in personal memories. Remembrance is a natural current that beats and breaks with the spring tides; the curious imagine a sensual undine on the wash, as the nasturtiums dress the barbed wire fences down to the wild sea.

My memories and interior landscapes are untamed. The back stoop of that tavern where I fed the squirrels while my grandfather drank in the dark, breaks into the exotic travels of Lafcadio Hearn. Tribal women in sueded shoes, and blonded hair, mince in my memories over the thresholds into the translated novels of Kawabata Yasunari, and Dazai Osamu.

Alice Beaulieu, in her sixties, married a blind man because he told her she looked beautiful; and now, in the white birch, with crows, bears, and a moist wind, their adventures in the suburbs to peddle brooms and brushes overturn the wisdom of modern families and their histories. The blind man and his old tribal stunner soothed lonesome women in those pastel suburban houses, the new tribal healers in the cities, and no one bought a broom from the blind man.

I had ordered a laminated miniature of my honorable discharge, bought a used car, a new suit, three shirts, a winter coat, and drove east to visit friends. I was an army veteran with two volumes of photographs to illustrate my stories that I had driven a tank, directed theater productions, survived a typhoon, and walked with the bears in the Imperial National Forest on Hokkaido. I was pensive and nineteen. Two months later I was a college student, by chance, and inspired by the novel *Look Homeward, Angel*. My dreams to be a writer, and much later the grammars, blossomed when my stories were praised by Eda Lou Walton, my first teacher of writing at New York University.

Matsuo Basho came to mind on the mound with the squirrels that late afternoon. In the distance he heard laughter, and smelled cigarette smoke; a hunter in a duck blind in a march behind the mound. Silent crows were on the trees, their eyes pinched the wind, and I squeezed the side of my nose, gathered the oil with my thumb nail and rubbed it into the dark grain of the rifle stock. I remembered laughter on a porch, through an open window, at the river, and snickers deep in the weeds behind the cabins at Silver Lake, a Salvation Army camp for welfare mothers. I taught their children how to paddle a canoe that summer, how to cook on an open fire without foil, and how to name seven birds in flight.

"I walked into the woods alone and found a place in the sun against a tree. The animals and birds were waiting in silence for me to pass. . . . When I opened my eyes, after a short rest, the birds were singing and the squirrels were eating without fear and jumping from tree to tree. I was jumping with them but against them as the hunter," I wrote in *Growing Up in Minnesota*.

I pretend in the last sentence to be an arboreal animal, a romantic weakness. I was neither hunter nor a tribal witness to the survival hunt. I was there as a crossblood writer and hunter in a transitive confessional, in my imaginative auto- biographies. I have never lived from the hunt, but I have been hunted, and cornered in wild dreams. I have shot squirrels and feasted on their bitter thighs, but I have never had to track an animal to the end, as I would to the last pronouns in my stories, to feed my families and friends.

I understand the instincts of the survival hunter, enough to mimic their movements; my compassion for animals arises from imagination and literature. My endurance has never been measured in heart muscles, livers, hides, horns, shared on the trail. My survival is mythic, an imaginative transition, an intellectual predation, deconstructed as masks and meta- phors at the water holes in autobiographies.

"Language is the main instrument of man's refusal to ac- cept the world as it is," wrote George Steiner in *After Babel: Aspects of Language and Translation.* "Ours is the ability, the need, to gainsay or 'un-say' the world, to image and speak it otherwise. . . . To misinform, to utter less than the truth was to gain a vital edge of space or subsistence. Natural selection would favor the contriver. Folk tales and mythology retain a blurred memory of the evolutionary advantage of mask and misdirection."

Survival hunters commiserate with animals, that much we have in common. I leapt over a fence to stop a man who raised his rifle to shoot two squirrels in the city. Elsewhere, an automobile had crushed the lower spine and pelvis of a red squirrel. I watched the animal scratch the cold asphalt with her front paws; she hauled her limp body to the wet maple leaves at the curb. Closer, I cried and the squirrel shiv- ered; then I warmed her with my hands, eased her into death, down to the mother sea.

I was having lunch with a psychic reader at the Swallow Restaurant in Berkeley a few years ago; we were sitting inside near the window. A finch hit the clear glass and dropped in shock to the cold concrete. I held the bird in my hands to keep him warm, his head on my thumb; then, a nictitating membrane moved, and as his muscles came alive, my hand opened. I moved closer to a shrub, the finch wobbled on my hand; he turned to me, once, twice, and then he flew into the leaves. My sensations were prominent, and then when I turned to continue our lunch, more than a dozen people watched me. My voice was a tremor, the audience had stolen my moment of peace with that bird, but not my stories.

John Berger wrote that the "opposite of to love is not to hate but to separate," in *And Our Faces, My Heart, Brief as Photos*. "If love and hate have something in common it is because, in both cases, their energy is that of bringing and holding together—the lover with the loved, the one who hates with the hated. Both passions are tested by separation." I learned that hunters, birds, and animals were never opposites, the opposite of both is separation. Both the hunter and the hunted are tested by their separation from the same landscapes.

Chester Anderson smoked too much when he edited the ten essays that were published in *Growing Up in Minnesota*. His borrowed books had sprouted markers, notes faded in his winter coat, and the thin manuscript of my thirteen autobiographical stories returned in a manila envelope, smelled of sweet pipe tobacco. The professor lowers one shoulder when he rides his bicycle in the wind, and he leans closer to listen at his desk; no one has been a more sensitive listener.

My first autobiographical stories were published by the University of Minnesota Press. The shadows were metaphors and vanished at seminars; personal memories shivered in the buckram and perished in public phrases; memories were measured and compared in a tournament of pronouns. The birds were healed, and now there were audiences.

A professor at Macalester College in Saint Paul, an agent provocateur in reflexive literature, said that my stories were not true. "These are not believable experiences," she announced in the chapel where several authors had gathered to read. Her haughtiness and peevish leer, broadened behind enormous spectacles, reminded me of that high school teacher who refused to honor one of my stories, she ruled, because an adolescent would not have such experiences.

Some stories choose their best time to be told, and other stories take their chances. Eight more autobiographical stories have bounced down to the end and chosen this time to be told.

Berkeley, California: James Baldwin was scheduled to read in the Bancroft Library at the University of California. I was honored to be with so many distinguished authors, scholars, and admirers; the great names in black literature and politics were there. The perfumes were rich and wild in that cool marble entrance hall; we waited and remembered characters, scenes, and ideas from his novels.

Baldwin arrived an hour late to be blessed by the audience; he told stories, the roar and praise of black literature. He was tired, but his face lightened at metaphors, his words and movements were considerate. He was wise, a gracious word dancer, and he was close to death with cancer. His smile held the entire audience.

I moved to the entrance, closer to the door; others had the same idea, to touch the author as he passed. Just behind me a woman and her child, a boy about two years old, crowded closer as the author approached the door. The boy was surrounded, buried in our legs. I moved aside, made room for the boy to see, and his mother coached him to greet the author. James Baldwin was close but the boy took me for the author; the boy was eager to please someone at the door and greeted me with his practiced speech. The boy held out his hand. His mother was nervous, but not unkind, and the boy was not sure what he had done. I crouched closer to the boy and directed his attention, through the prancing legs, to the great author. The boy was black and wore a bow tie. James Baldwin paused, leaned down, and held the boy's hand.

Mound, Minnesota: Wild Boy, a mixedblood member of the American Indian Movement, demanded the big-ticket items on his tour of the nation; for instance, he shouted, "Return the Black Hills." Wild once pursued a float in a parade to oppose an Indian Princess Contest. He reached for the back of the float just as a police officer closed in on him. The people on the street watched and laughed. Wild lost his glass eye just as the policeman raised his nightstick; the eye popped out and rolled on the asphalt to the curb. Wild found his eye at the feet of a spectator, polished it on his shirt, put it back in the socket, and chased the float to the end.

Wild hated my editorial essays about the American Indian Movement that had been published in the *Minneapolis Tribune*. We had avoided each other since the time he pursued me at an Indian education conference in Duluth, but there we were, at another education conference, ruled by chance, a trickster signature. Near the end of the conference we were alone in an enclosed courtyard.

"We could've killed you," said Boy.

"Fuck you, Boy."

"I'm just saying, you might be dead."

"You think your cup of tribal blood gives you the right to rule the world, well fuck you Boy, you got your head up your ass and you might lose it there." I was ready to end the battle right there, in a bourgeois courtyard at a conference center. My rage was seasoned, my bluster was on the rise.

"Listen, you're the best writer we got, but why do you have to write that shit about us, why don't you write the true stuff?" His hard voice and bluster had weakened.

"You'd like me even less if I told your lies, you never had it so good pretending to be a radical." I stopped and shouted at Boy, "You got nothing but a reservation head for blondes, and the greed of a white man."

"No, really, we need you," said Boy.

"Fuck you, Boy."

"Some day you'll need us to defend you."

"No thanks, but I'll keep your offer in mind." Boy had mellowed by the time we reached the end of the courtyard. I almost promised him a poem or a broadside in romantic blank verse.

Boy used narcotics. That evening at a conference seminar we saw the radical run nude in the courtyard. Later, he was seen in a women's toilet, and the next morning his clothes were found on the conference center grounds. Someone folded his clothes, and placed them at the door of his room. Boy had broken his sacred eagle feather in his wild tour that night.

Sioux Falls, South Dakota: Thomas James White Hawk was shaving in his cell on death row when South Dakota governor Frank Farrar announced the commutation of his sentence from death in the electric chair to life imprisonment. White Hawk had been in isolation at the South Dakota State Penitentiary since he had confessed, almost two years earlier, to the savage murder of James Yeado, a jeweler in Vermillion, South Dakota.

I traveled in South Dakota for more than six months to research and write about the case, and to organize a protest against capital punishment; the protest, not the court remedies, brought the commutation. Tourism was down because of the critical attention my essay brought to the state.

Three thousand copies of my essay on White Hawk, his family, education, the murder, and the responses of the community were mailed free to individuals and institutions around the world. White Hawk was a premedical student at the University of South Dakota when he murdered James Yeado. I reviewed the court hearings, attended the trial of William Stands, who was with White Hawk at the time of the crime, and asserted that White Hawk suffered from "cultural schizophrenia." My essay was published in the *Twin Citian magazine*, and later published with a collection of essays in *Tribal Scenes and Ceremonies*.

Joseph Satten, a psychiatrist from the Menninger Clinic, reported that White Hawk suffered from psychotic episodes and lapsed into "transient" dreams: "His Indian background would tend to make him place a high value on stoicism, emotional impassivity, withdrawal, aloofness, and the denial of dependence on others. In addition, the tendency of some in the dominant culture to devaluate Indians and the Indian culture would tend to accentuate his feelings of loneliness and suspicion." Satten supported my description of "cultural schizophrenia."

The South Dakota Board of Pardons and Paroles recommended in a written report to Governor Farrar that no further commutations be made in the future. Without the possibility of parole, White Hawk faces a natural death sentence in the state penitentiary. Many people in the state believe that is more than he deserves.

I visited White Hawk, with his lawyer Douglas Hall, at the state penitentiary in June 1987. I had not seen White Hawk for twenty years, and he never told me how he felt about my critical essay on the murder and his sentence. He said he would not have changed a word.

White Hawk was active in the Native American Church. Hall wanted to find some support for the discussion of parole, but even the idea was discouraged by the parole board. The warden and others in the penitentiary were impressed with White Hawk, but they do not make parole decisions. Everywhere, just beneath the surface of conversations, there were feelings of rage about the crime; the horrible murder of James Yeado and the brutal rape of his wife would not be forgiven with parole.

Thank you "for the good visits and for the support during our forthcoming fight. I can foresee quite a bit of trouble along the way because of the mental illness issue though. Let's just hope things won't be too tough," White Hawk wrote to his lawyer on May 10, 1987.

"I have done some heavy thinking and I have been unable to come up with any feasible method for altering Gerald Vizenor's journal to suit our purposes now. . . . Vizenor's work was superbly written and the only elements which I believe we could alter at all would be the placement of the transcript quotes he used. Otherwise, I would change nothing.

"I have submitted my name to attend the Sun Dance in Green Grass, South Dakota this summer. I am having second thoughts about even appearing at the board in September if the same board refuses to trust me enough to leave the prison again. But we can discuss this later, if necessary. Just keep going!"

Minneapolis, Minnesota: I held a summer seminar on Native American literatures at the University of Minnesota. Fifteen people attended class four times a week for five weeks.

In the fourth week of class an Indian student made a determined point about a particular author and was not pleased when other students seemed to disagree with his point. The Indian student was silent most of the time, but surly when he did speak. The next day in class the Indian student teased the students who had discussed his point the day before, and then drew a revolver. He placed the weapon on the seminar table and said, "Now, let's see how much you want to disagree."

Naturally, the students were silent; the gun was loaded. Then, in a few minutes, the students discussed another author with pure pleasure until the bell rang at the hour. I rushed to my office to call the police, to file a complaint and have the student removed from the university; however, I changed my mind before the police responded. I considered the headline in the student paper, "Indian Professor has Wounded Indian Veteran Arrested in Class." I assumed he was a decorated veteran because one of his legs had been amputated; he used crutches.

The Indian student arrived about ten minutes late to class, which gave me time to make an offer to the other students. We had one week of class left, and if the students agreed we could continue; when the Indian student arrived, the others agreed to leave the chair on his right open for me, his weak side. If he reached for his revolver again, I would knock him over on the floor. The class continued, the Indian student sat on my left, the class discussions were faultless, and the quarter ended four days later with great applause.

A few weeks later at breakfast, a special tribal gathering once a week to gossip and tell stories, I was about to tell my story about the wounded veteran and his seminar enforcer; however, that story did not choose to be told, it was not the right time or place for some reason. At the end of the meal an old friend told me how happy his son was with my class at the university.

"Which class?"

"Literature, this summer."

"Really?" I could not remember the name of his son.

"You know he lost his leg."

"He's your son?"

"Yes, he loved your class, said it was one of the best he ever had at the university, and you know he's had his troubles there in the past few years," he said and filled my cup with coffee.

"Haven't we all," I said and brushed his shoulder.

"He lost his leg to cancer, the report's not good, it's a terminal case, and we don't know how long he'll last, but he's looking good right now." I had come so close to making life even more miserable for a good friend.

Bismarck, North Dakota: Leo Landsberger was so conservative that he was drummed out of the John Birch Society in North Dakota; he was a candidate for governor twenty years ago on the Taxpayers' Revival ticket and lost the election. He promised less government, reduced taxes, stopping trade with Communist countries, elimination of the socialist employment services, and withdrawal from the United Nations.

Landsberger praised George Wallace, the independent presidential candidate, and said he was a "better Republican than all the others put together." He attended the rally in Minneapolis, and just before the square dance that turned into a police riot, he saw me and marched down the aisle. He was tired, or was he troubled about my story?

"I thought you'd be here," he said to me.

"Why here?"

"You got a nose for conservatives, don't you?"

"You mean the size?"

"You wrote a good story," he said and inhaled a cigarette.

"I thought you were coming down to chew me out."

"I can do that too, but you were fair, and that's more than anybody could ask for in a paper like yours," he said in a cloud of cigarette smoke. His hands were hard and stained; he had been a farmer before he became active in the John Birch Society.

Landsberger sat behind his desk in the basement of his home for three hours, chain-smoked cigarettes, and answered my questions for a feature news story in the *Minneapolis Tribune*. The walls were lined with bound volumes of investigations, and conservative literature. The four telephones on his desk never rang during the interview. He had the books, the ambition, the telephones, and a harsh dose of prairie conservatism, but he did not have constituents. I admired the temper he earned as a farmer, but he was a terminal believer in political monotheism. He said, "Wallace is not a racist, he is a segregationist, and that is constitutional."

Communists were everywhere, he said, in government agencies local and national. "When Joe McCarthy passed away there was nothing to stop a Communist takeover. We are living in one vast insane asylum. The John Birch Society is a fighting power, but what good will the members be behind barbed wire?"

"Leo, you smoke too much," I said and invited him to dinner.

"For all I know, this is Communist tobacco." He pinched another Camel cigarette out in the ashtray. He chose an old railroad hotel restaurant with linen, silver, and mirrors on the walls and pillars. He ate roast beef and mashed potatoes, and told me stories about certain people who were eating at the restaurant. I watched his many images in the mirrors. I understood the prairie in him but not the politics.

Bena, Minnesota: "Bena is a wicked town," said Pauline Wetzel, the minister of the Mission Alliance Church. "Even the Episcopals have given up." The railroad village, located on the Leech Lake Reservation, was once a trade center, salt pork and sewing machines for red pine, but the trees and population have been down for a generation. About two hundred people live in the village on the southern bay of Lake Winnibigoshish.

Twenty years ago the "wicked town" had the reputation of being the "Little Chicago" of the north woods. John Plattner, Cass County attorney then, said there is no question that Bena has the worst crime rate in the state. "Bena is the most sinful city in Minnesota," he said. "There is only one part-time deputy in a place where more than ten percent of the population has been committed for serious crimes. Bena is like no other place in the world."

John Clement Beaulieu, my granduncle, lived there in a one room house on a sand road, and he said it was true what they said about his town. Bena was wicked, and the town was like no place in the world, but he said that made it a great town for stories.

The constable, who was in his sixties then, was also the deputy sheriff for the area. He lived in a house trailer outside of the village. I drove out to see him because he had his telephone disconnected. The path to the trailer was covered with chicken bones; several mongrels faced me in the windows, but they were more eager to smell a stranger than protect the trailer that smelled of chicken skin and wet feathers. The constable said he would not arrest people anymore because he had to drive them twenty miles to the jail in Cass Lake.

"They puke in the back of my car, and I gotta smell that, and nobody pays me to clean up after drunk criminals, so that's the end of it," said the constable. "If they want somebody bad enough they know where to find him, and they can use one of their cars."

The constable was a teetotaler, but most of his time was given to dealing with people who were drunk. "Sometimes I just have to take them all out in the ball field and let 'em fight it out."

"How can people call you if there's an emergency?"

"They want me to babysit with some of these bastards,"

said the constable. He had the telephone removed several years ago. "They know where to find me if they need me."

Al and Joyce Lindquist owned the liquor store in Bena. "We tried a restaurant, but people would rather drink than eat. I sure love the people here, they've been good to us."

Bernadine Kirt lived in a red house with birch trees and flowers in the front lawn. She and her daughters helped my granduncle work out the first genealogies of the Beaulieu and Vizenor families. They loved his stories, and he loved their regular meals. I loved their house, the stories, the meals, and the generous humor of the family. I wrote about that wicked town but the town was never wicked to me. Social workers, not criminals or drunks, ruined that town; they found a place that was secular enough to save them from their methods.

Bernadine was a member of the Bena Better Blossom Garden Club, the only organized social life in Bena. Her husband worked for the mayor and drove an oil truck. "Bena is the damndest place in America," she said and laughed. "There's no social poise, no standards for anything. Bena is the great evener. We are independent individuals, we don't have to keep up to anybody."

Ellsworth, Wisconsin: The Plains Book Bus was a fantastic celebration of poets and their books; the bus, loaded with small press publications, planned poetry readings and tours to rural towns. I was honored to meet the bus in Ellsworth, a two-restaurant town.

The local bank provided space in the parking lot and electrical service to light the book shelves. My haiku books and other publications were on display at the side entrance to the camper bus. Meanwhile, a television crew met me there to film my presentation for a film, *A Nest of Singing Birds*, to be shown on public television.

The adventure began on Main Street with no preparation. I stopped a man who delivered the local paper and asked him what would happen if I read my poems out loud in the Coast to Coast store. That encounter was filmed, a spontaneous conversation in the best humor, but the footage was never used because the man was ruled retarded and the editors were concerned that the town should not be represented by a retarded man who delivered papers. I protested that he made more sense than some other people in town, and besides, he was concerned about me as a poet.

"I wouldn't do that," he said in a gentle tone of voice.

"Why not?"

"Well, not poems."

"How about the Coast to Coast store?"

"No, not there."

"Why not?"

"They might think you were queer."

"But my poems are short."

"I like your poems," he said.

"But you haven't heard them," I said.

"I like you."

"Join me for pie and coffee, and we can try my poems out in the restaurant down the street." The film crew followed us and taped our conversation.

The owners, an older couple, gave us permission to film me in their restaurant of several tables and a counter with a dozen stools. We occupied the stools that afternoon. I ordered strawberry pie and asked the owner's daughter to listen to my short poem and then respond: "Whatever comes to your mind." Sound levels were tested, lights were adjusted, and then my haiku poem was recorded over the counter.

> Fat green flies
>
> Square dance across the grapefruit,
>
> Honor your partner.

I said the poem twice and the owner's daughter listened to each word, and with each word a smile spread across her face. She turned to her parents for recognition, shrugged her shoulders, and then she said, "Well, that's not what we do with flies around here, mister." That scene was part of a public television production.

Excelsior, Minnesota: Melvin McCosh directed me to the attic of his enormous bookstore in what was once a retirement center, more than twenty rooms were crammed with books. The attic was haunted by thousands of remainders, books that had been abandoned by publishers; there on the right, in the second aisle, were several cases of *Slight Abrasions*, a dialogue in haiku between Jerome Downes and Gerald Vizenor.

Downes wrote in the first round of our dialogue: "Vizenor's book, blueflies on the yellow grain, grey mice behind the door." I replied in haiku: "Wet poppy seeds, hugging the dendrite Irish web, Downes' poems." The second round in the dialogue started with my poem: "We are leaves, down after a heavy rain, showing our teeth." Downes responded: "Wet hair, rain like dew on his body, listen to the rain." The haiku encounter ended with a house cat, and winter rug that was burned in the spring.

"Shorter, but not much better," said McCosh. He pushed the mongrels back from the sausage and cheese on the table. He carried thick pencils and collected stories and titles on index cards; he was seldom alone in his institution. The terse bibliophile was surrounded by mongrels and writers who waited on his stories. He wore oversized clothes, and buried his fingers in his beard when he listened.

McCosh bought the last copies of *Slight Abrasions* from the publisher for less than the cost of the laid finish paper. The books in the attic were a lure to stories, a reminder that he had read my longer poems thirty years earlier. He opened his first bookstore in a house and then he moved to a narrow storefront in Dinkytown near the University of Minnesota.

I was a veteran with short hair, a sophomore in the late fifties with a mission to be a writer. I searched the shelves of his bookstore at least twice a week to meet new authors. Albert Camus, Jean-Paul Sartre, Dylan Thomas, Nikos Kazantzakis, and Alan Watts, were there in the same season.

McCosh seldom smiled but he teased his customers in a slow and low tone of voice. New students, for instance, would wander into his store at the start of each quarter and ask: "Do you have psych one?"

"Would you be asking for a book?"

"Yes, for my class."

"Would you happen to know the title?"

"Intro to psych," the student would answer.

"Never heard of that book."

"It's on the list," the student would plead.

"Did someone write this book?"

"I don't know."

"What is the book about?"

"Psych one."

"Never heard of that book."

"But it's on my list."

"The university bookstore has introductions," he would announce and then touch his wild white beard. The University of Minnesota was a new world to some students from rural communities where there were no bookstores. McCosh might have been their first humane encounter with a trickster at the university. The students would wait in silence to be saved by the gentle man with the white beard. He teased sophomores, and writers too, but we avoided courses that were introductions.

McCosh read my descriptive and romantic poems one cold autumn morning in his bookstore. I had asked his advice about publication and copyright. He leaned closer, his fleet fingers turned the yellow pages in silence, too soon to read each word, and then he announced that *South of the Painted Stones*, my first collection of poems, must be protected by copyright. I was too eager to believe that he was pleased with my poems. No doubt about it, my poems would need protection.

"Indeed, you must copyright these poems."

"Thank you, McCosh."

"Do you want to know why?"

"Well, yes, of course."

"These poems are bad, so bad, that one day, when you are a better writer, you'll need the copyright to protect your reputation, to keep these poems out of circulation," said Mc-Cosh.

"That bad?"

"Indians are buried in precious poems." McCosh pinched a narrow black cigar; the smoke burned my nose. He was right about my poems, but then he was righteous about other peculiarities. For instance, he sold blocks of books, rows of old books glued together to suburban fans on their way to university football games. The books satisfied a primal need, he teased, to block the standard bookcases built in tract houses.

One Sunday morning, late that summer, he drove his car over a crushproof cigarette box and proved the obvious. I was there with hundreds of other people, some of whom had never been in his bookstore, to celebrate the comic end of another consumer myth. The crushed box was suspended in the window of his bookstore.

TOP Gerald Vizenor with Ronald Libertus at Bear Island, Leech Lake Reservation, Minnesota, 1997

RIGHT Gerald Vizenor, Berkeley, 1999

TOP *Gerald Vizenor with Louis Owens, Oakland, California, 1998*

BOTTOM *Diane Glancy introduces Gerald Vizenor, Macalester College, Honorary Degree, 1999*

TOP Gerald Vizenor with Kimberly Blaeser, author of Gerald Vizenor: Writing in the Oral Tradition, *Birchbark Books, Minneapolis, 2006*

BOTTOM Gerald Vizenor with Justice Gary Strankman, Peace Memorial Park, Hiroshima, Japan, 2000

Gerald Vizenor, University of California, Santa Cruz, 1988

Gerald Vizenor, conference lecture, Kobe, Japan, 1993

Gerald Vizenor with Bill Lawrence, Publisher of Ojibwe News, *Saint Paul, Minnesota, 1999*

Gerald Vizenor with his wife Laura Hall, Santa Fe, New Mexico, 2005

Gerald Vizenor, Santa Fe, New Mexico, 2005

TOP Gerald Vizenor, Cochin, Kerala, India, 2005.
BOTTOM Gerald Vizenor, Morikami Japanese Gardens, Delray Beach, Florida, 2009.

RIGHT Gerald Vizenor with David Bradley, artist, Santa Fe, New Mexico, 2007.

BELOW Pierre Cayol, artist, with Gerald Vizenor, Saint Paul de Mousole, Saint-Rémy-de-Provence, France, 2009.

LEFT *Gerald Vizenor with A. Robert Lee, editor of* Loosening the Seams: Interpretations of Gerald Vizenor, *London, England, 2009.*

BELOW Gerald Vizenor with Laura Hall, Cambridge, England, 2009.

Gerald Vizenor with Deborah Madsen, author of Understanding Gerald Vizenor, *Cambridge, England, 2009.*

Gerald Vizenor with Professor Carme Manuel, translator of Almost Ashore *into Catalan, University of Valencia, Spain, 2009.*

Gerald Vizenor at Oradour-sur-Glane, France, 2009. Nazi soldiers murdered Jean-Baptiste Beaulieu, the village blacksmith, and more than six hundred other citizens on June 10, 1944. Only a few citizens survived the genocide.

Erma Vizenor, President of the White Earth Nation, with Gerald Vizenor, delegate and principal writer of the new Constitution, at the final Constitutional Convention, Shooting Star Casino Hotel, Mahnomen, Minnesota. The Constitution of the White Earth Nation was ratified by delegates on April 4, 2009.

Gerald Vizenor, a mixedblood member of the Minnesota Chippewa tribe, is a professor of literature and American Studies at the University of California, Santa Cruz. He has also taught at the University of California, Berkeley, the University of Minnesota, and Tianjin University in China. Vizenor wrote the original screenplay for *Harold of Orange*, which won the Film-in-the-Cities national screenwriting award and was also named "best film" at the San Francisco American Indian Film Festival. His second novel, *Griever: An American Monkey King in China*, won the Fiction Collective Prize and the American Book Award sponsored by the Before Columbus Foundation. In 1989, he received the California Arts Council Literature Award.

Vizenor has published several collections of haiku poems; *Matsushima: Pine Islands* is the most recent. Selections of his poems and short stories have appeared in several anthologies, including *Voices of the Rainbow* and *Words in the Blood*. The University of Minnesota Press has published Vizenor's *Crossbloods: Bone Courts, Bingo, and Other Reports, Bearheart: The Heirship Chronicles*, and *Griever: An American Monkey King in China*. Minnesota also has published his novel *The Trickster of Liberty* and three of his books on the American Indian experience: *Wordarrows, Earthdivers*, and *The People Named the Chippewa*.

BOOKS PUBLISHED BY GERALD VIZENOR:

Interior Landscapes: Autobiographical Myths and Metaphors, Second Edition, State University of New York Press, 2009.

Native Liberty: Natural Reason and Cultural Sovereignty, selected essays, University of Nebraska Press, 2009.

Quasi En Terra, Catalan translation of *Almost Ashore* by Carme Manuel Cuenca, Editorial Denes, Poesia Edicions De La Guerra, València, Spain, 2009.

Native Storiers: Five Selections, edited with an introduction, University of Nebraska Press, 2009.

Des Nouvelles des Indiens d'Amérique du Nord, French translation of *Native Storiers*, introductory essay and editor, Éditions Métailié, Paris, 2008.

Survivance: Narratives of Native Presence, introductory essay and editor, University of Nebraska Press, 2008.

Father Meme, a novel, University of New Mexico, 2008.

Crâneurs, French translation of *Chancers*, Éditions du Rocher, Paris, 2007.

Literary Chance: Essays on Native American Survivance, Biblioteca Javier Coy d'studis nord-americans, Universitat de Valencia, España, 2007.

Almost Ashore: Selected Poems, Salt Publishing, Cambridge, England, 2006.

Bear Island: The War at Sugar Point, University of Minnesota Press, 2006.

The Trickster of Liberty: Native Heirs to a Wild Baronage, University of Oklahoma Press, February, 2005. First published by the University of Minnesota Press, 1988.

Hiroshima Bugi: Atomu 57, University of Nebraska Press, November 2003.

Postindian Conversations, Literary Conversation with A. Robert Lee, University of Nebraska Press, 1999, 2003.

Wordarrows: Native States of Literary Sovereignty, Introduction to a New Edition, University of Nebraska Press, 2003. First published as *Wordarrows: Indians and Whites in the New Fur Trade*, University of Minnesota Press, 1978.

The Everlasting Sky: Voices of the Anishinaabe People, Introduction to a New Edition, Minnesota Historical Society Press, Saint Paul, 2001. First published as *The Everlasting Sky: New Voices from the People Named the Chippewa,* Crowell Collier Press, New York, Collier Macmillan, London, 1972.

Chancers, a novel, University of Oklahoma Press, Norman, 2000,

Cranes Arise, original haiku poems, Nodin Press, Minneapolis, 1999.

Raising the Moon Vines, original haiku, Second Edition, Nodin Press, Minneapolis, 1999.

Manifest Manners: Narratives of Postindian Survivance, Preface to a New Edition, University of Nebraska Press, Lincoln, 1999. First published as *Manifest Manners: Postindian Warriors of Survivance,* Wesleyan University Press, 1994.

Fugitive Poses: Native American Indian Scenes of Absence and Presence, University of Nebraska Press, The Abraham Lincoln Lecture Series, 1998. Translated into Japanese, 2003.

Hotline Healers: An Almost Browne Novel, Wesleyan University Press, University Press of New England, 1997.

Native American Literature, an anthology, editor, HarperCollins College Publishers, 1995.

Shadow Distance: A Gerald Vizenor Reader, autobiography, fiction, stories, essays, and other selections, Wesleyan University Press, 1994.

Harold of Orange / Harold von Orangen, bilingual edition of "Harold of Orange," a screenplay, translated by Wolfgang Hochbruck, et al, Osnabrueck Bilingual Editions, Eddingen, German, 1994.

Dead Voices: Natural Agonies in the New World, a novel, University of Oklahoma Press, 1993. Paperbound edition, 1993.

Summer in the Spring: Anishinaabe Lyric Poems and Stories, new edition, edited and interpreted, University of Oklahoma Press, 1993. First published as *anishinabe nagamon,* and *anishinabe adisokan,* by Nodin Press, Minneapolis, 1970.

Narrative Chance: Postmodern Discourse on Native American Literatures, editor, with an essay, "Trickster Discourse: Comic Holotropes and Language Games," reprinted in a paperbound edition by the University of Oklahoma Press, 1993. First published by the University of New Mexico Press, 1989.

Touchwood: A Collection of Ojibway Prose, editor, New Rivers Press, 1987, second printing, 1994.

Parolefrecce, translation of *Wordarrows* by Maria Vittoria D'Amico. Italian edition in the literature series "Indianamericana." Edited by Laura Coltelli, University of Pisa, 1992.

The Heirs of Columbus, a novel, Wesleyan University Press, University Press of New England, 1991; paperbound edition 1992.

Landfill Meditation, collection of short stories, Wesleyan University Press, University Press of New England, 1991.

Interior Landscapes: Autobiographical Myths and Metaphors, University of Minnesota Press, Minneapolis, 1990.

Crossbloods: Bone Courts, Bingo, and Other Reports, a collection of essays, University of Minnesota Press, Minneapolis, 1990. This new edition includes several revised essays on the American Indian Movement that first appeared in a *Minneapolis Tribune* editorial series, and *Tribal Scenes and Ceremonies*, Nodin Press, 1976.

Griever: An American Monkey King in China, novel, Fiction Collective Award, 1986, American Book Award, 1988, second edition published by the University of Minnesota Press, 1990.

Bearheart: The Heirship Chronicles, novel, new revised edition, University of Minnesota Press, 1990. First published as *Darkness in Saint Louis Bearheart*, Truck Press, 1978.

The Trickster of Liberty: Tribal Heirs to a Wild Baronage, novel, University of Minnesota Press, 1988.

Matsushima: Pine Islands, collected haiku poems, Nodin Press, 1984.

The People Named the Chippewa: Narrative Histories, University of Minnesota Press, 1983, second printing, 1987.

Earthdivers: Tribal Narratives on Mixed Descent, University of Minnesota Press, 1983.

Wordarrows: Indians and Whites in the New Fur Trade, University of Minnesota Press, 1978; second printing, 1989.

Tribal Scenes and Ceremonies, Nodin Press, Minneapolis, 1976.

The Everlasting Sky: New Voices from the People Named the Chippewa, Crowell Collier Press, New York, Collier Macmillan, London, 1972.

Thomas James White Hawk, investigative narrative on the trial, capital punishment, and commutation of the death sentence of Thomas James White Hawk, Four Winds Press, 1968.

Empty Swings, Haiku, Nodin Press, Minneapolis, 1967.

Slight Abrasions: A Dialogue in Haiku, Nodin Press, Minneapolis, 1966.

Seventeen Chirps, Haiku, Nodin Press, Minneapolis, 1964, paperbound edition, 1968.

Escorts to White Earth: 100 Year Reservation 1868 to 1968, Four Winds, Minneapolis, 1968.

Raising the Moon Vines, Haiku, Callimachus Publishing Company, Minneapolis, 1964. Second Edition, Nodin Press, Minneapolis, 1968.